D1088512

Landmark Essays

Landmark Essays

on
Writing Across the
Curriculum

Edited by Charles Bazerman and David Russell

Hermagoras Press
1994

Landmark Essays Volume Six

Copyright © 1994 Hermagoras Press

Published 1994 by Hermagoras Press,
P.O. Box 1555, Davis, CA 95617

Cover design by Kathi Zamminer

Typesetting and camera-ready production
by Graphic Gold, Davis, California
Manufactured in the United States of America
by KNI Inc., Anaheim, California

ISBN 1-880393-09-3

2 3 4 5 6 7 8 9 0

Acknowledgements

Thanks to our many colleagues who offered suggestions for the essays to be included and who commented on drafts of our introduction.

About the Editors

Charles Bazerman is professor of Literature, Communication, and Culture at Georgia Institute of Technology. He has published widely on rhetorical and genre theory, the teaching of writing, and the rhetoric of science and technology. His books include *Constructing Experience* (Southern Illinois University Press), *Shaping Written Knowledge: The Genre and Activity of the Experimental Article in Science* (University of Wisconsin Press, 1988), and *The Informed Writer*, 5th edition (Houghton Mifflin). He has co-edited with James Paradis *Textual Dynamics of the Professions* (University of Wisconsin Press, 1991). He is currently working on a study of the discursive practices that were part of incandescent light emerging into the daily life-world, tentatively titled *The Languages of Edison's Light*, and a new textbook for first-year writing classes.

David R. Russell is associate professor of English at Iowa State University, where he teaches in the Ph.D. program in Rhetoric and Professional Communication. He has published widely on writing-across-the-curriculum. His book *Writing in the Academic Disciplines, 1970-1990: A Curricular History* (Southern Illinois University Press, 1991) examines the history of American writing instruction outside of general composition courses. His currently writing a book on Activity Theory and genre acquisition, editing a collection of essays describing the uses of writing in nine national education systems, and collaborating on a multimedia program to simulate writing activities in the disciplines.

Table of Contents

Section 4: Writing in the Disciplines

Preface

Writing Across the Curriculum as a Challenge to Rhetoric and Composition

by Charles Bazerman and David Russell

Rhetoric, as a general teaching, while preaching locality of action and guidelines for handling that locality, has tended from the beginning to a universality. Rhetoric has offered a generalized *techne* with only limited categories, appropriate for all discursive situations, at least for those that were not excluded from the realm of rhetoric. Nonetheless, from its beginnings, rhetoric limited its interests to certain activity fields such as law, government, religion, and, most important, the education of leaders in these activity fields. Thus rhetoric excluded from its realm the activities and discourses not perceived to be relevant to the goals of these fields, as well as excluding those people not empowered in those fields. Rhetoric has traditionally ignored other discourses, forums, and populations, or has appropriated their knowledges/ discourses only as necessary for its own circumscribed activities and goals. At the same time, rhetoric tended to view the discourse of its own powerful forums—the public legislative body, the courts, the speech of the leader to followers on ceremonial occasions—as a privileged, even a universal, discourse, worthy to be the sole focus of study and teaching.

When forums for public discourse were fewer and varieties of wisdom discourses were not far removed from each other or from rhetoric's chosen forums, such a generalization of discourse would be both descriptively and prescriptively accurate. All discourse heading toward the same or similar forum was responsive to the same communicative dynamics and needed to gain a hearing in the same communicative environment. However, beginning in the Europe of the late middle ages, philosophy retreated from the public forums of the politically powerful to become differentiated in various branches of an academic inquiry—first through natural philosophy's trans-formation into the physical and biological sciences, then through the trans-formation of social philosophy and philosophy of the mind into psychology, sociology, anthropology, economics and the other social sciences.

The discourses of learning retired behind university walls, into quiet seminar rooms, and into obscure journals. Indeed at various moments state politics was glad to be rid of philosophic controversy, handing it over to specialized practitioners who would keep dangerous and divisive questions to themselves, from the Jesuits to the Royal Society to modern experts. Although often these developments went on outside the gaze of rhetorical theory, there were sporadic attempts from the time of the ancients through the Enlighten-ment to provide theory and guidance to direct the development and practice of these discourses. The history of rhetoric's attempts to cope with these differentiating discourse practices through the eighteenth century is sketched out in the Introduction.

In the last two centuries these specialized discourses dealing with matters of knowledge and power have become increasingly differentiated from each other, organizing themselves institutionally in ways that further decreased the communication among them. In the United States, particularly, numbers of disciplinary and professional workers have increased at rates far more rapid than the already rapid general population growth, so that the size of any of the current specialized networks of communication is likely to be greater than that of all the combined intellectuals of Europe in the seventeenth century. During its first forty years, the membership of the Royal Society, including lay people as well as virtuosos, averaged under 200 at any one time, and the circulation of the early *Philosophical Transactions* was about 1000 copies—figures that today would define only the smallest of professional societies and scholarly journals. Currently in the United States alone there are about 1400 scientific and technical societies, 3200 educational and cultural societies, and 15,000 professional societies in all. Membership in individual societies can be as large as the 135,000 in the American Academy for the Advancement of Science.

Certainly not all intellectuals or social leaders or ordinary citizens have been happy with this differentiation of disciplinary discourses and the removal of knowledge-forming, -reproducing, and -applying discourse from the forums of discourse accessible to all—newspapers, popular magazines, trade books, mass electronic media. Rhetorical studies have themselves specialized in the last hundred and twenty years, becoming isolated in bye corners of the academy (primarily in speech departments), maintaining allegiance to the forums of political power. But rhetorical studies have continued teaching generalized technes, decrying the decline of political speech, and calling for what they have sometimes termed a "revival of public discourse." Specialized discourses have alternately been placed beyond the realm of rhetoric (and therefore of little rhetorical interest) or quite conventionally describable in traditional rhetorical terms (and therefore only of limited interest).

During that same period of emergent specialization, the teaching of writing was separated from rhetoric to become an adjunct of literary studies, justified by the role of belles-lettres in literacy education espoused by much enlightenment and romantic rhetorical theory. The formal teaching of writing in composition courses, which became increasingly defined as preparation of students for the intellectual life of the academy and the professions, none-theless was largely subordinated to the specializing professional ideals of literary studies. Literary studies, as did other disciplines, defined and refined its own practices of communication and its own tastes, which came to inform composition practice and isolate writing pedagogy from the other specialized discourses residing in the university. In the primary (and often the only) site of systematic writing instruction, the language of the literati was valued above the other literacies exercised in the academy and was taught as if it ought to be the general language of the literate professional life.

Yet, even though rhetoric and composition were isolated from the discourses surrounding them in the rest of the academy, these other language practices created an increasing challenge over the years. Despite the rejection of these surrounding discourses in increasingly shrill terms as inferior and reductionist, many of these discourses attained a social standing and epistemological status that made them powerful and appealing. Students who were attracted to the subject matters of the natural and social sciences and professions inevitably were drawn into these arcane ways of writing despite the firmest injunctions of their professors of literature, even as literary studies developed its own increasingly arcane ways of writing. Although the faith in literary language was maintained within literature and other humanities departments, literary language was often rejected by students who wandered in foreign disciplines. Even residual professions of faith to symbols of cultivation (perhaps expressed through denunciation of the barbaric writing of colleagues) could barely hide that what was taught about in literature department writing courses had only limited significance for disciplinary writing practices learned sub rosa in daily professional life, through apprenticeship.

The sporadic attempts in the earlier part of this century to prepare students systematically for their non-humanistic discourses—in particular the growth of the progressive education movement and development of specialties of technical and business writing—are documented in section 2. The section begins with David Russell's historical sketch of those attempts and their culmination in the Writing-across-the-Curriculum (WAC) movement. The section ends with an early call for cooperation among instructors in all disciplines. It is a 1913 article (widely reprinted at the time) by James Fleming Hosic, a Deweyan progressive who had founded the National Council of Teachers of English two years earlier. He surveys various "ways of securing co-operation of departments in the teaching of English composition" and proposes their adoption nation-wide—a proposal that was largely ignored for more than sixty years.

The WAC movement, which began in the 1970's, gave new focus and energy to the sporadic local attempts to focus attention on student writing outside composition courses. The WAC movement had its intellectual roots largely in the British classroom research and theorizing of James Britton and his colleagues at the London School of Education from 1966 to 1976, which is summarized in the selection by Martin, D'Arcy, Newton, and Parker that begins section 3. Since the Anglo-American conference at Dartmouth in 1966 on the teaching of English, there had been extensive transatlantic contact among researchers. In 1976 the findings of the first National Assessment of Education Progress in writing touched off a flurry of "Why Johnny Can't Write" articles in the U.S. popular press. And a few institutions responded by setting up writing-across-the-curriculum programs, inspired by the British research, and supported by the field of composition studies, just emerging in the U.S. in response to open admissions policies.

These early WAC programs took many forms, but the most common were and still are (1) workshops to encourage faculty in all disciplines to use writing more effectively in their courses (courses which in many institutions are designated "writing-intensive") and (2) courses taught by faculty or teaching assistants from the English department that introduce students to the kinds of writing done in other disciplines. Faculty writing workshops are the subject of "How Well Does Writing Across the Curriculum Work?" by Toby Fulwiler. In 1977 at Michigan Technical University, he and others started one of the most influential workshop-centered programs with a faculty writing retreat held in a logging camp. WAC courses sponsored by English departments are the subject of James Kinneavy's 1983 essay, which grew out of his program proposal for the University of Texas (partially implemented) and his work on a textbook, *Writing in the Liberal Arts Tradition*, that employs his humanistic rationale for WAC. Susan McLeod's report on a 1988 national survey concludes the section, and shows how far the WAC movement had spread by the late 1980s and how multifarious its curricular forms had become.

These curricular experiments spawned a whole range of new research on the teaching and learning of writing throughout the university, which section 4 takes up. This research focused on the real writing of real students in disciplinary classrooms. It applied theories and methods from ethnographic, historical, sociological, psychological, and cultural studies to the problematics of writing and learning. In the U.S., theorizing on WAC was launched with Janet Emig's 1977 essay, "Writing as a Mode of Learning," which begins section 4. Influenced by Britton and the British, Emig draws upon a surprisingly wide range of theorists, from Vygotsky and Luria in the Soviet Union to Dewey, Bruner, and Moffett in the U.S. Her thesis—revolutionary for many at the time—is that writing in academic settings does not merely improve writing, it improves learning, through a variety of cognitive and social processes. Students should not only learn to write but write to learn. This became the central working assumption of the WAC movement and spawned a host of studies to understand how (and if) that happens.

Early survey-based studies, including those of Britton's group, tended to characterize teachers and classrooms as rather homogeneous in their use (or misuse) of writing. But in the 1980s, researchers involved in WAC programs began to employ naturalistic, qualitative research methods drawn from anthropology and sociology to examine the roles writing plays in teaching and learning within specific disciplinary and curricular settings. They found crucially important differences not only among disciplines but also, as Anne Herrington's 1985 article shows, among courses within a single discipline— or even among courses offered by a single instructor. Herrington's essay also illustrates these researchers' use of several research methods to build a more dynamic and useful representation of writing in institutional settings, "triangulating" the results of surveys, analyses of student texts, classroom observations, and interviews with students and teachers. Employing ethnographic methods drawn from anthropology, Lucille McCarthy's essay, "A Stranger in Strange Lands," follows a first-year college student struggling to negotiate the differences among disciplinary cultures through the writing assignments in his various courses. The insights that these close-range studies provided led, in the late 1980s, to more comprehensive cross-disciplinary classrooms research. The selections in this and the next section are among the more prominent research statements, but they also point toward extensive other work that has been carried out and continues to grow in sophistication and range (see the Supplemental Bibliography).

When researchers began to pay serious attention to the classroom discourse in the disciplines, the next task was to investigate the disciplinary discourses that lay beyond the classroom, in the day-to-day writing of academics and professionals in many activity fields. For the first time, one might say, scholars in rhetoric and composition took as the object of descriptive and interpretive (not prescriptive and normative) study the discourse of other disciplines. This discipline-oriented research has been designated Writing in the Disciplines (WID) to distinguish it from the education-oriented WAC. Charles Bazerman's 1981 essay, "What Written Knowledge Does: Three Examples of Academic Writing," begins section 5 because it launched this tradition of research into the rhetoric of disciplinary and professional discourses. Significantly, it was published not in a rhetoric or composition journal but in a social sciences theory journal, indicating how interdisciplinary this work would become. It relies on the findings, tools, and problematics of many fields, from language studies to the history, sociology, and psychology of science, as well as studies of technical writing and communication.

Greg Myers' interpretation of two biologists' grant proposals traces the evolution of the documents as the scientists negotiate, through their writing, the complex social processes of their discipline: reviewers, granting agencies, fellow scientists. As we watch the documents and the project develop over time, those social processes are revealed through their dynamic interplay within an activity field. Berkenkotter, Huckin, and Ackerman's essay extends the diachronic analysis to the rhetorical development of a graduate student, a novice being socialized into a discipline. In a sense, it brings us back to the questions that motivated the study of writing and rhetoric in the disciplines in the first place: How do students learn (or fail to learn) the specific kinds of writing they will need in their future activities, professional and otherwise? And how can pedagogical arrangements improve that learning?

Given the history of rhetoric and composition, WAC and WID cannot but present many challenges, yet to be addressed. In this collection we present some landmarks, showing where WAC and WID have gone; full integration with the traditional concerns and activities of rhetoric and composition lies in the future. What kind of rhetoric would be appropriate to a highly differentiated society? What advice can we give about writing when the forms and forums of writing are complex and many, in pursuit of widely diverging human projects?

Although the current multiplicity and specialization of written discourse does not fit the ideals of traditional rhetorical teachings, this is what is. It deserves study. The needs of individuals and groups having to write in these complexes of language ought to be addressed, because of their importance to a world entering the information age, because mastery of those discourses is essential for entering into those powerful activities and social roles that expertise confers in modern cultures, and because these discursive activities might be made more accessible to non-experts, to allow more democratic scrutiny and dialogue. Opening professional discourses to analysis and teaching may also help open those professions to many who are excluded when those discourses are taught exclusively through apprenticeship, tacitly, sub rosa.

If there is a way to a more inclusive public discourse, it is through the specialized discourses engaging each other and the forums of politics and mass media. To be successful, such engagements must respect the dynamics that made these discourses distinctive, even while locating the common tasks and interests that bind them together and to the common weal. New forums and mechanisms must be created to allow a public discourse to emerge within our culture of specialization. We need to study interface discourse, where specialties meet each other and meet the forums of public decision making. Expert testimony, congressional witnesses, and media coverage of disciplinary research are but a few of the interface sites that need investigation.

WAC and WID have opened up a number of prospects that were impossible to see when rhetoric and composition confined their gaze to relatively few discursive activities. We do not know where this will lead, but can suggest that the rhetorical landscape is becoming more complex and interesting, as well as more responsive to life in the complex, differentiated societies that have emerged in the last few centuries. We hope this collection of landmarks will reveal to scholars and researchers a range of possibilities for the study of disciplinary discourse and its teaching, and suggest to them new prospects for the future and for the better.

Introduction

The Rhetorical Tradition and Specialized Discourses

by Charles Bazerman and David Russell

The problem of the specialization of discourse/knowledge/work—or what we might broadly call the differentiation of organized human activities—has been a nagging presence within Western rhetoric and formal education since their beginnings in ancient Athens and Rome. But specialization has only sporadically emerged as a crisp problem in the Western tradition of rhetorical theory. In this essay, we point to some textual loci where rhetorical theory has attended to the issue of the specialization of discourse and offer a preliminary account of why such attention has been so rare.

In the fifth century b.c.e. several specialized fields of activity began to codify their knowledge in written form, often as a means of staking out some social practice and defending it as their exclusive privilege. Rhetoric, with its handbooks of codified practice, and medicine, with the Hippocratic corpus of texts, were perhaps the first to defend their claims publicly in writing. Technical manuals or treatises on agriculture, music, mathematics, geometry, and many others followed. These fields of activity were called *technai*, a term that implied some reasoned practice, distinct from others, an acquired art or skill, expertise. The writing of each activity field (that resorted to writing), each techne, had its own specialized vocabulary and conventions, which were accessible to outsiders in various degrees. There were many other technai, of course, such as shipbuilding, that were passed along orally to children and apprentices. But significantly, it is those practices about which knowledge or social value was disputed among the upper social classes that have left written records (Führmann).

As there are professional rivalries today, so there were battles among technai in the fifth century b.c.e., as one group of practitioners challenged the knowledge or skill of another group to win social credit in some activity field. For example, the physicians in the Hippocratic tradition challenged the ritual healers for control of health care and eventually won, at least among the upper classes. For our purposes, the most important battle was over control of the higher education of male property owners, a battle fought most conspicuously in Athens and, later, in Rome between the rhetoricians and the philosophers. What kind of knowledge, and therefore discourse, was best for young men to learn given the institutional activities they would participate in for the maintenance of power: the Athenian assembly and the Roman political and legal system? And how could such discourse best be taught? Because the subject matter of rhetoric—and its successful practice—are not as clearly limited and self-evident as they are in, say, architecture, the relation of rhetoric (and also philosophy) to other activity fields became an issue. What, if anything, is the subject of rhetoric?

Ancient rhetorical theorists generally coped with these differentiating discourse practices and the challenge to define their own techne by claiming the ability to speak on any subject for the purpose of persuading a jury or ruling body or public assembly to take some course of action *and* the ability to teach others to do so, or at least those who had sufficient talent. The other fields were to be "the handmaids of oratory," as Crassus puts it in Cicero's *De Oratore*. All knowledge is available for the orator to use to accomplish some purpose in his own activity field—not as an object of study proper or a means of furthering the goals of the specialized field itself. Given rhetoric's pragmatic, instrumental approach and its limited, though high-status, activities and goals, the discourses of other activity fields were not of specific interest to rhetorical theorists. But this response was severely tested by the Platonic philosophical tradition, which accused the rhetoricians of arrogating all knowledge without possessing any of their own.[1]

The Sophists

In general, the sophists viewed rhetoric as a techne, a universal art of communication applicable to any subject—though apparently only in appropriate forums. Philostratus recounts that the preeminent sophist, Gorgias, coming to the theater of Athens:

> had the boldness to say, "suggest a subject," and he was the first to proclaim himself willing to take this chance, showing apparently that he knew everything and would trust to the moment to speak on any subject. (DK A 82 1a)

In his few extant writings, Gorgias indeed speaks on a wide range of subjects including astronomy, metaphysics, law, literary criticism, and diplomacy, as well as the social commentary in the "Encomium of Helen."

By the same token, for Gorgias all technai are fundamentally rhetorical, persuasive. This is as true of scientists (astronomers, in his example) as it is of orators and philosophers:

> To understand that persuasion, when added to speech, is wont also to impress the soul as it wishes, one must study: first, the words of astronomers (*meterologon*) who, substituting opinion for opinion, taking away one but creating another, make what is incredible and unclear seem necessary and true to the eyes of opinion; then second, logically necessary debates in which a single speech, written with art

---

[1] On the ancient and enduring battle between rhetoric and philosophy, see Barnes, "Is Rhetoric an Art?"; Vickers, *In Defense of Rhetoric*; and Roochnick, "Is Rhetoric an Art?".

but not spoken with truth, bends a great crowd and persuades; [and] third, the verbal disputes of philosophers in which the swiftness of thought is also shown making the belief in an opinion subject to easy change. (DK B 82 11, 13)

Though Gorgias argues that all technai rely on persuasion, and he claims to be able to speak persuasively on any subject, he apparently confined his speaking to certain forums, and in that sense did not claim all knowledge, expertise in any activity field, but only the art of using all knowledge in his specific forums. The sophists were interested in the uses of discourse for training young men to speak persuasively in legal and political forums, though that training might involve acquiring some knowledge in a number of activity fields useful to public speakers—grammar, logic, law, history, poetry. Gorgias, like the other sophists, trained young men to speak in those powerful but circumscribed forums, not to speak to groups of specialists in other activity fields. Rhetoric became the art of *civic* discourse and what came to be known as liberal education.

Isocrates, sometimes called the father of liberal education, distanced himself from the sophists in many ways. But he too insisted the students be taught knowledge of many types in his influential school. Rhetorical education became broad in its available subjects, but remained limited in the social roles for which it prepared students—leadership roles in law, public administration, higher education, religion. It is liberal not only in the sense that it is free to range over all knowledge to accomplish its goals but also in the sense that it directly serves only those with the wealth to be freed from the need to pursue some mundane specialty in order to earn their bread. Rhetorical study of an Isocratean cast, supported by knowledge of other areas, set the pattern for higher education in classical times and beyond.

Plato

Plato's dialogues repeatedly question the Sophists' claim to speak with authority on specialized areas of knowledge and work. Socrates argues these kinds of technical knowledge/discourse are the legitimate function only of those adept in these specific arts or technai. Rhetoric, in Socrates' view, is not an art (techne), much less a universal one; each art has its own kind of knowledge and its own kind of discourse, and one cannot learn them by learning rhetoric.

Socrates: Now, does the medical art, which we mentioned just now, make men able to understand and speak about the sick?

Gorgias: It must. . . .

Socrates: And moreover it is the same, Gorgias, with all the other arts; each of them is concerned with that kind of speech which deals with the subject matter of that particular art?

Gorgias: Apparently. (*Gorgias* 450a)

Rhetoric, Socrates goes on to conclude, has no particular subject and therefore nothing of value to teach. Socrates makes a firm distinction between true knowledge and the mere appearance of knowledge. Rhetoric, in his view, is not concerned with true knowledge but only with appearances, mere *doxa* or opinion, the ways knowledge of specialists in some activity field can be used for legal or political purposes extrinsic to that activity field. Only through specialized discourse among experts who debate competing arguments among themselves (dialectic), can human beings get beyond mere opinion to truth.

> Socrates: When the city holds a meeting to appoint doctors or shipbuilders or any other set of craftsmen, there is no question then, is there, of the rhetorician giving advice [on these appointments] and clearly this is because in each appointment we have to select the most skillful person. (*Gorgias* 455b)

If knowledge comes from the discourse of specialists on some clearly limited subject, and if rhetoric has no such clearly limited subject matter, then the sophists cannot be entrusted to teach the young. Rhetoric can only be a bag of tricks for deceiving non-experts. In the *Gorgias* and the *Phaedrus*, Plato suggests that the proper role of rhetoric lies in specialists correcting errors among non-experts, for the good of society. Higher education for civic leadership must not be left to rhetoricians but to philosophers, those who concern themselves with—perhaps specialize in—virtue.[2]

Aristotle

Aristotle attempts to overcome the problems raised by the Sophists and Plato by proposing three kinds of knowing. In the realm of rhetoric, knowledge is contingent on circumstances and persuasion is the goal, as in politics, law, and ethics. In the realm of dialectic, one seeks universal truths, as in natural philosophy or metaphysics. And in the realm of demonstration, one has already discovered these truths or first principles, as in any technai in which certain knowledge (first principles) have been arrived at syllogistically—mathematics being the preeminent example (Johnstone; Moss). The rhetor may use expert knowledge gleaned from dialectic or demonstration, but such knowledge comes into play only as part of attempts to find means of persuasion in civic forums. Though the rhetor cannot speak *as an expert* on all subjects, he can speak persuasively *about* all subjects as they affect the situations that arise in particular cases in the activity fields concerned with practical decision-making: law, politics, and so on.

---

[2] David Roochnick's *The Tragedy of Reason: Toward a Platonic Conception of Logos* analyzes the vexed problem of the status of philosophy as a techne of virtue and its relation to rhetoric in the Platonic dialogs.

> Let rhetoric be [defined as] an ability, in each [particular] case, to see
> the available means of persuasion. This is the function of no other art;
> for each of the others is instructive and persuasive about its own
> subject: for example, medicine about health and disease and geometry
> about the properties of magnitudes and arithmetic about numbers and
> similarly in the case of the other arts and sciences. But rhetoric seems
> to be able to observe the persuasive about "the given," so to speak.
> (*Rhetoric* 1.2.1)

Although dialectic (through its characteristic form of argument, the syllogism)
and rhetoric (through its characteristic form of argument, the enthymeme)
allow human beings to discuss any subject or find available means of
arguments on any subject, rhetoric and dialectic must both borrow from other
fields for their subject matter. Although every kind of knowledge uses
arguments (and thus dialectic or rhetoric), we tend to lose sight of the
rhetorical strategies the closer we get to subject matter (the first principles) of
a field of activity.

> The more [speakers] fasten upon [the subject matter] in its proper
> sense, [the more] they depart from rhetoric or dialectic. [*Rhetoric*
> 1.2.20]

Aristotle deals with this problematic relation of rhetoric (and dialectic) to
special knowledges (technai) by erecting categories of argument. He divides
resources for finding arguments (*topoi*) into two kinds, common topics [*koinei
topoi*] that can be applied to any field of knowledge and "specific" topics
[*idia* here, later *idia topoi* and *stoikheia*] that are used only in a specific field.

> The former [the common *topoi*] will not make one understand any
> genus [kind of knowledge]; for they are not concerned with any
> underlying subject. As to the latter [the specifics], to the degree that
> someone makes better choice of the premises, he will have created
> knowledge different from dialectic and rhetoric without its being
> recognized; for if he succeeds in hitting on first principles [of a field],
> the knowledge will no longer be dialectic or rhetoric but the science
> of which [the speaker] grasps the first principles. [*Rhetoric* 1.2.1358a]

This distinction allows Aristotle to steer his usual course between two
extremes: on one hand the Socratic denial that rhetoric has a subject and can
be taught, on the other hand the Sophistic insistence on the central place of
rhetorical persuasion in human affairs. When people confine themselves
closely to a specialized field of human activity, they discover knowledge for
the purposes of that field, knowledge which is not that of those whose activity
is the study of discursive argument. Thus, rhetoric was separated from
specialized knowledges and discourses. Subsequent rhetorical theory paid
little attention to Aristotle's specific topics, perhaps because, as Carolyn
Miller points out, Aristotle's theory provided no stable place for them between
the common topics and the "first principles" of each field.

Cicero

Cicero renews the debate over the relationship between rhetoric and specialized knowledge in *De Oratore*. Like Gorgias and Isocrates, he argues (through the debate between Crassus and Antonius) that the orator must study all kinds of specialized knowledge, but only as they are necessary for political or judicial discourse, not as an expert speaking to experts.

> Attainments in other sciences are drawn from recluse and hidden springs; but the whole art of speaking lies before us, and is concerned with common usage and the custom and language of all men; so that while in other things that is most excellent which is most remote from the knowledge and understanding of the illiterate; it is in speaking even the greatest of faults to vary from the ordinary kind of language, and the practice sanctioned by universal reason. (Bk I Ch. iii)

As need arises, an orator can consult an expert on any subject so he can speak "most eloquently on those matters of which he shall have gained a knowledge for a special purpose and occasion." But the orator seeks specialized knowledge for his own ends, not for the specialized work of a profession. For the goals of the orator are not those of any other profession. Though the orator should have wide general knowledge, drawn from the close study of great literature, arcane professional discourse is of no interest to the orator—indeed is a detriment to effective persuasion in his forums. Cicero thus affirms the importance of wide knowledge and thus of liberal education, and he particularly recommends legal training, for obvious reasons. But he ignores Aristotle's specific topics as a resource for invention and looks down on arcane discourse as mere pedantry unbecoming an orator-gentleman—a theme that would be revived in the Renaissance along with Ciceronian rhetoric and Roman rhetorical education (Leff, "Topics").

Quintilian

Quintilian summarizes the previous arguments over the scope of rhetoric and comes down firmly on the side of Cicero and the orators. To those who argue, as Socrates does, that rhetoric is limitless and therefore no techne at all, Quintilian replies that many arts, such as architecture, are characterized by the same multiplicity and employ "whatever is useful for the purpose of building," regardless of whether other arts also use them (II xxi 8). And to those who argue, "If an orator has to speak on every subject, he must be the master of all the arts," Quintilian quotes Cicero: "In my opinion no one can be an absolutely perfect orator unless he has acquired a knowledge of all important subjects and arts." But, as a practical teacher, Quintilian is forced to hedge, and his hedge says much about the relationship between the rhetor and other disciplines and professions:

> I however regard it as sufficient that an orator should not be actually ignorant of the subject on which he has to speak. For he

cannot have a knowledge of all causes, and yet he should be able to speak on all. On what then will he speak? On those which he has studied. Similarly as regards the arts, he will study those concerning which he has to speak, as occasion may demand, and will speak on those which he has studied.

What then?—I am asked—will not a builder speak better on the subject of building and a musician on music? Certainly, if the orator does not know what is the question at issue. Even an illiterate peasant who is a party to a suit will speak better on behalf of his case than an orator who does not know what the subject in dispute may be. But on the other hand if the orator receive instruction from the builder or the musician, he will put forward what he has thus learned better than either, just as he will plead a case better than his client, once he has been instructed in it. *The builder and the musician will, however, speak on the subject of their respective arts, if there should be an technical point which requires to be established. Neither will be an orator, but he will perform his task like an orator*, just as when an untrained person binds up a wound, he will not be a physician, but he will be acting as one. . . .

It is suggested that such topics never come up in panegyric, deliberative, or forensic oratory? When the question of the construction of the port at Ostia came up for discussion [in the Senate], had not the orator to state his views? And yet it was a subject requiring technical knowledge of the architect. Does not the orator [in murder trials] discuss the question whether livid spots and swellings on the body are symptomatic of ill-health or poison? And yet that is a question for the qualified physician. Will he not deal with measurements and figures? And yet we must admit that they form a part of mathematics. For my part I hold that practically all subjects are under certain circumstances liable to come up for treatment by the orator. *If the circumstances do not occur, the subjects will not concern him.* (II xxi 14-19, italics added)

In this passage, we are in the world of the law-court and the legislative body, where, like today, experts are called upon to give expert testimony that attorneys and legislators use in their arguments, and where those experts must "translate" their expert knowledge into discourse for the non-specialists and so function, to that extent, as orators (though without training and experience in those forums).

Even in antiquity, activity fields, with their specialized knowledges and discourses, were too various for one person to know all of them. But for those close to the seats of power, where rhetoric remained, one need only know enough of other activity fields' work and words to carry on one's administrative duties and successfully maintain or advance one's cultural and economic position. There were of course many who had received formal rhetorical education, whether those of the upper class or those associated with it (educated slaves, freedmen, or foreigners), who entered into specialized activity fields other than rhetoric. But rhetorical theory did not take an active interest in these activities and their discourses because its realm, its goals, lay elsewhere. The value of other fields was thus only instrumental, a means of winning a judgment from those who also were not involved in the specialized activity.

The Greco-Roman rhetorical education system proved remarkably resilient and useful. The genres of formal administrative correspondence became increasingly important as the oral institutions of senate and courts lost power and a centrally-administered empire expanded, but rhetoricians did not (with one unimportant exception) theorize this written form of discourse (Murphy 195-96). Schools continued to teach the old rhetorical theory and turn out a homogeneous cadre of imperial functionaries.

Rhetoric Through the Middle Ages

Even after the breakup of the Roman empire and its legal and political institutions made the old rhetorical training for law and politics less directly relevant, the traditional educational system was adequate for the task of preparing administrators to communicate, without formal training in the specific genres that evolved (Leff, "Material" 76). Vestiges of the Greco-Roman education system continued to train clerics to carry on correspondence for the church and for illiterate rulers, often through the use of *formularies*, books of model letters (Murphy 199).

But by the twelfth century, social structures for organizing specialized knowledge had begun to evolve, and with them specialized discourses. The craft guild structure of the middle ages facilitated the growth of knowledge and specialized discourses in many activity fields. These knowledges were primarily oral and untheorized. Moreover, the guilds maintained a protective secrecy that would have deterred rhetorical theory from investigating them even if rhetoric had had a reason to do so (Goldstein 112, 124-26; Shelby). But it did not have such a reason. In the twelfth century, the first universities took shape, modeling their structure on the guilds (*universitas* is a medieval Latin term for guild; hence the granting of the *master's* degree). They developed specialized written discourses in three powerful professional specialties: law, theology (including philosophy), and medicine. Rhetoric was relegated to lower levels of teaching, but it continued to profoundly influence at least two of these activity fields: law and religion.

Rhetorical theory was important to the study and teaching of law largely through the profound influence of Cicero and the renewed study of Roman law. Rhetoric and law were taught together in the early middle ages. Later, when rhetoric was relegated to lower levels of instruction, rhetorical theory influenced law through the study of letter writing (*ars dictaminis*) and the preparation of legal documents (*ars notaria*) (Murphy 112). The growing need for legal, commercial, political, and ecclesiastical correspondence led to the creation of courses in *dictamen* (letter writing) at monastic schools and, slightly later, at law schools (Bologna and Orleans). Competition for students among two groups, monastic or ecclesiastical schola and secular masters, led teachers of dictamen to produce theoretical texts to justify their practice and maintain their territory and status. Eventually, letter writing came to require a sophistication and precision that could only be met by professional specialists: the notaries, who organized themselves into guilds (see Murphy chap. 5).

In theology and philosophy, rhetoric also became preparatory to professional study. Though rhetoric lost status, rhetorical theory nevertheless profoundly influenced the teaching and theorizing of preaching—and hence, indirectly, the professional training and practice in theology and philosophy (see Murphy chap. 6). Codified manuals of preaching practice linked classical rhetorical concerns to theological concerns, but insisted on the unique nature of theological discourse. Thomas of Salisbury (c. 1210) wrote, "The sacred page has its own special topics (*loci*) beyond those of dialectic and rhetoric" (quoted in Murphy 323).

Renaissance Rhetoric and Specialization

The combination of social, political, and intellectual changes called the Renaissance further complicated the relationship between the formal study of rhetoric and communicative practices in specialized fields. The printing press and improved communication made it feasible to disseminate texts on increasingly specialized topics. By disseminating guild and university knowledge, the printing press made specialized discourses accessible to those outside the narrow circle of initiates (or those with access to manuscripts). Artisans and scholars of all types evolved specialized conventions of written discourse and national and international channels of communication, not only in the traditional university subjects but also in practical arts and technologies: martial arts, mining, herbal lore, shipbuilding, metalworking, cookery, alchemy, and so on (Eisenstein).

The fourteenth century humanist revival of classical learning and education—already well under way before the Gutenburg revolution—renewed and promoted the study of rhetoric. But in some ways, the humanist revival of classical rhetoric militated against the acceptance of specialized discourses as objects of rhetorical study and the broadening of rhetorical theory to include the study of those discourses that the coming of the printing press helped to create and disseminate. First, humanist education was above all literary, focusing on the development of an excellent style and with it, according to the ideal, an excellent character. Ciceronian prose was held up as the compositional ideal, zealously taught in the new humanist schools modeled on Quintilian's. Humanists, while pursuing highly specialized philological study, disdained the specializations of late medieval scholasticism, against which they were struggling for control of education. Humanists showed little interest in building upon the advancements late medieval scholasticism had made in law, medicine, and philosophy, much less in seriously examining their discourses, which were regarded as crude by Ciceronian standards

(Bolgar 282-95).

Second, humanists preserved the Aristotelian distinction between rhetoric (the realm of civic discourse) and natural philosophy (the realm of dialectic and demonstration). A late sixteenth-century Jesuit commentator on Aristotle's *Rhetoric* described how to study a techne:

> First one should learn the proper meanings of ambiguous words and the terminology of that art; then one should perceive the first principles on which the entire discipline depends. After that one should learn the subject matter in a general way, the several parts, causes, and properties; following that one should descend to particulars. One should do this in physics, metaphysics, and ethics, and in other arts, and in all of learning (quoted in Moss 14).

Rhetoric, in this view, is not relevant to the business of learning knowledge arrived at through dialectic and demonstration.

Third, the revival of the Ciceronian ideal of the orator-statesman the *uomo universale* or Renaissance man, as he was later to be called, was associated with the education of the ruling class of the new nation states, the courtier rather than the cleric or artisan. The courtier was expected to be versed in all knowledge—not, to be sure, as a technical specialist or pedant "too much dipped in the inkhorn," but as an advisor to rulers or a ruler himself, who could use that broad classical knowledge for the good of the state. For humanist practitioners of rhetoric, as Brian Vickers put it, "Rhetoric is essential to governors and counselors because it can persuade men to do what you want them to do. . . . But it leads humanists, whatever their language and status, on to a further and more dangerous position: rhetoric is useful, the rival disciplines are useless" ("Practicalities" 135). Humanists often ridiculed specialized discourse (Rabalais comes first to mind) and rarely theorized it. The Ciceronian ideal, combined with its pedagogical emphasis on close reading of literary texts in the classical languages and development of literary style through imitation, set the pattern for higher education until well into the twentieth century, and left to the academic specialties that came to be called the *humanities* a legacy of isolation from the developing sciences (Grafton and Jardine).

Nonetheless, in the short run, the humanist revival of rhetoric exerted a positive and profound influence on learned disciplines and on technical knowledges. Humanism, as Paul Oskar Kristeller has consistently pointed out, was only one current of renaissance culture, though it was the one that most consciously appropriated rhetoric to its ends (*Renaissance*). And many humanists took an active interest in the knowledges, if not the discourses, of artisans, especially in fields essential to Renaissance rulers, such as commerce and military technology (navigation, engineering, ballistics, metallurgy) (Rossi). Students educated in humanist schools profoundly influenced the genres and styles of specialist treatises (Kristeller, "Impact" 18). "It is not exaggeration to say that the rules of the classical oration were applied to every kind of discourse" (Abbott 108). The Ciceronian dialogue and the *institutio* of Quintilian became important genres in a wide range of disciplines, including the new science. Humanists searched out, edited, and translated classical texts on natural philosophy and many practical arts, then applied to them a sophisticated textual method that stimulated critical and, in many cases, empirical inquiry. Finally, developments in rhetorical theory itself, such as Ramus's rationalization of curriculum, paved the way for the modern academic specialization of teaching and learning (Ong 162-64). And while rhetoric did not investigate the specialized modes of discourse emerging in sciences and technology, rhetorical modes of thought instilled in students at humanist schools may well have contributed to the formation of modern scientific method itself (Slawinski). As studies of the impact of rhetoric on Renaissance science are undertaken, such as Jean Dietz Moss's recent *Novelties in the Heavens: Rhetoric and Science in the Copernican Controversy*, and Maurice Slawinski's "Rhetoric and Science/Rhetoric of Science/Rhetoric As Science," we can better understand the interplay of Renaissance rhetoric and specialization before the revolutions wrought by Bacon, Galileo, Newton, and Locke.

Bacon and the Language of Inquiry

Francis Bacon, while showing many continuities with the intellectual world of the early Renaissance, redefined the relationship of rhetoric and other discourses of the intellectual and practical worlds. He, like Aristotle, had an extensive vision and interest in the wide ranges of symbolic activity, of which rhetoric was only a part, but unlike Aristotle, Bacon saw natural philosophy enmeshed in communicative practices, and therefore needing reflection on the best means for knowledge formulation and communication. His rhetoric for popular communication stood side by side with his discussion of philosophic language, and neither were separated into isolated practices. They were elucidated in compendious works like the *Magna Instauratio* and *The Advancement of Learning* and in the comprehensive vision of an integrated society, as in the *New Atlantis*. Moreover, while each kind of discursive practice had its own needs and methods, the knowledge gained in one would influence the others. He was concerned with how practical arts might communicate secrets to the savants, how the savants might communicate knowledge to the community, how the knowledge of human nature could inform rhetorical practice, how public rhetoric could be practiced ethically and wisely in awareness of the illusions humans were heir to. And he was concerned how the needs of the polity and economy could be transmitted to the inquirers into the mysteries of nature.

Thus, while his rhetoric in *The Advancement of Learning* articulated many traditional principles, it did not espouse persuasion at any cost, nor did it accede to common belief. Rather it attempted to free daily language from what Bacon called sophistries. Moreover, Bacon advised that rhetoric be informed of what he called the four idols, even though they could not be easily eliminated from public discourse. The analysis of the four idols was to become the cornerstone of his thinking on method for interpreting nature, or natural philosophy, as presented in the *Novum Organum*. Three of the four idols specifically entail the ways we represent knowledge to each other in language, and thus form a contrastive basis for a rhetoric for science—those kinds of representations that must to the best of our abilities be removed from language of inquiry. Nonetheless, Bacon recognized that these idols are deeply ingrained in the condition of being human, and so never to be totally eliminated except by true method—the method of induction:

    XXXIX. There are four classes of Idols which beset men's minds. To these for distinction's sake I have assigned names, calling the first class Idols of the Tribe; the second, Idols of the Cave; the third, Idols of the Market-place; the fourth, Idols of the Theatre.

    XL. The formation of ideas and axioms by true induction is no doubt the proper remedy to be applied for the keeping off and clearing away of idols. To point them out, however, is of great use, for the doctrine of Idols is to the Interpretation of Nature what the doctrine of the refutation of Sophisms is to common Logic.

    XLI. The Idols of the Tribe have their foundation in human nature itself and in the tribe or race of men. For it is a false assertion that the sense of man is the measure of things. On the contrary, all perceptions as well of the sense as of the mind are according to the measure of the individual and not according to the measure of the universe. And the human understanding is like a false mirror, which, receiving rays irregularly, distorts and discolours the nature of things by mingling its own nature with it.

    XLII. The Idols of the Cave are the idols of the individual man. For every one (besides the errors common to human nature in general) has a cave or den of his own, which refracts and discolours the light of nature, owing either to his own proper and peculiar nature, or to his education and conversation with others, or to the reading of books, and the authority of those he esteems and admires, or to the differences of impressions, accordingly as they take place in a mind preoccupied and predisposed or in a mind indifferent and settled, or the like. So that the spirit of man (according as it is meted out to different individuals) is in fact a thing variable and full of perturbation, and governed, as it were by chance. Whence it was well observed by Heraclitus that men look for sciences in their own lesser worlds and not in the greater or common world.

    XLIII. There are also Idols formed by the intercourse and association of men with each other, which I call Idols of the Marketplace on account of the commerce and consort of men there. For it is by discourse that men associate, and words are imposed according to the apprehension of the vulgar. And therefore the ill and unfit choice of words wonderfully obstructs the understanding. Nor do the definitions or explanations, wherewith in some things learned men are wont to guard and defend themselves, by any means set the manner right. But words plainly force and overrule the understanding, and throw all into confusion, and lead men away into numberless empty controversies and idle fancies.

XLIV. Lastly, there are Idols which have immigrated into men's minds from the various dogmas of philosophies and also from wrong laws of demonstration. These I call Idols of the Theatre, because in my judgment all the received systems are but so many stage-plays, representing worlds of their own creation after an unreal and scenic fashion. . . . (*Novum Organum*, 19-21)

In expanding upon each of the idols, he identifies that most directly associated with language as that which is most difficult to overcome:

LIX. But the Idols of the Market-place are the most troublesome of all, idols which have crept into the understanding through the alliances of words and names. For men believe that their reason governs words, but it is also true that words react on the understanding, and this it is that has rendered philosophy and the sciences sophistical and inactive. Now words, being commonly framed and applied according to the capacity of the vulgar, follow those lines of division which are most obvious to the vulgar understanding. And whenever an understanding of greater acuteness or more diligent observation would alter those lines to suit the true division of nature, words stand in the way and resist the change. Whence it comes to pass that the high and formal discussions of learned men end oftentimes in disputes about words and names, with which (according to the use and wisdom of the mathematicians) it would be more prudent to begin, and so by means of definitions reduce them to order. Yet even definitions cannot cure this evil in dealing with natural and material things; since the definitions themselves consist of words, and those words beget others, so that it is necessary to recur to individual instances, and those in due series and order. . . .

LX. The Idols imposed by words on the understanding are of two kinds. They are either names of things which do not exist (for as there are things left unnamed through lack of observation, so likewise are there names which result from fantastic suppositions and to which nothing in reality corresponds), or they are names of things which exist, but yet confused and ill-defined and hastily or irregularly derived from realities. . . . (*Novum Organum*, 31-32)

His positive method for inquiry included specific procedures of representation, including making lists of all possible causes and eliminating them. His procedures led him to specific recommendations for writing natural histories laid out in his *Historia Naturalis*. Further, his vision of the *New Atlantis*, the structure of Salomon's house, which produces knowledge of nature for the benefit of the community, identified specific communicative or symbolic practices to be carried out by classes of knowledge workers who work along with those devoted to experimental practices:

> For the several employments and offices of our fellows, we have twelve that sail into foreign countries, under the names of other nations (for our own we conceal), who bring us the books and abstracts and patterns of experiments of all other parts. These we call Merchants of Light.
>
> We have three that collect the experiments which are in all books. These we call Depradators.
>
> [three collectors of experiments and practices, called mystery-men; three that try new experiments, called "Pioneers or Miners."]
>
> We have three that draw the experiments of the former four into titles and tables, to give the better light for the drawing of observations, and axioms out of them. These we call compilers.
>
> [three who find practical application of experiments, called Dowry-men; three who direct new experiments of a higher light, called lamps; three who carry out these new experiments, called Inoculators]
>
> Lastly, we have three that raise the former discoveries by experiments into greater observations, axioms, and aphorisms. These we call Interpreters of Nature. . . .
>
> . . . And this we do also: we have consultations, which of the inventions and experiences, which we have discovered shall be published, and which not; and take all an oath of secrecy for the concealing of those which we think fit to keep secret. (*New Atlantis* 488-9).

Two of Bacon's themes continued through the eighteenth century: concern for the symbolic practices of natural philosophy, and the placement of natural philosophy within the entire range of human symbolic practices. His third concern for communication of the practical arts largely fell by the wayside in the Royal Society's failure to enlist artisans, a failure that was not remedied until the professionalization of engineering in the nineteenth century, which then gave rise to reflective concern for technical writing in this century.

The New Rhetoric of Seventeenth Century Science

The concern for philosophic language led to a rhetoric of science that denied rhetoricity while proclaiming constant vigilance to self-cleansing. The general strategy, following Bacon, was to expunge philosophic language of the features of language that were believed to mislead, leaving a pure philosophic language. Thus we get the famous strictures of the Royal Society, as expressed by Sprat in his history.

> There is one more thing about which the Society has been most sollicitous, and that is, the manner of their Discourse: which unless

they had been very watchful to keep in due temper, the whole spirit and vigour of their Design had soon been eaten out by the luxury and redundance of speech. . . .

[The ornaments of speaking] were at first, no doubt, an admirable Instrument in the hands of Wise Men, when they were onely employ'd to describe goodness, Honesty, Obedience in larger, fairer, and more moving Images, to represent Truth cloth'd with Bodies, and to bring Knowledg back again to our very senses, from whence it was first deriv'd to our understandings. But now they are generally chang'd to worse uses. They make the fancy disgust the best things, if they come sound and unadorn'd; they are in open defiance against Reason, professing not to hold much correspondence with that but with its Slaves, the Passions; they give the mind a motion too changeable and bewitching to consist of right practice. Who can behold without indignation how many mists and uncertainties these specious Tropes and Figures have brought on our Knowledg? How many rewards which are due to more profitable and difficult Arts have been still snatch'd away by the easie vanity of fine speaking? . . . It will suffice my present purpose to point out what has been done by the Royal Society towards correcting of its excesses in Natural Philosophy, to which it is, of all others a most profest enemy.

They have therefore been most rigorous in putting in execution the only Remedy that can be found for this extravagance: and that has been a constant Resolution to reject all the amplifications, digressions, and swellings of style, to return back to the primitive purity and shortness when men deliver'd so many things almost in an equal number of words. They have exacted from all their members a close, naked, natural way of speaking; positive expressions; clear sense; a native easiness; bringing all things as near the Mathematical plainness as they can; and preferring the language of Artizans, Countrymen, and Merchants, before that of Wits, or Scholars.

The prescriptions for style were accompanied by attempts to develop a philosophic vocabulary that referred only to objects that existed along the proper natural divisions and relations, while eliminating those words that described phantasms. The most famous of these projects was John Wilkins' *An Essay Towards a Real Character and a Philosophical Language.*

Although these attempts to develop a specialized language for natural philosophy consistently identified themselves as specifically nonrhetorical, nonetheless the actual communicative practices did not turn into Swift's parody in *Gulliver's Travels* of the Grand Academy of Lagado where savants suggested eliminating words altogether in favor of pointing to objects which we would carry about with us. Rather, the philosophic experimenters in the Royal Academy developed highly skillful ways of representing events so as to compel assent about their facticity and about the empirical grounding of generalizations constructed upon the textually represented fact. The rhetorical problems perceived by Boyle, Newton, and the contributors to the *Philosophic Transactions of the Royal Society* laid the groundwork for the modern rhetorical practices of the sciences (see Bazerman *Shaping*; Shapin and Schaffer; Dear). Thus while explicitly distancing themselves from the rhetorical tradition, the scientists of the latter seventeenth and eighteenth centuries established new canons and procedures of argument.

While most of the founders of modern science followed a rhetorical strategy of appearing to eschew rhetoric and rise above the weakness of the language, others recognized that they necessarily had to work with the frail medium of language and other human, created representations of realities they had no unmediated access to. All empirical knowledge was seen by them as necessarily only probable, and therefore open to argument (see Shapiro; Hacking). Christian Huygens' reflection on arguing from induction from his *Treatise on Light* (1690) is a typical expression of the concern about probable argument in empirical science:

> There will be seen in [this Treatise] demonstrations of those kinds which do not produce as great a certitude as those of Geometry, and even differ much therefrom, since whereas Geometers prove their propositions by fixed and incontestable Principles, here the Principles are verified by the conclusions to be drawn from them; the nature of these things not allowing of this being done otherwise. It is always possible to attain thereby to a degree of probability which very often is scarcely less than complete proof. To wit, when things have been demonstrated by the Principles that have been assumed correspond perfectly to the phenomena which experiment has brought under observation; especially when there are a great number of them, and further, principally, when one can imagine and foresee new phenomena which ought to follow from the hypotheses which one employs, and when one finds that therein the facts correspond to our prevision. But if all these proofs of probability are met with in that which I propose to discuss, as it seems to me they are, this ought to be strong confirmation of the success of my inquiry; and it must be ill if the facts are not pretty much as I represent them.

And philosophers like Hobbes, Locke, Hume and Berkeley further called into question our abilities to formulate knowledge with certainty, given the idiosyncrasy of our experiences and associations by which we turned sense impressions into articulated concepts; these inquiries opened up issues of language and knowledge that were to puzzle a number of eighteenth century rhetorical thinkers—most notably Joseph Priestley and Adam Smith.

Joseph Priestley and Adam Smith

Both Priestley and Smith saw the problem of knowledge formulation not only as a problem of individual sense experience and cognition, but also as a problem of public communication and cooperation—both in the formulation of knowledge and its use throughout society. In this they followed on Bacon's concerns for seeing the production of natural philosophic knowledge within the framework of the entire life of society. Hobbes viewed natural philosophic discourse as continuous with society, so much so that it was heir to all the uncertainties of political rhetoric, which allowed him to treat Aristotelean rhetoric as universal (See Shapin and Schaffer). Hobbes himself wrote the first English translation of Aristotle's *Rhetoric*, modifying it only by some excisions and a very few elaborations.

Adam Smith, from his earliest *Lectures on Rhetoric and Belles Lettres* (first delivered in 1748), was concerned about the communicative practices that held society together, the way scientific production occurred within society and was transmitted throughout society, and the rhetorical means by which knowledge could be produced and could gain public credibility so as to inform policy choices. His rhetoric added to the traditional categories of rhetoric a new category of didactic rhetoric aimed at producing conviction rather than simple persuasion. This didactic discourse "proposes to put before us the arguments on both sides of the question in their true light, giving each its proper degree of influence, and has in its view to perswade us no farther than the arguments themselves appear convincing." (Lecture 12, p. 63). Thus true persuasion was a measured cooperative endeavor rather than the result of agonistic struggle. After a discussion of the various techniques and methods of didactic discourse, however, Smith commented,

> The Didacticall method tho undoubtedly the best in all matters of Science, is hardly ever applicable to Rhetoricall discourses. The people, to which they are ordinarily directed, have no pleasure in these abstruse deductions; their interest, and their practicability and honourableness of the thing recommended is what alone will sway with them. . . . (Lecture 24, p. 146)

Smith continued his reflections upon the special discourses of knowledge production in his second work, *The History of Astronomy*. This essay proposes a relativist method of natural philosophic investigation, which considers knowledge production as creating chains of associations among the various experiences we have recorded—thus placing emphasis on coherence of philosophic accounts to relieve the anxieties raised among humans by the multiplicity of apparently incoherent experiences.

> Philosophy is the science of the connecting principles of nature. Nature, after the largest experience that common observation can acquire, seems to abound with events which appear solitary and incoherent with all that go before them, which therefore distuyrb the easy movement of the imagination; which makes its ideas succeed each other, if one may say so, by irregular starts and sallies; and which thus tend, in some measure, to introduce those confusions and distractions we formerly mentioned. Philosophy, by representing the invisible chains which bind together all these disjointed objects,

endeavours to introduce order into this chaos of jarring and discordant appearances, to allay this tumult of the imagination, and to restore it, when it surveys the great revolutions of the universe, to that tone of tranquillity and composure, which is most agreeable in itself, and most suitable to its nature. Philosophy, therefore, may be regarded as one of those arts which address themselves to the imagination. (*Essays on Philosophic Subjects*, 45-46)

He admired the monumental coherence of Newton's writings, which makes the universe appear indeed harmonious in its nature, even though he knew that Newton's writing was only a coherently plausible story.

In his later work Smith attended to the personal internal discourse that produces moral knowledge, and in his most famous work, *An Inquiry into the Wealth of Nations*, he built a system of political economy based on the symbolic communication of money, justifying it in publicly persuasive terms to urge its adoption as policy, and laid the groundwork for a technical discourse of economics to support the policy he espoused.

Likewise, Priestley, despite philosophic skepticism and associationist psychology, established discourses of knowledge production and transmission as being of a special character, needing particular practices for their success—practices developed with both cognitive and social considerations in mind. In *A Course of Lectures on Oratory and Criticism*, first delivered in 1762 when he was twenty-nine, Priestley considered the particular rhetorical character of many different kinds discourses that extended beyond those traditionally considered rhetorical, including texts of philosophy, mechanics, geometry, natural philosophy, natural history, political history, geography, biography, and fiction and romance. (See especially lectures 6 through 10).

Priestley's own books in various areas of knowledge self-consciously reflected on their own rhetorical methods, which were frequently original to serve special purposes of advancing knowledge within the community. His books of natural philosophy in particular were self-consciously crafted to establish cooperative communal relationships and build the community of natural philosophy, rather than to structure public struggles as agonistic persuasion. Especially in his first scientific work, *The History and Present State of Electricity*, he gave an explicit description and rationale for the rhetorical practice of the book, which he encouraged others to follow. He was particularly concerned with the full and detailed representation of all empirical experiences, the methods and reasoning processes by which they were produced, and the synthetic summary of work. Such synthesis aimed to allow all inquirers full access to all empirical experiences, theories, apparatuses and methods side by side to make the practices and experiences of the field democratically open to novices. In addition to recommendations for histories of accounts of experiences (what we now call reviews of literature), codifications of findings, syntheses of theories, accounts of procedures and descriptions of apparatus, he offered specific reflections about how experiments should be written up as personal paths of reasoning, trial, and discovery, with the intent of demystifying the research process.

To make this account [of experiments] the more useful to such persons as may be willing to enter into philosophical investigations, I shall not fail to report the real views with which every experiment was made, false and imperfect as they often were . . . And Though an account of experiments drawn up on this plan be less calculated to do an author honour as a philosopher; it will, probably, contribute more to make other persons philosophers, which is a thing of more consequence to the public.

Many modest and ingenious persons may be engaged to attempt philosophical investigations, when they see that it requires no more sagacity to find new truths, than they themselves are masters of; and when they see that many discoveries have been made by mere accident, which may prove as favorable to them as others. Whereas it is great discouragement to young and enterprising geniuses, to see philosophers proposing that first, which they themselves attained to last; first laying down the propositions which were the result of all their experiments, and then relating the facts, as if every thing had been done to verify a true preconceived theory.

This synthetic method is, certainly, the most expeditious way of making a person understand a branch of science, but the analytic method, in which discoveries were actually made, is most favorable to the progress of knowledge. (*The History and Present State of Electricity* II, 165-166)

Priestley and Smith's broad visions of complex social worlds mediated by language thus included specialized communities of knowledge producers and transmitters, who would be aided by explicit reflections on and guidelines for their discourse. Moreover, their complex enlightenment rhetorics recognized Belles Lettres as a new vehicle of public discourse and attended to the style, taste, and personae constructed in contemporary literature. But their vision of complex differentiated discourses including specialized esoteric and popular modes of communication was not transmitted to nineteenth century America to inform education for the new country.[3]

Blair, Campbell, Whately and the Emergence of Nineteenth Century Rhetoric

As has been frequently told, Hugh Blair, George Campbell and Richard Whately were the vehicles for the transmission of the rhetorical tradition to North America (see, for example, Johnson). These three absorbed something of the communicative psychology of Priestley and Smith, but they reduced into a reified and uniform psychology of defined faculties a more capacious

---

[3] For further examination of the rhetorical visions of Priestley and Smith, see Bazerman, "How Natural Philosophers Can Cooperate," and "Money Talks."

approach that tried to gain principled understanding of how the variety of human experience helped form the particulars of each person's skills, perceptions, interpersonal relations, and associative landscapes. This reduction undermined Priestley's and Smith's concerns for the historical and sociological particulars surrounding communicative acts, with the attendant concerns for the structure of communities that are the sites of various forms of rhetoric. Thus a sociologically differentiated rhetoric returned to a universal rhetoric based on a universalized psychology.

Blair's *Lectures on Rhetoric and Belles Lettres* (first delivered in 1760) and Campbell's *The Philosophy of Rhetoric* (1776) did retain strong interest in Belles Lettres as a new realm of public discourse and a repository of taste that informed individual development. Moreover, Blair's work showed substantial interest in history (see lectures 35 and 36) and a lesser concern for philosophical writing (the opening of Lecture 37), but Whately's *Elements of Rhetoric* (1828) fully renarrowed the domain of rhetoric to public oratory and the pulpit. Only Whately, the last of this triad and the most purely clerical, gave a principled reason for the narrowed concerns, returning to the classical position that specialized forms of knowledge can provide evidence for rhetorical arguments, but are not themselves fields of rhetoric. For Blair and Campbell, the narrowing seemed more a reflection of narrower personal interests, neither having the broad social vision or interests that motivated Enlightenment reformers like Locke, Hume, Priestley, or Smith.

The modern historian of rhetoric, Wilbur Samuel Howell, laments the loss of the eighteenth century rhetoricians' interest in a wider range of discourse and how those specialized practices ought to influence popular discourse: "Twentieth century rhetoric . . . has greatly suffered as a result." Perhaps as we enter the information age the challenge of Writing Across the Curriculum and research in Writing in the Disciplines will reopen questions first seriously addressed by eighteenth century rhetoricians confronting their entry into an age of science. But now the questions must encompass a greatly enlarged science and many other forms of specialized knowledge and professional work emerging since 1800 and institutionalized in the modern university and system of the professions. Moreover, at the end of the twentieth century, we must also confront the new media of communications that are reorganizing knowledge production, dissemination, and application. We should not again put these questions of specialized discourse aside. The exigency is great.

Works Cited

Abbott, Don Paul. "Rhetoric and Writing in Renaissance Europe and England." *A Short History of Writing Instruction*. Ed. James J. Murphy. Davis, CA: Hermagoras, 1990. 95-120.

Aristotle. *On Rhetoric: A Theory of Civic Discourse*. Tr. George A. Kennedy. New York: Oxford University Press, 1991.

Bacon, Francis. *Essays, Advancement of Learning, New Atlantis and other Pieces*. R. F. Jones, ed. New York: Odyssey Press, 1937.

Bacon, Francis. *Novum Organum*. New York. P. F. Collier & Son, 1902.

Barnes, Jonathan. "Is Rhetoric an Art?" *DARG Newsletter* 2 (1986): 2-22.

Bazerman, Charles. "How Natural Philosophers can Cooperate: The Literary Technology of Coordinated Investigation in Joseph Priestley's *History and Present State of Electricity.*" *Textual Dynamics of the Professions*. Ed. Bazerman and Paradis. Madison: University of Wisconsin Press, 1991.

Bazerman, Charles. "Money Talks: The Rhetorical Project of the Wealth of Nations." *Economics and Language*. Ed. W. Henderson, T. Dudley Evans and R. Backhouse. London: Routledge, 1993.

Bazerman, Charles. *Shaping Written Knowledge*. Madison: University of Wisconsin Press, 1988.

Blair, Hugh. *Lectures on Rhetoric and Belles Lettres*. 2 Vols. Carbondale: Southern Illinois University Press, 1965.

Bolgar, Ray R. *The Classical Heritage and Its Beneficiaries*. Cambridge: Cambridge University Press, 1963.

Campbell, George. *The Philosophy of Rhetoric*. Carbondale: Southern Illinois University Press, 1963.

Cicero. *Cicero on Oratory and Orators*. Tr. J. S. Watson. Carbondale: Southern Illinois University Press, 1970.

Dear, Peter. "Totius in Verba: Rhetoric and Authority in the Early Royal Society." *Isis* 76 (1985): 145-61.

Eisenstein, Elizabeth L. *The Printing Press as an Agent of Change*. 2 vols. Cambridge: Cambridge University Press, 1979.

Führmann, Manfred. *Das Systematische*. Gottingen: Vandernhoeck, 1960.

Goldstein, Thomas. *Dawn of Modern Science*. Boston: Houghton, 1980

Gorgias. *The Older Sophists*. Ed. Rosamond Kent Sprague. Columbia: University of South Carolina Press, 1972.

Grafton, Anthony, and Lisa Jardine. *From Humanism to the Humanities*. London: Duckworth, 1986.

Hacking, Ian. *The Emergence of Probability*. Cambridge: Cambridge University Press, 1975.

Hobbes, Thomas. *Briefe of the Arte of Rhetorique*. London, 1637.

Howell, Wilbur Samuel. *Eighteenth-Century British Logic and Rhetoric*. Princeton: Princeton University Press, 1971.

Huygens, Christian. *Treatise on Light*. Trans. Silvanus Thompson. Chicago: University of Chicago Press. 1945.

Johnson, Nan. *Nineteenth-Century Rhetoric in North America*. Carbondale: Southern Illinois University Press, 1991.

Johnstone, Christopher Lyle. "An Aristotelian Trilogy: Rhetoric, Politics, and the Search for Moral Truth." *Philosophy and Rhetoric* 13 (1980): 1-24.

Kristeller, Paul O. *Renaissance Thought and Its Sources*. New York: Columbia University Press, 1979.

Kristeller, Paul O. "The Impact of Early Italian Humanism on Thought and Learning." *Developments in the Early Renaissance*. Albany, NY: State University of New York Press, 1972. 120-57.

Leff, Michael C. "The Material of the Art in the Latin Handbooks of the Fourth Century A.D." *Rhetoric Revalued*. Ed. Brian Vickers. Binghamton, NY: Center for Medieval and Early Renaissance Studies, 1982. 71-78.

Leff, Michael C. "The Topics of Argumentative Invention in Latin Rhetorical Theory from Cicero to Boethius." *Rhetorica* 1 (1983): 23-44.

Miller, Carolyn. "Aristotle's 'Special Topics' in Rhetorical Practice and Pedagogy." *Rhetoric Society Quarterly* 17 (1987): 61-70.

Moss, Jean Dietz. *Novelties in the Heavens: Rhetoric and Science in the Copernican Controversy*. Chicago : University of Chicago Press, 1993.

Murphy, James J. *Rhetoric in the Middle Ages*. Berkeley: University of California Press, 1974.

Ong, Walter. *Rhetoric, Romance, and Technology*. Ithica: Cornell University Press, 1971.

Plato. *Gorgias*. Tr. W. R. M. Lamb. Loeb Classical Library. London: Heinemann, 1932.

Priestley, Joseph. *A Course of Lectures on Oratory and Criticism*. London, 1777.

Priestley, Joseph. *The History and Present State of Electricity*. 2 vols. London, 1767.

Quintillian. *Institutio Oratoria*. 4 vols. Tr. H. E. Butler. Cambridge, MA: Harvard University Press, 1920.

Roochnick, David. *The Tragedy of Reason: Toward a Platonic Conception of Logos*. New York: Routledge, 1990.

Roochnick, David. "Is Rhetoric an Art?" *Philosophy and Rhetoric* (forthcoming).

Rossi, Paolo. *Philosophy, Technology, and the Arts in the Early Modern Era*. New York: Harper, 1970.

Shapin, Steven and Simon Schaffer. *The Leviathan and the Air-Pump: Hobbes, Boyle, and the Experimental Life*. Princeton: Princeton University Press, 1985.

Shapiro, Barbara. *Probability and Certainty in Seventeenth-Century England*. Princeton: Princeton University Press, 1983.

Shelby, Lon R. "The 'Secret' of Medieval Masons." *On Pre-Modern Technology and Science*. Ed. Bert S. Hall and Delno C. West. Malibu: Undena, 1976. 201-19.

Slawinski, Maurice. "Rhetoric and Science/Rhetoric of Science/Rhetoric As Science." *Science, Culture, and Popular Belief in Renaissance Europe*. Ed. Stephen Pumfrey, Paolo L. Rossi, and Maurice Slawinski. Manchester, UK: Manchester University Press, 1991. 71-99.

Smith, Adam. *An Inquiry into the Nature and Causes of the Wealth of Nations*. Oxford: Clarendon, 1976.

Smith, Adam. *Essays on Philosophical Subjects*. Oxford: Clarendon, 1980.

Smith, Adam. *Lectures on Rhetoric and Belles Lettres*. Oxford: Clarendon, 1983.

Sprat, Thomas. *History of the Royal Society*. London, 1667.

Swift, Jonathan. *Gulliver's Travels*. London, 1726.

Vickers, Brian. *In Defense of Rhetoric*. Oxford: Oxford University Press, 1988.

Vickers, Brian. "On the Practicalities of Renaissance Rhetoric." *Rhetoric Revalued*. Ed. Brian Vickers. Binghamton, NY: Center for Medieval and Early Renaissance Studies, 1982. 133-42.

Whately, Richard. *Elements of Rhetoric*. Carbondale: Southern Illinois University Press, 1963.

Wilkins, John. *An Essay Toward a Real Character and a Philosophical Language*. London, 1688.

Section 1:
Twentieth Century Beginnings

American Origins of the Writing-across-the-Curriculum Movement

by David R. Russell

Writing has been an issue in American secondary and higher education since written papers and examinations came into wide use in the 1870s, eventually driving out formal recitation and oral examination.[1] Significantly, that shift coincided with the rise of academic disciplines and the reorganization of secondary and higher education by disciplines, each with its own text-based discourse conventions to carry on its professional work and select, evaluate, and credential students. But from the first "literacy crisis," in the 1870s—precipitated by the new discipline-specific writing requirements and the entry of students from previously excluded groups into the nascent mass education system—the academic disciplines have taken little direct interest in writing, either by consciously investigating their own conventions of scholarly writing or by teaching their students those conventions in a deliberate, systematic way—despite a century-long tradition of complaints by faculty members and other professionals about the poor writing of students (Daniels; Greenbaum). Given the traditional separation of writing instruction from postelementary pedagogy in the American mass education system, the birth and unprecedented growth of the writing-across-the-curriculum movement in the last decade and a half is surprising. But the WAC movement has deep, though rarely exposed, roots in the recurring debates over approaches to writing and to pedagogy—especially in the American tradition of progressive education.

From its birth in the late nineteenth century, progressive education has wrestled with the conflict within industrial society between pressure to increase specialization of knowledge and of professional work (upholding disciplinary standards) and pressure to integrate more fully an ever-widening number of citizens into intellectually meaningful activity within mass society (promoting social equity). Language, particularly the written language that organized and facilitated the differentiation and rationalization of industrial society, lay at the very center of the conflict between disciplinary standards

---

Reprinted from *Writing, Teaching and Learning Across the Curriculum*. New York: MLA, 1992. Reprinted with permission.

[1] This account draws heavily on my *Writing in the Academic Disciplines, 1870-1990: A Curricular History*, especially chapters 2 and 9.

and social equity, exclusion and access. But the role written knowledge plays in preparing students for (or excluding them from) disciplinary communities was rarely addressed systematically, either by the disciplines and the professional interests they represented or by progressive education, which itself became professionalized in education departments and public school bureaucracies. Rhetoric departments died out, writing instruction was marginalized, and the issues of student writing remained largely submerged, reappearing only when the conflicts between disciplinary standards and social equity, exclusion and access, became most visible—usually when previously excluded groups pressed for entry into higher education and thus into professional roles.

Faculty members and administrators have long agreed that every teacher should teach writing (a cliché as old as mass education), but since the turn of the century, the American education system has placed the responsibility for teaching writing outside the disciplines, including, to a large extent, the discipline of "English" or literary study (Berlin 32-57; Stewart; Piché). Writing came to be seen not in broad rhetorical terms, as a central function of the emerging disciplines, but in two reductive (and conflicting) ways, neither of which engaged the intellectual activity of disciplines. Writing was thought of, on the one hand, as a set of elementary transcription skills unrelated to disciplinary activity ("talking with the pen instead of the tongue," as the 1892 Harvard Committee on Composition and Rhetoric put it) or, on the other hand, as a belletristic art, the product of genius or inspiration rather than of the mundane social and professional activity of the disciplines (Russell, "Romantics"). In the great middle lay most of the writing done by students and professionals, academic or "real-world." But this writing was largely dismissed by the sciences, with their positivist orientation, and by the humanities, with their belletristic orientation, as an arhetorical, unproblematic recording of thought or speech, unworthy of serious intellectual attention, beneath systematic consideration in the inquiry and teaching of the disciplines.

Since the 1870s, writing instruction in America has largely been separate from other instruction and has been relegated to lower levels: to first-year composition courses taught primarily by junior, temporary, or graduate student instructors; to one relatively small component of the secondary English curriculum (composition units); or even to the primary schools. Instead of being an integral part of teaching and learning, writing instruction has gradually been confined to the margins of postelementary mass education, an adjunct to the "real" work of the disciplines and thus of secondary and higher education.[2] And in the disciplines, the organizing units of post-elementary education, writing was thus able to remain largely transparent,

---

[2] On the marginalization of composition in higher education, see, for example, Berlin 31 and Stewart. On composition in secondary schools, see Applebee, *Tradition* 32-34 and Piché.

unexamined. The discursive practices of each academic field are so embedded in the texture of its disciplinary activity that they have not, until very recently, become an object of study or teaching within the disciplines. The American Historical Association, for example, has rarely devoted its attention to the question of how students learn to write (or write to learn) history, apart from occasional mentions in its reports on secondary instruction (e.g., Beard 227). Even the MLA, the professional association representing scholarship in written texts and the discipline most often considered responsible for teaching composition, disbanded its pedagogical section—the section devoted to writing instruction—as early as 1903 and rarely concerned itself with questions of writing instruction (much less of writing instruction in other disciplines) until the 1960s (Stewart; Applebee, *Tradition* 198-204).

Several essays in this volume suggest reasons for this lack of rhetorical self-consciousness within disciplines. As Charles Bazerman says, following Bruno Latour, the "overt teachings of a discipline . . . may ignore or even suppress knowledge of the contexts and forces in which the field operates and that shape the knowledge of the discipline." And as Judith A. Langer points out, even when faculty members conceive of their discipline's knowledge as a dynamic social and rhetorical process, they may continue to teach as if that knowledge were static and arhetorical. This transparency of writing has created a central contradiction in the American mass education system: its organizing principle—disciplinary specialization—recognizes no integral role for writing, and in many ways the disciplines have resisted the sharing of responsibility for writing instruction; yet schools and colleges are expected to teach students to write in ways sanctioned by the disciplines.

United States mass education has found ways of living with this contradiction. The 1870s literacy crisis led to the creation of that characteristically American institution, general composition courses, which effectively relieved faculty members outside of English and rhetoric departments of any direct responsibility for teaching writing (Douglas). Around the turn of the century, with yet another influx of students from previously excluded groups, institution-wide speaking and writing requirements were dropped, relieving teachers of the obligation to assign and evaluate extended writing (Wozniack). By the 1940s, American secondary and higher education had almost entirely given up externally graded written examinations, its last institutionally mandated site for writing in the disciplines, in favor of "new type" or "objective" tests (Kandel). As a result, the disciplines were no longer responsible for communally arriving at standards for student writing; the assigning and evaluating of even brief writing was almost entirely at the discretion of individual faculty members, who had few incentives from their institutions or from their disciplines to pursue these tasks.

But even before institution-wide writing requirements and external essay examinations faded, the mass education system had settled into a restrictive conception of school writing that allowed disciplines to live comfortably with the contradiction of writing as the responsibility of every discipline and of no discipline. Instead of viewing writing as a complex and continuously developing response to a specialized, text-based, discourse community, highly embedded in the differentiated practices of that community, educators came to see it as a set of generalizable, mechanical "skills" independent of disciplinary knowledge, learned once and for all at an early age. Writing skills could be taught separately from content, as a mere adjunct or service to a curriculum (in freshman composition, for example) or to a single course (in a research paper, for example). And because secondary and higher education is organized around specialized content, the generalized skills came to be subordinate. Moreover, this narrow conception of writing and learning fit well with the industrial model American schools adopted. Progress could be measured in the number of errors reduced per dollar invested, and students could be tracked and taught according to their "deficiencies." Thus, writing instruction past the elementary school was viewed as mere remediation of deficiencies in skill rather than as a means of fostering a continuously developing intellectual and social attainment intimately tied to disciplinary learning (Dixon 1-4; Rose; Piché; Russell, "Cooperation").

In the light of these narrow views of writing and learning, it is not surprising that all but a handful of the many cross-curricular efforts to improve student writing launched over the last hundred years merely asked general faculty members to correct students' mechanical and grammatical errors or, more commonly, to refer "deficient" students to a "remedial" program run by composition instructors.[3] Nor is it surprising that most efforts to improve student learning in the disciplines had little to say about the role that writing might play in pedagogy. The skills model of writing offered no intellectually interesting reason to connect the process of learning to write with one's students' (or one's own) intellectual or professional development—with the activities of a discipline, in other words.

Progressive Education and Its Discrediting

The few attempts progressive educators made to introduce a developmental model for writing instruction across the curriculum are important, however, for they form the backdrop of the current WAC movement. From the birth of progressive education, in the 1890s, some curricular reformers in that tradition have seen writing and speaking in developmental terms—a "growth," as Dewey's early colleague Fred Newton Scott put it (464)—and railed against the "remedial racket" (Porter G. Perrin's term [382]). Dewey himself considered language central to learning, a means of organizing experience in progressively more sophisticated and meaningful ways. Unlike "child-centered" progressives, such as Hughes Mearns, Dewey argued that

---

[3] At the secondary level, these were called "hospitals" or, later, "labs" (both terms reflect the medical model on which remediation is based). At the college level, the most influential program was Harvard's Committee on the Use of English by Students (1915-50), which policed student writing with the aid of faculty members in the disciplines.

students' use of language must lead systematically from the experience of the individual to the collective experience of the culture as represented by the organized disciplines. Education must begin with the student's experience, Dewey argued, but it cannot end there, as many of his child-centered followers assumed. "The next step," Dewey wrote in his most impassioned attack on the excesses of his followers, "is the progressive development of what is already experienced into a fuller and richer and also more organized form, a form that gradually approximates that in which subject matter is presented to the skilled, mature person" (148). New experience must be continually and consciously related to old experience—the individual's personal history, certainly, but also the culture's experience preserved in the organized knowledge of the disciplines. Language plays a central role in this "continuous spiral" of progressively wider and "thicker" engagement with the culture (53). "There must be some advance made in conscious articulation of facts and ideas," Dewey insisted, for there to be "connectedness in growth" (50). Thus curriculum and instruction—particularly beyond elementary school—must consciously and carefully weave together the interests of the learner with the structures and activities of the disciplines through increasingly more sophisticated uses of language, balancing in a range of discourse the personal and private experience of the student and the public and impersonal knowledge of the community (or, in the modern world, communities of disciplinary specialists). In this view, progressive education must not be "child-centered" but rather, to borrow James Britton's coinage, "adult- and child-centered," engaging the world of the learner with the world of the discipline the teacher represents (re-presents) ("English Teaching" 204-05).

However, neither the disciplines, on the one hand, nor progressive education, on the other hand, explored in any systematic way the role of language in disciplinary learning to achieve such a balance. The disciplines, at the most powerful and influential levels of their activity (in research universities and professional organizations), concerned themselves primarily with specialized, high-level teaching and research, turning their attention to secondary education and introductory courses only in times of crisis.[4] Progressive reformers in education departments, isolated in their own embattled discipline, championed child-centered teaching and radical curricular change in order to overcome the dominance of the disciplines, not to foster ongoing dialogue with them (Cremin 183-85; for recent developments, see Clifford and Guthrie). Largely ignoring Dewey's insistence on the importance of disciplinary knowledge, progressive reformers attempted to transcend disciplinary traditions through "correlation" of subject matter in core courses organized around student experiences instead of around "fixed-in-advance"

---

[4] Academia's reaction to Sputnik is only the most obvious instance. See, for example, the history of university involvement with secondary physics and chemistry courses (Hurd, *New Directions 80-86*).

knowledge (Weeks). Students' writing would grow out of their experience and escape the confines of teacher-made assignments requiring the usual academic conventions. For the most radical of the child-centered progressives, unfettered freedom of expression became an educational end in itself (a doctrine Dewey called "really stupid" [Dewey et al. 37]). Predictably, administrators, parents, and disciplines (including English) rejected "correlation" as unworkable, chaotic, or downright subversive (this despite many successes) (Applebee, *Tradition* 122-23, 144-46; Aikin; Wright; Smith, Tyler, and the Evaluation Staff). Correlation threatened to overthrow the disciplinary structure that organized modern education (and modern knowledge) rather than mediate between that structure and the experience of students.

In the years following World War II, progressive education was thoroughly discredited in the public eye, and experiments in cross-curricular writing instruction returned to the familiar skills model, this time with a new emphasis on practical "communications." At hundreds of institutions, English and speech departments cooperated to train the newest influx of previously excluded students—returning GIs—in the "four skills," listening, reading, speaking, and writing. But the "communications movement," as it was called, rarely involved other departments; indeed, the communications approach offered no intellectually satisfying reason for departments to take an active role in language instruction, because it treated writing as a generalizable skill, unrelated to the specialized intellectual and professional activities of the disciplines (Berlin 92-107; Applebee, *Tradition* 156-60).

However, a handful of institutions actively involved faculty members in the disciplines, most notably the University of California at Berkeley in its Prose Improvement Committee (1947-64). This university-wide committee supervised the training of TAs from about a dozen disciplines in assessing and tutoring the writing assigned in large lecture courses. The committee explicitly rejected the skills model and adopted instead a specifically developmental perspective, which saw writing as central to disciplinary teaching and learning (Russell, "Writing across the Curriculum"). In the committee's final report before it disbanded (for lack of departments willing to use its services), the chair, Ralph Rader, wrote:

> When student writing is deficient, then, it is deficient . . . in ways having directly to do with the student's real control of the subject matter of his discipline and not in ways having to do with the special disciplines of English or Speech departments. To raise the level of student writing . . . would be in effect to raise the student's level of intellectual attainment in the subject matter itself. To say this is to indicate . . . the reason for the lack of response to the committee program: faculty are by and large satisfied with the intellectual attainment of their students. The Committee is suggesting, then . . . that the faculty should not be so easily satisfied. (5)

Though such interdisciplinary efforts were rare, the communications movement did spur renewed interest in composition and rhetoric within

English departments and, more important, gave rise to a professional association for writing teachers, the Conference on College Composition and Communication. CCCC provided a forum for discussion and research of issues outside the purview of the MLA (as then organized) and became the seedbed for the WAC movement and research into writing in the disciplines (Bird).

The 1960s: Language and Equity

Though the WAC movement did not appear in the United States until the mid-1970s, the fundamental institutional, social, and theoretical shifts that gave rise to the movement took shape in the 1960s. The decade left its greatest legacy for WAC through far-reaching changes in the structure and social role of mass education. Higher education began a vast building project. The number of institutions increased by more than one-fourth in the decade, and the number of students more than doubled, from 3.6 million in 1960 to 8 million in 1970 (Bureau 166). The expanded higher education system trained and credentialed students for new roles or roles that had traditionally required no post-secondary training. Institutional and disciplinary differentiation increased apace and, with it, linguistic differentiation. Academics began speaking of *interdisciplinarity* and sought ways of understanding the discipline-specific "discourse communities" that specialization created (King and Brownell; Sherif and Sherif).

Though the expansion in higher education allowed selective institutions to become even more selective and research-oriented (many such institutions dropped or reduced composition requirements), it also brought a host of students into higher education who had previously been excluded (R. Smith). But there were few institutional structures for dealing with the needs of these new students, including the need for writing instruction to help them enter specialized academic discourse communities. Moreover, the ratio of students to regular faculty members increased dramatically, as the system increasingly relied on graduate students or part-time teachers for instruction in composition and other fields (a result of the vastly expanded research mission of higher education under the influence of corporate and state funding) (Jenks and Riesman). Many faculty members felt that standards were declining, that the new students could not do "college-level" writing (presumably the writing that instructors assigned in the disciplines). In turn, many undergraduates felt alienated from the increasingly specialized teaching staff in the new "multiversities." Faculty members and students did not speak (or write) the same language, and there were few opportunities, formal or informal, to learn specialized discourses.

The social turmoil of the 1960s also highlighted the role of language in education. The campuses exploded in a rash of political upheavals. Racial desegregation forced secondary and higher education to address the problem of teaching long-excluded social groups who did not write the dominant form of English. In this highly charged political environment, educators had to confront volatile issues of language and access, language and learning, that had been largely submerged when higher education placed disciplinary standards over equity and access. The NCTE funded the Task Force on Teaching English to the Disadvantaged in 1964, and the federal government funded programs for teaching reading and writing to inner-city youth (Applebee, *Tradition* 225-28). The late 1960s also witnessed a small revival of child-centered progressive thought, which had been central to discussions of writing and pedagogy in the 1920s and 1930s. Writing teachers in the child-centered progressive tradition, such as Ken Macrorie (*Uptaught*) and Peter Elbow (*Writing without Teachers*), sought to overturn the skills model of composition, just as the broader "open classroom" movement and other late 1960s progressive reform efforts sought to overturn the industrial model of specialized education (see Kohl; Postman and Weingartner). However, progressive reformers in the 1960s, like their predecessors, did not systematically address the issue of writing pedagogy and disciplinarity.

In the wake of Sputnik, federal funds were appropriated for curricular reform along disciplinary lines. Disciplines, including English, again turned their attention to pedagogy and found in the theories of Jerome Bruner a rationale for discipline-centered secondary and undergraduate teaching. Bruner's emphasis on the structure of the disciplines was in one sense a corrective to the progressives' insistence on the experience of the student. But Bruner, no less than Dewey, conceived of education in developmental and transactional terms, though he relied more heavily on Continental theorists, mainly Piaget, rather than on the American progressive tradition. And like Dewey, Bruner emphasized inductive teaching (the "discovery" method), affective and intuitive factors in learning, and, significantly, the role of language in ordering experience (M. J. Smith). Unfortunately, pedagogical reformers in the disciplines focused on Bruner's notion of a "spiral curriculum," which would teach the central concepts of a discipline "in some intellectually honest form to any child at any stage of development," and paid less heed to his insights into the role of language and of inductive teaching in formulating such curricula (Bruner 13). The curriculum materials produced by research-oriented university instructors in the federally funded projects of the late 1950s and early 1960s were concerned primarily with *what* to teach and *when*, rather than *how* to teach it and *why*. The sciences, where funding was most generous, paid little attention to laboratory writing, though in some cases the typical "cookbook" lab manuals were expanded to include more white space for students to write (Hurd, *New Directions* 30). In English, which in 1964 belatedly received federal funding, a national curriculum research effort, Project English, developed traditional skills-oriented composition curricula that lacked an integral relation not only to other disciplines but also to the other two parts of the English disciplinary "tripod": literature and language (though the student-oriented process approach of Wallace W. Douglas at the Northwestern University site and the materials for "disadvantaged" students at the Hunter College site were important exceptions) (Shugrue).

In 1966, just as the federally funded English projects were drawing to a close, the American English profession's confidence in its traditional pedagogy and disciplinary focus was deeply shaken by a month-long encounter with British colleagues at the Dartmouth Seminar, a meeting of some fifty educators jointly sponsored by the MLA, the NCTE, and the young British professional association the National Association for the Teaching of English. As one participant put it, the two delegations found they had "passed each other in mid-Atlantic" (Dixon 72). While American education since World War II had generally been moving away from the progressive tradition toward a pedagogy centered on disciplinary rigor, standard curricula, and standard "objective" evaluation, the British school reformers had been moving in the opposite direction, toward pedagogy centered on informal classroom *talk,* dramatics, and expressive writing. Echoing American progressives of the 1920s and 1930s, the British pedagogy stressed not structured disciplinary knowledge but experience-centered "awareness" leading to personal development, and adherents attacked standard examinations (in their tradition, as in earlier American practice, primarily essay tests) and hierarchical imposition of curriculum by disciplines (Dixon 81-83).

In a working paper, British researcher Harold Rosen raised the central question of what relation informal, personal writing bore to the more formal and impersonal writing required in the disciplines, a question Britain's Schools Council was just beginning to investigate (Dixon 87; Muller 106). But the Dartmouth Seminar did not take up the question of writing in the disciplines (indeed, none of its many working groups was specifically concerned with composition, though several groups dealt with it peripherally) (Muller 98). Discussions of "practical" writing in the disciplines went against the grain of the conference, with its concern for liberating students from "the System, the Machine" (160). A few participants felt that the conference overemphasized individual experience and personal development at the expense of public and disciplinary claims. As Herbert J. Muller wrote in his report on the seminar, "I think John Dewey, now much maligned in America, took a more comprehensive, balanced view of education, with a clearer eye to both practical and intellectual interests, and to individuality as something that can be fully developed only in and through community" (176). But even the conference's critics agreed that Dartmouth had effectively reopened the crucial theoretical and policy issues that the American antiprogressive emphasis had stifled, and several of the conference participants—James Britton, Douglas Barnes, Harold Rosen, and James Moffett, among others—would, in the coming decade, create and shape the WAC movement.

First Stirrings of WAC

During the 1960s, the interest in writing instruction evident in the 1950s communications movement coalesced into a revival of rhetoric as an academic discipline, giving institutions recognized experts who would design and implement curricular reforms in writing instruction (Berlin 120-28). Researchers in composition embraced native theorists such as Bruner and began to discover Continental and British theorists who would be central to WAC initiatives in the 1970s. Composition research acquired a new disciplinary rigor and produced studies of the rhetorical, cognitive, and social dimensions of writing, studies that in the mid-1970s would provide an intellectual basis for WAC (Berlin, ch. 7).

Though composition was still marginalized in English departments and in the wider institutions, the late 1960s stress on increased access invigorated efforts in the progressive tradition to initiate students into academic communities through language instruction. The City University of New York, for example, found it politically necessary to begin its open admissions policy five years ahead of schedule. At CUNY Mina Shaughnessy became interested in writing and access; she eventually rose to a deanship and pioneered the study of "basic writing," a highly influential developmental approach to teaching academic writing to students from previously excluded groups. Shaughnessy's research and curriculum reform brought respectability to an area that had been regarded as intellectually uninteresting and reshaped the remedial writing lab tradition along developmental lines (Lyons).

Across the river at Brooklyn College, Kenneth A. Bruffee began, in 1972, a program of undergraduate peer tutoring for students in all courses, through a writing lab staffed by undergraduates from many disciplines (Bruffee, "Brooklyn"). And across the continent in that same year, at California State at Dominguez Hills, a similar program was initiated to train undergraduate writing tutors assigned to particular courses in the disciplines (Sutton). Research conducted in the 1960s had shown that American college students suffered from "an indifference to ideas, and the irrelevance of their education to their associations and relationships with other students" (Clark and Trow 67, qtd. in Bruffee, "Brooklyn" 449). These peer tutoring programs and the continuing research by Bruffee and others explored the potential for using writing to link students' experience with their learning in a collaborative environment—an important theme of the future WAC movement.

Also in the early 1970s, in a few small private liberal arts colleges with selective admissions (Carleton, Central, Grinnell), writing programs sprang up that encouraged faculty from disciplines outside English to use writing in their courses. In the previous decade, selective colleges had been able to raise admissions standards and reduce or even eliminate composition courses, as the new or expanded institutions with lower standards enrolled the less well prepared students (Wilcox 94-102). But in the late 1960s and early 1970s, as pressure for widening access increased, private colleges began rethinking their admissions policies—and their writing programs. Again the "skills" orientation prevailed, with remedial labs a common model. But a few colleges organized cross-curricular programs to deal with rising enrollment of students whose writing the faculty considered inadequate. After its enrollment doubled within a few years, Carleton College, in Northfield, Minnesota, began a "college writing proficiency requirement" to show "formal recognition of the fact that teachers in departments other than English may assume the responsibility of judging a student's ability to read and write well" (Larsen 8). Students could satisfy the proficiency requirement by writing for courses in departments other than English. In 1974, under the leadership of Harriet W. Sheridan, Carleton offered faculty members a two-week conference on evaluating and using writing in their pedagogy. And instead of the usual remedial lab, Sheridan began a "writing fellows" program, which trained undergraduates to tutor their peers on writing assignments from courses in the disciplines.

At Central College in Pella, Iowa, a group of faculty members led by Barbara E. Fassler Walvoord began meeting in a week-long seminar, held once each semester, to discuss student writing. In 1975, Central received federal funding under a grant from HEW for "special services for economically disadvantaged students" to hire a full-time coordinator for a college-wide reading and writing program (which later included a peer tutoring program funded by Exxon). As at Carleton, the heart of the program was departmental responsibility for certifying majors as competent in reading, writing, and (in Central's case) oral communications, supported by workshops to help instructors in the disciplines foster and evaluate student writing (Walvoord; "Development").

The most important predecessor of the American WAC movement—certainly at the secondary level—was the Bay Area Writing Project (later the California and National Writing projects). In 1971, seven years after the demise of the Prose Improvement Committee, the University of California at Berkeley began another developmental program to improve college students' writing, this time by focusing on writing instruction in secondary schools. But instead of using the "top-down" approach of the federally sponsored curriculum reforms of the 1960s, with their prescribed "teacher-proof" materials and content-centered disciplinary emphasis, Berkeley adopted a collegial, interdisciplinary, "bottom-up" approach reminiscent of the Prose Improvement Committee, organized around workshops in which secondary teachers shared experiences, presented successful methods, and together investigated the roles writing could play in their classrooms, all the while writing a good deal themselves. The BAWP staff—usually from English, not education, departments—found opportunities to expose participants to writing research and theory without claiming to have definitive answers. The first workshops began in 1974 and were so popular that two years later the California Department of Education (with help from a federal grant for compensatory education) made the BAWP approach its statewide staff development model (causing some friction with education departments) (Clifford and Guthrie 317-18). Writing projects proliferated nationwide, with some sixteen sites in California and sixty-eight in other states by 1979 ("Bay Area").

Most of the participants were English teachers, though teachers from other disciplines also attended the workshops. But the project's developmental approach to writing as an integral part of learning (not a separate skill) transcended disciplinary boundaries. And more important, its collegial workshop environment, with faculty members discussing writing and learning (while writing themselves), helped free composition from the remedial stigma—and would become a hallmark of the WAC movement.

The Newest Literacy Crisis: A Movement Coalesces

These and other similar programs might have remained scattered experiments but for yet another national literacy crisis—this one in the mid-1970s—that produced the most dramatic institutional demand for writing instruction since the mass education system founded composition courses a century before. The public outcry was precipitated by alarmist press reports of declining writing ability, based (tenuously) on the results of the 1974 National Assessment of Educational Progress. The NAEP test of student writing, administered every five years, seemed to show that student writing had declined since the first administration in 1969. In fact, the results were inconclusive. The 1979 administration produced higher results than those from either 1969 or 1974 in many areas, and NAEP officials called for "caution in making global statements about writing." But in 1974, caution was the first casualty in a war on "illiteracy," laxness, and waste in schools and colleges. A *Newsweek* cover story, "Why Johnny Can't Write," concluded that, "willy-nilly, the U.S. educational system is spawning a generation of semi-literates" (58). Academics joined the chorus. NEH chair Ronald Berman saw in the NAEP evidence of "a massive regression toward the intellectually invertebrate" (qtd. in Daniels 138). The immediate target of the attacks was the supposed permissiveness of schools in the wake of the late 1960s reforms. But like similar literacy crises in the 1870s, 1910s, and late 1940s, the mid-1970s crisis coincided with widening access to previously excluded groups. And like its predecessors, the mid-1970s uproar led to a renewed emphasis on mechanical correctness and "skills"—now dubbed "back to the basics"—accompanied by the usual remedial drill that is America's almost reflexive response to a perceived lack of writing competence.

However, unlike the previous literacy crises, this one drew a more considered response in some quarters. America now had a corps of writing specialists to provide leadership, a resurgence of interdisciplinary interest in rhetoric, a growing body of research on writing, sources of public and private funding to support experiments, and a theoretical basis to allow for more than the usual remedial and cosmetic changes in response to the public outcry.

The British tradition of teaching, research, and curricular reform in language instruction, which had so challenged American English educators in 1966, proved to be the catalyst for the American WAC movement almost a decade later. American reformers borrowed the term "writing across the curriculum" from the British Schools Council research effort to map the ways language is used for learning, a project begun about the time of the Dartmouth Seminar and drawing to a close in 1975. But more important, Americans drew heavily on the British theoretical and research models rather than go directly to their own progressive tradition of language instruction (though of course there was much cross-fertilization). American reformers quickly adopted and adapted Britton's classification of discourse into trans-actional, expressive, and poetic functions, particularly his valorization of expressive discourse in pedagogy (echoing the American child-centered progressives' earlier emphasis on "creative expression"), and they borrowed British methods of qualitative research: a descriptive inquiry more philo-sophical than quantitative, attentive to the discourse of students and teachers, broadly humanistic, and free of the "educationist" perspective so suspect in American higher education.

The report of the Schools Council project, entitled *The Development of Writing Abilities (11-18),* was published just as America was in the throes of its latest literacy crisis (Britton, Burgess, Martin, McLeod, and Rosen). A few influential secondary school reformers attempted to spread the theory and concept of WAC as a developmental alternative to the remedial skills orien-tation. But the main thrust of American reform was in higher education, unlike in Britain, where WAC reforms were (and largely are) at the secondary level. There were CCCC convention sessions on WAC in 1976 and 1977, led by program organizers such as Walvoord and Sheridan. Robert Parker and others organized an NEH summer institute at Rutgers in 1977 to bring the new theories and classroom practices to fifty college faculty members. Future leaders of the WAC movement such as Toby Fulwiler were exposed to the new British writing research. Perhaps more important, they saw illustrated in the teaching of Lee Odell, Dixie Goswami, and other institute instructors the collegial workshop method that was the hallmark of the Bay Area Writing Project faculty development model and of British research methods (a National Writing Project workshop was meeting down the hall from the NEH seminar).

That same year, Janet Emig, a Rutgers education professor whose work on the development of secondary students' writing was heavily influenced by the British approach, published a seminal essay, "Writing as a Mode of Learning," that wove together the British research, the Continental theories of Vygotsky, Luria, and Piaget, and American theorists such as Dewey, Bruner, and George Kelly. Emig's essay announced the central themes of the emerging WAC movement: that writing has "unique value for learning," not only in English but in all disciplines, and that it is "a central academic process" (127-28).

The Movement Gains Momentum

In the highly charged political atmosphere of the new literacy crisis, Elaine Maimon and Toby Fulwiler began widely influential programs at Beaver College (a small liberal arts college of eight hundred students) and Michigan Technological University (a public regional university of six thousand). Both were junior English faculty members with training in literature, not composition, who, in the long tradition of the marginalization of composition, had just been named composition directors.

Maimon's dean called her in, confronted her with the *Newsweek* exposé, and charged her with the task of improving student writing. Inspired by the research and experimentation going on elsewhere (particularly the Carleton program), she began working with colleagues in other disciplines who were interested in improving pedagogy through writing—biologist Gail Hearn, for example, was working on an NSF-sponsored project to study ways to improve students' laboratory observations. They began collaborative teaching and research experiments and read widely in the new literature on writing and learning. Maimon and her colleagues eventually convinced the college's Educational Policy Committee to adopt a developmental strategy involving many faculty members instead of a marginalized remedial approach. With an NEH grant, in 1977 she launched the first of many faculty workshops on writing. These workshops treated writing (and teaching) as a serious intellectual and scholarly activity intimately related to disciplinary interests, not as a generalizable elementary skill (the first workshop was led by Sheridan, using Aristotle's *Rhetoric* as its central text). "The teaching of writing," as Maimon put it, "is scholarly not scullery" (5).

At a very different kind of institution, Michigan Tech, Fulwiler and his department chair, Art Young, responded to faculty calls for a junior-year examination on grammar and mechanics by creating a WAC program to involve technical and scientific, as well as humanities, faculty members in writing instruction. With a General Motors grant (ordinarily given to improve technical instruction), they conducted the first of their influential writing retreats for fifteen volunteer faculty members at a mountain lodge in northern Michigan. Fulwiler used Britton's theoretical formulation and the BAWP's workshop style to emphasize the uses of expressive language—often in journals or "learning logs." Young called the response to the first retreat "heartwarming if not epidemical" (5). And future retreats led by Michigan Tech faculty members at other institutions around the country made this "consciousness-raising" model of WAC one of the most prominent.

WAC soon spread to the new open admissions colleges and community colleges, to the expanding regional universities, and to major state universities and consortia of colleges and secondary schools. The national interest in literacy made WAC programs frequent beneficiaries of corporate and government funding. And WAC became popular among administrators in higher education, not only as a means of responding to the public demand for better student writing but also as a faculty development program and, in broader terms, as a means of encouraging a sense of academic community.

However, the widespread ferment in discussions of writing and learning did not produce a single movement with an overarching philosophy or organizational structure. As WAC programs proliferated in secondary schools, colleges, and universities around the country, they reflected the enormous structural variety of American postelementary education. Some programs were merely general composition courses that taught belletristic essays on subjects treated in other disciplines (e.g., Stephen Jay Gould and Loren Eiseley); others were tutoring programs or expanded writing labs; still others were organized around an institution-wide writing examination or a writing requirement satisfied by taking certain "writing-intensive" courses offered by several departments.

But the WAC programs had certain similarities. Though they were almost always organized by composition instructors from English departments, not by those from other disciplines, they were usually supervised by an inter-disciplinary committee. WAC initiatives were (and largely are still) outside the regular departmental structure of academia—and therefore subject to the vagaries of personnel, funding, and priorities. They depended for their success on the individual commitment of faculty members (and individual administrators) in a grassroots pedagogical reform movement—not on the support of departments and disciplines (McLeod, *Strengthening*; Fulwiler and Young). As Fredrick Rudolph, a leading historian of American college curric-ulum, has said of interdisciplinary programs, "Unless handsomely funded and courageously defended, efforts to launch courses and programs outside the departmental structure [have] generally failed" (251). Yet by the early 1980s, scattered theories and experiments had become a national movement, with publications, conferences, and a growing number of programs. As with previous literacy crises, the one in the mid-1970s faded when pressures for widening access abated in the 1980s. Other movements across the curriculum took the spotlight—"core curriculum," "cultural literacy," "ethics across the curriculum," and so on. But unlike the ephemeral responses to various literacy crises of the past, the WAC movement carried on its slow work of reform, despite cuts in outside funding, competition from other educational movements, and reduced emphasis on expanding access to higher education. Indeed, a 1988 survey of all 2,735 institutions of higher education in the United States and Canada found that, of the 1,113 that replied, 427 (38 percent) had some WAC program, and 235 of these programs had been in existence for three years or more (McLeod, "Writing").

Progressive Pedagogy and the Disciplines

The rapid growth of WAC in higher education was in the deepest sense a response to the demands for writing instruction created by increasing enrollment, particularly of previously excluded groups, but those demands were not new and do not in themselves explain the unique structures Ameri-can higher education evolved in the WAC movement or the movement's comparative longevity. Significantly, the late 1970s and early 1980s responses to the newest literacy crisis often went beyond the usual remedial correctives or administrative measures that had characterized WAC's many antecedents. The reasons for WAC's success are complex. The movement's strength and longevity (in comparison with earlier efforts to involve faculty members in improving students' writing) is the result, in part, of the fact that reformers found a new way to revive progressive alternatives to traditional pedagogy. They were able to face the issues of writing and specialization, which had lain submerged for a century, and evolve a broader version of progressive pedagogy, one that recognized the importance of disciplinary knowledge and structure for effecting reforms. Though WAC did not entirely change the ground of the argument over writing from "skills" to "development," it certainly staked out another, higher ground for discussions of writing, one that linked writing not only to learning and student development but also to the intellectual interests of specialists. Today it is possible to discuss writing in the disciplines as more than a favor to the English department or as a means of evaluating students' content knowledge. Unlike its predecessors, WAC (in its most common forms) did not attempt to substitute some overarching educational or philosophical program or a millennial hope of doing away with disciplinary boundaries and enshrining some version of "plain English," as reformers from both the left and the right had advocated for almost a century. Instead, WAC acknowledged differences among disciplines and tried to understand them, without trying to dismiss or transcend them.

Student-centered progressive education had in the 1960s reemerged as an option for faculty members outside education departments, but in the late 1970s the old battles between student-centered and discipline-centered teaching were broadened to consider the nature of education in a society organized by specialization—and by specialized written discourse. (Maimon called Dewey "the presiding ghost" in Beaver College's efforts to make writing an issue in the whole curriculum.) For Maimon, Fulwiler, and many other WAC proponents, the emphasis was not on writing improvement as an end in itself, or even (at least initially) as a means of improving communication. Rather, they stressed the power of writing to produce active, student-*and* teacher-centered learning. WAC was a tool for faculty development, for reforming pedagogy, though of course improved writing was an important benefit. For many college faculty members—unlike secondary teachers, who take education courses and attend faculty development meetings—WAC workshops provided their first opportunity to discuss pedagogy (much less writing) in an institutionally sponsored forum. And because the discussions centered on writing, an activity embedded in every disciplinary matrix, faculty members could bring to bear their resources as specialists, addressing the unique curricular and pedagogical problems of their disciplines. WAC programs produced a collegial environment out of which fruitful research as well as pedagogical and curricular reform grew. For example, the first book on WAC, C. Williams Griffin's *Teaching Writing in All Disciplines,* included essays by a physicist, F. D. Lee, and a finance professor, Dean Drenk.

The WAC movement of the 1970s, unlike its predecessors, was also able to draw on an emerging discipline of rhetoric and composition for its organizational and theoretical base, outside education departments and traditional literary study. In the 1970s, graduate study in rhetoric and composition began within English departments (some forty PhD programs existed by 1987); scholarly books, journals, and conferences proliferated (Chapman and Tate). After a century of marginalization, the study of writing could be viewed as a serious intellectual activity. The whole WAC enterprise was thus able to treat rhetoric and composition as a research area, a field worthy of serious intellectual activity, intimately related to disciplinary inquiry—an important source of credibility in American higher education, where research is often valued over teaching. There were conflicts, of course—over "jargon," "turf," pedagogical approach, and other issues. But for the faculty members participating in WAC programs, at least, writing could not so easily remain transparent, either in their pedagogy or in their own research (Fulwiler, "How Well"; Maimon).

WAC programs gave rise to research projects on rhetoric and argument in many disciplines and to cross-disciplinary comparative studies. And from the late 1970s, the WAC movement drew strength from research, in several disciplines, into the social and rhetorical nature of disciplinary inquiry and discourse, research carried on in such diverse fields as history, anthropology, and the sociology of science, as well as in linguistics, cognitive psychology, and literary theory (see McCloskey; Myers, "Social"; Broadhead and Freed; J. B. White; H. White; Yates; Fleck; Latour). By recognizing the disciplinary organization of knowledge (and thus of postelementary education), WAC has been able to appeal to faculty members from many departments, whose primary loyalty and interest lay in a discipline, not in a particular educational philosophy or institution. And by carrying on cooperative research with faculty members in many disciplines, progressive reformers today, unlike their forebears, at last have the means to explore the ways students and teachers can create that balance between the individual student's experience and the collective experience that a discipline and its teachers represent. Since the late 1970s in America, such cooperative research has sought to find those language experiences that engage students with disciplinary communities (see Jolliffe; McCarthy and Walvoord; see also Kaufer and Geisler; Herrington; Anderson et al.; Anson, "Classroom"; Berkenkotter, Huckin, and Ackerman).

These were great accomplishments: to reopen issues of pedagogy that had been largely unexplored for decades and to make visible those issues of writing and learning that had been largely transparent in the disciplines. But WAC thus far has only begun to explore those issues that lie behind its basic assumption: that language, learning, and teaching are inextricably linked. To understand the ways students (and teachers) learn through writing will be an unending project, for to arrive at such understanding means negotiating—and continually renegotiating—the relations between the many interests that have a stake in the ways language is used in education: students and faculty members, with their diverse backgrounds and goals; institutions on a huge spectrum and hierarchy; disciplines with various and sometimes competing professional interests; and, of course, social organizations of many kinds, which depend on postelementary institutions to educate (and often select) their members.

The WAC movement, like the tradition of progressive education it is ultimately a part of, was born out of a desire to make the mass education system more equitable and inclusive but, at the same time, more rational in its pursuit of disciplinary excellence and the differentiation of knowledge and work that drives modern (and postmodern) society. Thus the WAC movement, like its progressive antecedents, must negotiate the claims of both equity and disciplinary standards, social unity and social specialization. Through these negotiations it may be possible to realize the vision of Dewey: that curricula would be arrived at by means of open communication and rational engagement, not by fiat; that new institutional structures would be created, new pedagogical traditions evolved, continually to balance the experience of the learner with the demands of the disciplines through discourse—of students, teachers, disciplines, and the wider culture.

Works Cited

Aikin, Wilford M. *The Story of the Eight Year Study.* New York: Harper, 1942.

Anderson, Worth, Cynthia Best, Alycia Black, John Hurst, Brandt Miller, and Susan Miller. "Cross-Curricular Underlife: A Collaborative Report on Ways with Academic Words." *College Composition and Communication* 41 (1990): 11-36.

Anson, Chris M. "The Classroom and the 'Real World' as Contexts: Re-examining the Goals of Writing Instruction." *MMLA* 20 (1987): 1-16.

Applebee, Arthur N. *Tradition and Reform in the Teaching of English: A History.* Urbana: NCTE, 1974.

"Bay Area Writing Project/California Writing Project/National Writing Project: An Overview." University of California at Berkeley, School of Education. Urbana, IL: ERIC, 1978 (ED 184 123).

Beard, Charles A. *The Nature of the Social Sciences: In Relation to Objectives of Instruction.* New York: Scribner's, 1934.

Berkenkotter, Carol, Thomas N. Huckin, and John Ackerman. "Conventions, Conversations, and the Writer: Case Study of a Student in a Rhetoric Ph.D. Program." *Research in the Teaching of English* 22 (1988): 9-43.

Berlin, James A. *Rhetoric and Reality: Writing Instruction in American Colleges 1900-1985.* Carbondale: Southern Illinois U P, 1987.

Bird, Nancy K. "The Conference on College Composition and Communication: A Historical Study of Its Continuing Education and Professionalization Activities, 1947-1975." Diss. VPI, 1977.

Britton, James. "English Teaching: Retrospect and Prospect." *Prospect and Retrospect: Selected Essays of James Britton.* Ed. Gordon M. Pradl. London: Heinemann, 1982. 201-215.

Britton, James, Tony Burgess, Nancy Martin, Alex McLeod, and Harold Rosen. *The Development of Writing Abilities (11-18).* London: Macmillan, 1975.

Broadhead, Glenn, and Richard C. Freed. *The Variables of Composition: Process and Product in a Business Setting.* Carbondale: Southern Illinois U P, 1985.

Bruffee, Kenneth A. "The Brooklyn Plan: Attaining Intellectual Growth through Peer-Group Tutoring." *Liberal Education* 64 (1978): 447-68.

Bruner, Jerome S. *The Process of Education.* Westminster, MD: Random, 1963.

Bureau of the Census. *Historical Atlas of the U.S.* Washington: GPO, 1975.

Chapman, David, and Gary Tate. "A Survey of Doctoral Programs in Rhetoric and Composition." *Rhetoric Review* (1987): 124-83.

Clark, Burton and Martin Trow. "The Organizational Context." *College Peer Groups.* Ed. Theodore M. Newcomb and Everett K. Wilson. Chicago: Aldine, 1966. 17-70.

Clifford, Geraldine Joncich, and James W. Guthrie. *Ed School: A Brief for Professional Education.* Chicago: U of Chicago P, 1988.

Committee on Composition and Rhetoric. "Report of the Committee on Composition and Rhetoric." No. 28 (1892). Bound in *Reports of the Visiting Committees of the Board of Overseers of Harvard College* 1902.

Cremin, Lawrence A. *The Transformation of the School: Progressivism in American Education.* New York: Vantage, 1961.

Daniels, Harvey. *Famous Last Words: The American Language Crisis Reconsidered.* Carbondale: Southern Illinois U P, 1983.

"The Development of the Communication Skills Program at Central College, Pella, Iowa." Central College Archives, 1985.

Dewey, John. "Progressive Organization of Subject Matter." *John Dewey: The Later Works, 1925-1933.* Ed. Jo Ann Boydston. 16 vols. Carbondale: Southern Illinois University Press, 1981-1989.

Dewey, John, Albert C. Barnes, Laurence Buermeyer, Mary Mullen, Violette de Mazia. *Art and Education.* 2d ed. Merion, PA: Barnes Foundation, 1947.

Dixon, John. *Growth Through English: A Report Based on the Dartmouth Seminar, 1966.* Reading, UK: National Association for the Teaching of English, 1967.

Douglas, Wallace W. "Notes Toward an Ideology of Composition." *ADE Bulletin* 43 (1974): 24-33.

Elbow, Peter. *Writing Without Teachers.* New York: Oxford U P, 1973.

Emig, Janet. "Writing as a Mode of Learning." *College Composition and Communication* 28 (1977): 122-128.

Fleck, Ludwig. *Genesis and Development of a Scientific Fact.* Chicago: U of Chicago P, 1979.

Fulwiler, Toby. "How Well Does Writing Across the Curriculum Work?" *College English* 46 (1984): 113-25.

Fulwiler, Toby, and Art Young, eds. *Programs That Work: Models and Methods for Writing across the Curriculum.* Portsmouth, NH: Boynton, 1990.

Greenbaum, Leonard A. "A Tradition of Complaint." *College English* 31 (1969): 174-78.

Griffin, C. Williams, ed. *Teaching Writing in All Disciplines.* New Directions for Teaching and Learning, No. 12. San Francisco: Jossey, 1982.

Herrington, Anne. "Writing in Academic Settings: A Study of the Contexts for Writing in Two College Chemical Engineering Courses." *Research in the Teaching of English* 19 (1985): 331-61.

Hurd, Paul DeHart. *New Directions in Teaching Secondary School Science.* Chicago: Rand McNally, 1969.

Jenks, Christopher and David Riesman. *Academic Revolution.* Garden City, NJ: Doubleday, 1968.

Jolliffe, David, ed. *Writing in Academic Disciplines.* Norwood, NJ: Ablex, 1988.

Kandel, Issac A. *Examinations and their Substitutes in the United States.* New York: Carnegie Foundation for the Advancement of Teaching, 1936.

Kaufer, David S., and Cheryl Geisler. "Novelty in Academic Writing." *Written Communication* 6 (1989): 286-311.

King, Arthur R., Jr., and John A. Brownell. *The Curriculum and the Disciplines of Knowledge.* New York: Wiley, 1966.

Kohl, Herbert R. *The Open Classroom: A Practical Guide to a New Way of Teaching.* New York: Random, 1969.

Larsen, Erling. "Carleton College." *Options for the Teaching of English: The Undergraduate Curriculum.* Ed. Elizabeth Wooton Cowan. New York: MLA, 1975. 7-11.

Latour, Bruno. *Science in Action.* Cambridge: Harvard U P, 1987.

Lyons, Robert. "Mina Shaughnessy." *Traditions of Inquiry.* Ed. John Brereton. New York: Oxford U P, 1985. 171-189.

Macrorie, Ken. *Uptaught.* New York: Hayden, 1970.

Maimon, Elaine. "Writing, Learning, and Thinking at Beaver College." Address. College English Association. Savannah, GA, Mar. 1979 (ED 175 054).

McCarthy, Lucille Parkinson, and Barbara E. Fassler Walvoord. "Models for Collaborative Research in Writing Across the Curriculum." McLeod, *Strengthening.* 77-90.

McCloskey, Donald N. *The Rhetoric of Economics.* Madison: U of Wisconsin P, 1986.

McLeod, Susan H. "Writing Across the Curriculum: The Second Stage and Beyond." *College Composition and Communication* 40 (1989): 337-43.

McLeod, Susan H., ed. *Strengthening Programs for Writing Across the Curriculum.* San Francisco: Jossey, 1988.

Muller, Herbert J. *The Uses of English.* New York: Holt, 1967.

Myers, Greg. "The Social Construction of Two Biologists' Proposals." *Written Communication* 2 (1985): 219-45.

Neel, Jasper P., ed. *Options for the Teaching of English: Freshman Composition.* New York: MLA, 1978.

Perrin, Porter G. "The Remedial Racket." *English Journal* coll. ed. 22 (1933): 382-88.

Piché, Gene. "Class and Culture in the Development of High School English Curriculum, 1800-1900." *Research in the Teaching of English* 11 (1977): 17-25.

Postman, Neil, and Charles Weingartner. *Teaching As a Subversive Activity.* New York: Dell, 1969.

Rader, Ralph W., chair. "Report of the Committee on Prose Improvement, 1964-65," Papers of the Prose Improvement Committee, Department of English, University of California, Berkeley.

Rose, Mike. "The Language of Exclusion: Writing Instruction at the University." *College English* 47 (1985): 341-59.

Rudolph, Fredrick. *Curriculum: A History of the American Undergraduate Course of Study Since 1636.* San Francisco: Jossey, 1978.

Russell, David R. "The Cooperation Movement: Writing and Mass Education, 1890-1930." *Research in the Teaching of English* 23 (1989): 399-423..

_____. "Romantics on Writing: Liberal Culture and the Abolition of Composition Courses." *Rhetoric Review* 6 (1988): 132-48..

_____. "Writing Across the Curriculum and the Communications Movement: Some Lessons from the Past." *College Composition and Communication* 38 (1987): 184-94.

_____. *Writing in the Academic Disciplines, 1870-1990: A Curricular History.* Carbondale: Southern Illinois U P, in press.

Scott, Fred Newton. "English Composition as a Mode of Behavior." *English Journal* 11 (1922): 463-73.

Sherif, Muzafer, and Carolyn W. Sherif, eds. *Interdisciplinary Relationships in the Social Sciences.* Chicago: Aldine, 1969.

Shugrue, Michael F. *English in a Decade of Change.* New York: Pegasus, 1968.

Smith, Eugene R., Ralph Tyler, and the Evaluation Staff. *Appraising and Recording Student Progress.* New York, Harper, 1942.

Smith, Myrna J. "Bruner on Writing." *College Composition and Communication* 28 (1977): 129-33.

Smith, Ron. "Composition Requirements: A Report on a Nationwide Survey of Four-Year Colleges and Universities." *College Composition and Communication* 25 (1974): 138-48.

Stewart, Donald. "The Status of Composition and Rhetoric in American Colleges, 1880-1902: An MLA Perspective." *College English* 47 (1975): 734-46.

Sutton, Marilyn. "The Writing Adjunct Program at the Small College of California State College, Dominguez Hills." Neel 104-09.

Walvoord, Barbara E. Fassler. "The Interdepartmental Composition Program at Central College." Neel 84-89.

Weeks, Ruth Mary, comp. *A Correlated Curriculum.* NCTE Educational Monograph No. 5. New York: Appleton, 1936.

White, Hayden. *The Content of the Form: Narrative Discourse and Historical Presentation.* Baltimore: Johns Hopkins U P, 1987.

White, James Boyd. *Heracles' Bow: Essays on the Rhetoric and Poetics of the Law.* Madison: U of Wisconsin P, 1986.

"Why Johnny Can't Write." *Newsweek* 9 Dec. 1975: 58-65.

Wilcox, Thomas W. *Anatomy of Freshman English.* San Francisco: Jossey, 1973.

Wozniack, John Michael. *English Composition in Eastern Colleges, 1850-1940.* Washington, DC: University P of America, 1978.

Wright Grace S. *Core Curriculum Development: Problems and Practices.* U.S. Office of Education Bulletin No. 5. Washington: GPO, 1952.

Yates, JoAnne. *Control through Communication: The Rise of System in American Management.* Baltimore: Johns Hopkins U P, 1989.

Young, Art. "Teaching Writing Across the University: The Michigan Tech Experience." Address. College English Association Convention. Savannah, GA, Mar. 1979 (ED 176 928).

Effective Ways of Securing Co-operation of All Departments in the Teaching of English Composition

by James Fleming Hosic

The opportunity of discussing co-operation in the teaching of English composition before the Secondary Department as a whole is most welcome, for the subject is comparatively new, it is tremendously important, and it is one which English teachers cannot profitably discuss by themselves. By saying that the subject is new I do not mean to imply that no experiments have been tried or that there is no record of them. On the contrary, there are several documents which the seeker after educational experience may consult. But as compared with the question of electives or vocational guidance, the field is virgin soil.

I speak of the subject as tremendously important. So I believe it to be; no doubt all present share that opinion—or will do so on a moment's reflection. For we are here concerned with habits almost if not quite the most significant which any individual possesses, namely, language habits. No one will deny that the mastery of the vernacular is the supreme achievement of social beings, and probably no one will deny either that there is no other mastery so difficult, requiring as it does adjustments finer and more complicated than those demanded by any other aspect of human behavior. Moreover, these adjustments begin in early infancy, are operative during every waking hour, and have fairly established themselves by the time a child enters the high school. If now the pupil speaks and writes and reads well, it is necessary only that the new environment foster a growth well begun, not hinder it or destroy it. If, however, the entering student has made small progress in language or has accumulated a stock of bad practices, to save him will require the united efforts of all the teachers he may meet. How profoundly true this is appears in the doctrine, now widely accepted, that language habits are special, not general; that proficiency in a given situation gives no positive assurance that we shall find it in another. To illustrate from our common experience: Pupils often express themselves well in the English classroom, and very badly

Reprinted from *Journal of Proceedings and Addresses, National Education Association* 51 (1913): 478-85. Reprinted with permission.

elsewhere. It is in a sense true that unless all instructors teach English it is nearly useless for any to do so. Hence co-operation deserves our most serious consideration.

Difficulties To Be Overcome

By co-operation in English we mean the working together of all the teachers of a school to secure, on the part of their students, the correct and effective use of oral and written expression. We have glanced at the necessity of this; let us now consider, with some care, the difficulties which any plan of co-operation will involve.

1. *Uniform standards.*—There can be little progress in co-operating in English teaching so long as some departments support by example, or are at best indifferent to, language which others condemn or, what is equally destructive, while some departments offer no positive stimulus to accurate and adequate expression in speech and writing. It may be that the teacher of English is over-precise, a purist, and prizes too little the plain and straight-forward expression of the results of observation and thought. It may be that the teacher of science prides himself on his freedom from conventionality, and has scant respect for good usage. It is, at any rate, more than likely that each goes his own way, quite unfamiliar with the attitude of the other, while the pupil finds it easy to choose the path of least resistance.

One reason for such a state is the overspecialization of students in the universities and of teachers in the high schools. A strong reaction against a one-sided preparation which can result only in mutual lack of sympathy and support, and which tends to disintegrate the life of the pupil instead of unifying and harmonizing it, has already set in. It may be desirable to require each teacher in the large schools to give instruction in at least two departments in order to secure the necessary breadth and catholicity of interest. From the numerous suggestions concerning the preparation of high-school teachers which have come to my notice I quote the following, which is one of a series of resolutions presented by a special committee to the Conference of High Schools with the University of Illinois in November, 1913:

> All candidates for high-school teaching positions should have work in English extending thru at least two years, with emphasis upon oral and written composition. The committee is impelled to make this recommendation because of the deficiencies in English that so frequently characterize high-school teachers. The committee recognizes, however, that even the best technical training in English composition will not alone suffice to accomplish the desired results. In addition to this, every effort should be made in all classes to develop adequate habits of clear and concise expression, and to encourage effective standards of diction, syntax, and logical organization. We recommend that the conference urge upon college and university authorities the importance of emphasizing this phase of education in all classes in which intending high-school teachers are

enrolled.

(The last recommendation is an interesting confirmation of the necessity of co-operation in English, even in the college.)

2. *Common aims.*—But granting that the teachers of a school have been broadly and adequately prepared and that there exists among them reasonable agreement as to what standards of expression in language should be set up, difficulties will remain. Prominent among these is that of setting up common aims. Overspecialization is the chief stumbling-block here also. The teacher of physics wants to make scientists and the teacher of English wants to make novelists, while both should be eager to make men. Neither has time, or will take it, to visit the classes of the other, and no common interests are discovered. Moreover, co-operation is very generally viewed as one-sided. It is supposed to be a device for giving English a large place in the program or, on the other hand, a means by which teachers of other subjects may unload their manuscripts and escape the grind of correcting them. These objections must first be removed before the necessary willingness to co-operate can be secured.

It is not the business of the science teacher to give instruction in the principles of English composition. That subject has its technique, as all subjects have, and instruction in the technique of composition requires skill born of experience as is the case with any other sort of instruction. It will be sufficient if the science teacher will but require his pupils to employ to the full whatever command of language they possess. So far as correctness is concerned, it is certainly true that high-school pupils rarely make mistakes thru ignorance. They know what is right but fail to choose it. Teachers in departments other than English need not fear encroachment, then, for it is demanded only that they require the pupils to use the knowledge they possess. This doctrine may, however, be too narrowly interpreted. Many proceed on the supposition that co-operation in English means merely correcting bad grammar, bad pronunciation, and bad spelling, with the possible addition of insistence on neat manuscript. These are certainly desiderata. "These ought ye to have done, and not to have left the other undone." Language is almost identical with thought. Meagerness, confusion, and inexactness of expression are fairly indicative of like qualities of idea. When all is said that can be said for those who think by means of images, objects, drawings, or what not, the fact remains that almost all of our thinking is done with words. Hence, when the teacher of geometry insists on crystal clearness of statement, he is really making sure that the pupil has grasped the idea; when the teacher of history requires the evidence on a point to be properly arranged and adequately set forth, he has really brought the individual and the class to a complete consciousness of the facts involved, has secured full knowledge where half-knowledge lurked before. As soon as all teachers understand this and act accordingly, our problem will be practically solved. As it is now, we divine what is passing in the pupil's mind, supply the words which he cannot find, and hasten on, with a resulting lack of thoroness which is the most crying weakness of our schools. A few things properly mastered, a few steps carefully taken, would result in more knowledge and better training than we now secure by our hurried attempt to orient the boy in his teens in all the formulated and predigested experience of the race.

3. *Working conditions.*—But quite enough has been said about teachers. They are unable, however willing, to solve the problem alone. School officers and administrators must provide the necessary conditions. Suppose the English teacher meets a class of forty pupils each period of the school day. This is a situation somewhat worse than the average, but it is by no means unknown. How, in that case, will he give sympathetic attention to the interests of his pupils so that their practice in speaking and writing may react favorably on their work in other classes? How will he attend carefully to the individual so that his grasp of principles may be assured? How will he retain sufficient energy to consult with his colleagues and devise plans of assault on particularly stubborn fastnesses of metropolitan polyglot or rural *patois*? We write a course of study for the English teacher and crowd it with literary masterpieces—thought important for those who will attend college. Then we demand more than twice as much work of him as he can possibly do well and wonder why he does not succeed in vanquishing single-handed the foes of clear thinking and correct and clear expression which have been intrenched for years and which can now command aid and succor from all sides during every waking hour.

Ultimately the problem of co-operation is one for the principal, the superintendent, and the school board. It is primarily a question of economics. In a given school, then, co-operation in English must be brought about by the principal. He alone can see the problem from all sides; he alone is free, or ought to be, from predilection for one activity or interest; he should see his boys and girls as developing beings with whole, undivided lives; he is in a position not only to institute plans but to see that they are carried out and to judge of the results. Wherever any measure of success in co-operation has been secured, the principal has generally been the guiding force.

Successful Plans

This brings us at last to the point where we can speak, for a moment, of a few successful plans. Most notable, perhaps, is that now in operation in the Cicero Township High School near Chicago, Ill. This is a school in an industrial community. The parents are largely of foreign birth and not well to do. The pupils enter high school as much in need of training in the vernacular as can be found. What Principal Church is doing here will be done else-where—as soon as the importance of it is understood.

Mr. Church recognized the economic aspect of the problem and began reform by inducing his board to supply him with additional teachers. He has thus reduced the number of pupils assigned to a teacher of English to sixty. These teachers are on duty in their classrooms thruout the school day and afterward, to deal with individuals and discuss their oral and written work with them. The next step was to secure unanimity of effort in certain specific matters. This was attained by having the English teachers prepare a brief statement as to what other teachers might do to enforce the instruction they were giving; as, for example, the correcting of grammatical errors, the use, when appropriate, of full sentences, etc. Eventually it was found desirable to issue a monthly bulletin by means of which every teacher might know what instruction in English was being given and might demand that it be observed in his recitations. It was agreed that all departments should keep a separate and distinct record of the quality of the English used by each pupil, and the average of such marks was permitted to form 25 per cent of the composition grade given to the pupil at the end of the semester.

The effect is described by competent observers as wonderful. The entire school is pervaded by an atmosphere of good English, and the performance of the pupils, coming as they do from ill-educated homes, is comparable to that which may be found in the small high-grade private school.

Another typical example of successful co-operation is to be found in the Boston High School of Commerce. The principal, Mr. O. C. Gallagher, describes their plan as follows:

> To keep the pupils on the watch for accurate, effective, and smooth composition in all their work they were informed that at frequent, tho unstated, intervals their papers in other subjects would be corrected by their English teachers, to ascertain their observance of the principles taught in the English classes. The marks thus obtained are entered upon the regular composition work, and unsatisfactory papers are revised or rewritten—the same as unsatisfactory themes. In addition, teachers of other subjects are urged to send batches of papers whenever pupils seem to be growing careless—a condition that often prevails immediately after the correction of sets of papers in subjects other than English.

> The teacher of the other subject demands that the work be clear, and substantially correct in spelling, punctuation, and sentence structure. Failing to secure the first, he lowers the pupil's mark, and at his option, demands revision; failing to secure the second, he withholds all credit until the work is presented in a satisfactory form. The teacher of English insists that every piece of writing shall be regarded as an English theme to be corrected, revised, and rewritten, and to count in the making-up of the mark in English. The collection of papers at unexpected moments convinces most pupils of the unwisdom of taking chances; for even if the English teacher fails to collect a set, the teacher of the other subject is likely to send him any piece of slipshod work.

> Again, a conscientious attempt is made to teach pupils how to answer questions in other subjects. We correlate the English work in the first year with history; in the second, with commercial geography; in the third, with local industries and civil government; in the fourth,

with business law and economics. By drawing upon these branches for occasional subjects, and correcting the themes orally for sentence structure, unity, mass, and coherence, we try to train the pupils to bear in mind the principles of English while their attention is focused upon another subject. Similarly in connection with science, descriptions of apparatus and expositions of experiments are required, and the teacher of science is consulted as to the adequacy of the productions from a technical standpoint. With foreign languages the English department has found most need for co-operation in drill upon points of grammar as they are taken up in German and in French.

Besides "corrective" co-operation, there is such a thing as "preventive or anticipatory" co-operation, which is quite as important as the other. Since most teachers are interested in English as a means rather than as an end, the use of English must be made effective in recitation as well as in writing. Several subjects taken up in the first year of a secondary school lend themselves readily to such drill, especially history and elementary science. After consultation between the teacher of English and the teacher of history, the history textbook may be taken up in the English class, and the pupil taught how to make his English do the work that the author tried to have his do. What has the author aimed at? Did he hit it? Why? How? This brings the pupil to the outline; he must get his sights in line. Then the discharge—oral delivery. The class watch as markers, criticize the sighting, aiming, line of flight, and the hit. The aim is thus upon the English essentials of unity and coherence, in whole composition, paragraphs, and sentences.

The result is easier work for the teacher of history, for the teacher of English, and for the pupils, since the work in the English class is "a practical job." The pupils can measure the success of their effort in one class by their achievement in the other.

Reports from several other schools embody some of these ideas and suggest a number in addition. One of the most striking is that of keeping pupils on probation in English thruout the course. Delinquents who have been warned and who fail to improve are remanded to the English department for such further training as seems necessary. This may result in the establishing of a sort of hospital squad. Naturally pupils wish to get out of the hospital as soon as possible. Sometimes it is possible to require those who persist in making mistakes in externals such as spelling to take a course in typewriting. Again, certain teachers or departments find it possible to employ the same subject-matter for a part of the course. Science notebooks are made the basis of instruction in sentence structure in the English class, pupils engaged in shop work are taught how to organize notes on their projects in the form of analytical outlines, etc. The outside reading of the pupil is sometimes directed to lists of books which have been made up by all departments in conference, and care is exercised that only a reasonable amount of collateral reading is required of any pupil. Similarly the amount and distribution of written work are determined, the form of notebooks is agreed upon, etc. Of great importance is the compiling of a standard guide to the preparation and correction of manuscripts, which should reflect the practice of good publishers and which should be in the hands of all teachers and pupils and be consistently adhered to.

Various attempts have been made to work out a practicable method of grading so that due account may be taken of the value of substance on the one hand and externals of form on the other. Some years ago, G. H. Browne, head master of a preparatory school in Cambridge, Mass., established in his institution the custom of dual marking by means of a "numerator" and a "denominator." The mark above the line was to stand for substance in all papers, including those for the English teacher, while the mark below the line was to indicate excellence in "mother-tongue," that is, spelling, etc. Marks of the latter sort were sent in by all teachers, and averaged and reported to the parents. The effect is said to have been immediate and gratifying. Lately the practice of holding occasional conferences at which a few papers are examined, corrected, and graded by members from all departments has been growing in favor. Marking has been further systematized in a few cases by the working-out of some sort of scale after the general plan of that invented by professors Thorndike and Hillegas. These conferences are necessary and may be made the means of unifying and co-ordinating the activities of the different departments of a school to a remarkable degree.

To summarize: Co-operation in English composition, to be successful, must be organized and administered by the head of the school for the good of all. This will involve the setting-up of common aims and the establishment of suitable working conditions. Instruction in the technic of speaking and writing should be regarded as the work of the teachers of English. Teachers of other subjects should refuse to accept oral reports or written papers which are below the standards agreed upon. If the delinquent student fails to repair the deficiency, he should be reported to the principal and sent to the English department for further training. In matters of substance, particularly clearness and completeness, the teacher of each subject should point out the weakness, cause it to be removed, and apportion credit to the paper in accordance with the degree of success attained. By means of class visitation and conference, teachers of English and of other subjects should seek to join their efforts so as to accomplish the most effective training of the student in the arts of study and of expression with the greatest economy of his time and the most consistent unifying of his life.

Section 2:
Recent Programmatic and Institutional Projects

The Development of Writing Abilities

by Nancy Martin, Pat D'Arcy, Brian Newton, and Robert Parker

Every day in schools children write—in exercise books, in rough work books, on file paper, on worksheets. They write stories, recipes, poems, accounts of experiments; they answer questions on what they have just been told, what they have read, what they have seen or done. Why do they? What is all this writing for? What does it achieve?

When we asked pupils and students about their recent experience of writing in school we found, not surprisingly, that the teacher figured prominently in their recollections. He structures situations, he makes demands, he influences both implicitly and explicitly by his responses to what is offered. The teacher has his own ideas about what his subject is and what learning is and these inform his practice. He may be more or less aware of the criteria on which he bases his teaching but in either case his pupils soon know what pleases him. But what pleases the teacher, what he considers to be the appropriate language of his subject and the appropriate way of using it, may not be helpful—indeed may actually impede—the understanding of his pupils.

> Our history teacher used to make us put down—she gave us a load of facts to make into an essay. Well, I couldn't do that. When I was confronted with a whole list of facts I just couldn't do it and I failed my history exam and she told me I'd fail 'cos I couldn't do it.
>
> (Technical College student)

> I knew what he was on about but I only knew what he was on about in my words. I didn't know his words.
>
> (Technical College student)

> In my exams I had to change the way I learnt, you know. In all my exercise books I put it down the way I understood, but I had to remember what I'd written there and then translate it into what I think *they* will understand, you know.
>
> (Technical College student)

At secondary school it was always writing to please whichever

Reprinted from *Writing and Learning Across the Curriculum*, 12-34. Ward Lock Educational UK. 1976. Reprinted with permission.

teacher was taking you. The fifth form was the worst for writing essays—due to the teacher we had. They all had to be very descriptive and interesting to him otherwise they were no good. If you were given a question and wrote about something completely different, this was great for him. I didn't get on very well with him so this led to low marks anyway. I managed to fool him once or twice by copying pieces out of books. This didn't always work through.

(College of Education student)

What pleases the teacher is apparently of major importance to these pupils. After all, he can be judge, jury and hangman—and there is no appeal.

The teacher as the only audience for the pupil's writing is a point which will be discussed later. Meanwhile, it is clear that if the teacher sees writing mainly as a means of recording and testing this will inevitably influence the expectations and attitudes of his pupils.

We do all the experiments. She tells us what to do and we do it and then we have to write up in our books—method, result and conclusion.

(Third year pupil)

. . . our lessons consisted entirely of bending pieces of glass over bunsen burners and copying down endless notes of dictation. Our involvement in the learning procedure can be measured by the accuracy of my notes. Every time he dictated punctuation I wrote it down in longhand, taking 'cover' instead of 'comma' so that a sentence might read:

Common salt cover to be found in many kitchens cover is chemically made of sodium cover represented Na cover and chlorine cover represented Ch full stop

Dictation was similarly rife in other subjects.

(College of Education student)

In RS right up to the fifth year we were not allowed to make our own notes on the Apostles, everything was copied from the blackboard. This was a weekly exercise in neat writing and nothing else; we never discussed the work, nor was there any homework set. What I do not understand is why everybody passed the 0 level. Maybe there is some loose connection.

(College of Education student)

I don't like dictated notes because you haven't got no room for imagination. Really, when you're doing your English it's better than any other subject because you can use your imagination. You don't have to, you know, do what the teacher tells you to do.

(Fifth year pupil)

The implication that there is no room for imagination in subjects other than English might be disputed by the teachers of other subjects in that boy's school—but that is the message he has received after five years there.

What goes on in talk in the classroom may reinforce the pupil's view of how he should write:

> A lot of the time, though, some of my teachers said, you know, what's your opinion and everybody gave their opinion and they said, well, that's not really right. So—you've got to take down what the teachers says in the end.
>
> (Technical College student)

A major concern of some teachers was technical accuracy which took precedence—or so it seemed to the pupils—over content. Handwriting, spelling and punctuation were frequently referred to:

> Girl 2: I like the teachers marking it but they tend to mark the spelling and the English instead of the actual story—the content.
> Girl 1: Well, mostly they just mark spellings and they're so involved in getting all the spelling right that they forget the story and there's so many papers to mark they can't go over it twice.
> Girl 2: And they just make sure you've got the punctuation right and everything.
>
> (Third year pupils)

> BN: What sort of things does he write?
> Fiona: 'Good, but watch the punctuation'—things like that. And, um, 'Good idea, but spoilt by untidy writing'.
>
> (Third year pupil)

The power of the teacher was dramatically illustrated by the recollections of some of the students who could remember clearly how a single remark by a particular teacher influenced their feelings about writing for months—even years—afterwards. Sometimes the effect seemed beneficial, sometimes not, but either way it seems that teachers may often underestimate the effect that their opinions can have on their pupils.

> Jeanette: Well, it's mostly fairy tales I write about because Mr A- - - always commented I've got a good imagination for fairy tales, so I'm about pixies and fairies and goblins and things.
>
> (First year girl, comprehensive school)

> BN: You said you weren't any good at it (writing poems), didn't you?
> Sandra: No, I'm not very good at it.
> BN: Now why do you say that?
> Sandra: Because when I was at primary school I got a very low

mark for a poem that I'd done and the teacher put under-
neath it: poetry isn't your bright spark, or something, is it?
And that's what put me off, I think.

(Third year girl, comprehensive school)

My first notion of the change in emphasis between junior and
grammar school came when I had to write an essay on Neolithic man
for my first piece of history homework. I started 'My name is Wanda
and I am the son of the headman in our village.' The history master
read it out to the rest of the class in a sarcastic voice—everybody
laughed and I felt deeply humiliated. I got 3/20 for covering the page
with writing. I hated history after that until the third year.

(College of Education student)

The influence of the teacher, then, may be profound and is certainly
pervasive. All the more reason why he should be as fully aware as possible of
the options open to him in approaching his pupils' writing—in what he asks
them to do and in how he responds to what they have done. But the
opportunities for children to use writing more effectively can be widened
much more than this. If the teacher is concerned not only with *what* he asks
his pupils to do but also with *how* he allows them to respond (after all, why
shouldn't a history homework on Neolithic man begin 'My name is
Wanda . . .'?) then he may find that they discover their own strategies for
learning through writing. And if he also allows opportunities for pupils to
write for an audience other than himself—perhaps the class—then his pupils'
opportunities to experience different writing situations will have been
significantly widened.

The Development of Writing Abilities

What is the writing for? Who is it for? These were the two questions to
which the research team of the Schools Council Project The Written
Language of 11-18 Year Olds chiefly addressed themselves when they looked
at a sample of about 2000 pieces of school writing which they had collected
from 65 secondary schools. They wanted to find a way of describing how
writing was used in schools so that they could go on to define or track any
development in writing abilities (Britton *et al* 1975).

To do this, the Project developed in detail these two dimensions of
writing: 'Sense of audience' (*who* the writing was for) and 'Function' (*what*
it was for). Other dimensions are, of course, possible, and the research team
looked at, for instance, individual language resources. The results of their
analysis of the 2000 pieces of school writing and the implications which they
drew from their results are the foundations upon which the Development
Project Writing across the Curriculum 11-16 has worked.

The research team not only listed the different kinds of writing but they
also looked for the relationships between them. They made specific suggestions about the way writing ability develops, about the order of development

and the reasons for it. They suggested the relationships between the different functions of writing, the audience for which they were written and the mental processes required to produce them. In fact, they provided an approach which is valid for all areas of the curriculum—a 'writing across the curriculum' rationale.

So before presenting some of the work of the Development Project we need to summarize the model for looking at writing which the research team formulated.

A Sense of Audience—the Child and His Reader

A sense of audience—how the writer pictures his reader—is obviously very important in determining how the writing is done. A letter to a friend, to an acquaintance, to a newspaper may all be about the same subject but will be very differently written by any competent writer. Furthermore, another letter to the same friend on a different occasion may differ markedly from the first. If, for example, the first letter was to inform your friend about certain social events in which you knew he was interested and the second was to persuade him to take a particular course of action which you thought he might be reluctant to do, then you will be seeing your reader in different ways.

In school children write mostly for the teacher. But what makes for differences between pieces of writing is not just who the reader is but how the writer *sees* his reader. Different children see the same teacher in different ways, of course. But a child may also see his teacher as a different sort of reader on different occasions. (Sometimes teachers may make this explicit to the children—'. . . she doesn't care about the English side when we're writing stories. She just marks the story itself. But when we're told that she's going to mark the punctuation and that, y'know, it's all right then'–Third year girl, comprehensive school.)

In distinguishing between the different sorts of 'sense of audience' found in school writing, the writing research team suggested these main categories (for a fuller account of audience categories see Britton *et al* 1975):

1   Child (or adolescent) to self
2   Child (or adolescent) to trusted adult
3   Pupil to teacher as partner in dialogue
4   Pupil to teacher seen as examiner or assessor
5   Child (or adolescent) to his peers (as expert, co-worker, friend, etc.)
6   Writer to his readers (or unknown audience)

1   'Child to self' writing takes no account of the needs of any other reader— as in some diaries, notes and first drafts.
2   Writing for the teacher could come under any of the categories 2-4. In 'Child to trusted adult' the writing takes place because the reader exists for it who can be relied on to respond sympathetically. So the child may write about personal, deeply felt matters which he would not attempt to do without feeling very secure with his reader. For example:

If I think about what I would really like to do, I feel as if I want to curl into a ball and let everything go on without me. Knowing about it. Whichever way I turn, I feel trapped. College doesn't seem a release, it seems a new trap, another place where I have to conform to something . . .

(Carol 18)

3 'Pupil to teacher as partner in dialogue' covers writing which is recognisably part of an educational process. Here the dialogue is likely to be centrally concerned with the subject matter of school, although the writer's personal feelings about it may be included. The child still feels secure in the teacher's presence and is assuming that the teacher is there to help him, will be interested in what he is saying and is likely to respond to what he writes—hence, 'dialogue'. For example:

. . . If we look back through history at any one incident if that did not happen or if something else happened instead we could have a totally different way of life. I think that any main discisions that are taken should be aimed at the future. So it will not affect the future population in any ways that would harm their ways of life. Political discussions are very important to the future. If China was allowed to join the UN this could help the future tremendesly.

(John 14: 'China and the UN')

4 'Pupil to teacher seen as examiner or assessor' refers not only to exams but to all writing which the child appears to be producing simply to satisfy a teacher's demand and on which he expects to be judged or assessed— either for how well he has written or for what he has shown he knows. For example:

Tamworth was Peel's own consitutency. All the Tamworth Manifesto was, was what Peel said the Tories (or conservatives) would do. He said that Tories would support the Reform act and would not let past grievances exist any longer. These were the two most important things that Peel said, as they have been the Conservatives word upto this day and have not yet been broken.

(Janet 15: The Tamworth Manifesto)

5 'Child (or adolescent) to his peers (as expert, co-worker, friend etc.)'. Although the teacher may be a member of the audience for writing in this category, the focus is upon the peer group. For example:

The rooms were changed a lot and so also was Mr Comer. The way the rooms were changed was. The benches were in different orders and Mr Comers desk was pushed back to the blackboard. . . . Mr Comer was changed a lot two. The ways he was changed were, there was no 'are you at your bench' or no 'go to your bench and stay at it' or no 'Stay! at your bench.' Mr Comer also was going round giveing more of a helping hand than usual. The boys talked to Mr

Comer about the job and he wasn't the usual old cross looking black patch, He was happy took a joke and listend to a joke. If any-body was doing anything wrong he didn't catch them by the ear and blow his top, instead he told them where they were wrong and explined how to do it. Thes effects weren't of him on the following Monday.

(Cyril 12: reporting to his classmates about a woodwork
lesson which he had observed in his school)

6 'Writer to his readers (or unknown audience)'. Writing for an unknown or public audience expresses the writer's sense of the general value of what he has to say, and that he is not addressing himself to any particular audience. Some school writing comes into this category. For example:

. . . A child quarrels in order to assert itself, and frequently fails to do so. Its main desire is to have supremacy over something. It cannot, in all probability, have any power over an adult and so has to find its power in breaking things or being the leader of a gang. This wish stems from the animal kingdom, where survival of the fittest means that only the strongest, most powerful are successful. Animals only fight over serious matters, like where to live, and what to eat.

(Derek 15)

The research team classified their sample of scripts in terms of 'sense of audience' as follows:

Audience By Year (percentages of year sample)

	Year 1	Year 3	Year 5	Year 7
Self	0	0	0	0
Trusted adult	2	3	2	1
Pupil-teacher dialogue	51	45	36	19
Teacher examiner	40	45	52	61
Peer group	0	0	0	0
Public	0	1	5	6
Miscellaneous (translation, dictation, exercises ect.)	7	6	5	13

Audience By Subject (percentages of subject sample)

	English	History	Geography	RE	Science
Self*	0	0	0	0	0
Trusted adult	5	0	0	4	0
Pupil-teacher dialogue	65	17	13	64	7
Teacher examiner	18	69	81	22	87
Peer group	0	0	0	0	0
Public	6	0	0	0	0
Miscellaneous	6	14	6	10	6

*(The team considered that in any involved writing the self was a significant part of the writer's sense of audience. They therefore defined the category for their purposes as covering items obviously unconnected with an audience—rough work for instance.)

What is most striking about these figures is that writing for the 'Examiner' audience accounts for about half of all school writing. Even in the first year it was 40%. This does not necessarily mean that teachers *intended* the situation to be one of examination or assessment—but that is how the pupils saw the context for their writing. As we saw earlier, the way the teacher responds to writing will determine how the pupil sees the situation. And, of course, previous experience in school will set up expectations about writing. In addition it may also be that the whole atmosphere of the secondary school promotes the sense of constantly being assessed.

What this means, though, is that the single most important use for writing in secondary schools appears to be as a means of testing and not as a means of learning—and that this emphasis becomes stronger as the child moves up the school.

Of course teachers must assess their pupils' progress. But that so much of secondary school writing appears to be concerned with assessment is worrying because it suggests that the more important function of writing—its potential contribution to the mental, emotional and social development of the writer—is being neglected.

The emphasis on testing, on monitoring knowledge and performance, which the research figures indicate, suggests that most school writing is seen not as part of the learning process but as something which happens *after* the learning.

However, before looking at some examples of what effect changing the 'sense of audience' can have on writing in schools, we need to look at the second of the two dimensions developed by the writing research team, because then we can see how they interrelate.

Functions of Writing

Another major influence on the writer is his sense of what the writing is for. Our culture has developed distinct language forms which are typically associated with certain situations. For example, we know when we are listening to a story, or a speech, or are being persuaded to buy something—because we have internalised these kinds of language from our day-to-day encounters with them. When children come to write they draw on their pool of language experience which helps them to know what kind of language to use in certain types of situation. For instance, few children in an infant class are taught to begin their stories 'Once upon a time' or 'Once there was a . . .', but most of them do this because this beginning is so clear a 'marker' of stories which they have listened to or read.

Although the boundaries are not clear-cut, the writing research team suggested three broad categories of function to which recognisably distinct kinds of writing belong. What distinguishes them is that both writer and reader recognise the conventions that distinguish one 'job' from another. There are often linguistic differences, too, and these are indicators of the different functions—but the essential difference lies in the sorts of things the writer *takes for granted about his reader's response*. If, for instance, we read 'Once upon a time there was a flying horse', we know the writer is taking it for granted that we shall recognise a story and shall not quarrel about whether horses can fly. On the other hand, if we read 'The biggest aircraft company in America is the Northrop Corporation, trade name Boeing . . .', we might reasonably dispute this and refer to evidence which indicated that there was a larger aircraft company in America. But if we read 'When I write it is as if all the ideas in my head have come together into order and when I write I am reading them for the first time . . .', we recognise that the writer is assuming that we are interested in her and in her experience.

The three 'recognised and allowed for' functions of writing are represented by the research team as a continuum thus:

$$\text{Transactional} \leftarrow \text{Expressive} \rightarrow \text{Poetic}$$

The characteristics of each function can be defined as follows:

Expressive: in which it is taken for granted that the writer himself is of interest to the reader; he feels free to jump from facts to speculation to personal anecdote to emotional outburst and none of it will be taken down and used against him—it is all part of being a person *vis à vis* another person. It is the means by which the new is tentatively explored, thoughts may be half-uttered, attitudes half-expressed, the rest being left to be picked up by a listener or reader who is willing to take the unexpressed on trust.

The following extract from a personal log book written by Andrew, aged 12, illustrates many of the features of expressive writing:

Before what I'm about to write Mr T . . . told us what to do. It took a bit of getting through to some of the class and as they didn't understand they became restless and Mr T . . . had to interrupt what he was saying and deal with them. He shouldn't have to do this because they should know that if they don't understand they should listen again to what he is saying and perhaps they'll know what he's talking about. The student teacher who worked with us in English and Enquiry is quite a nice woman and she helps us do our work, she has a good voice when reading aloud and you can understand her. When the class starts throwing pencils over an argument, she gets upset and sometimes leaves the room, I think she should be much firmer with the class and then with a bit of luck they might obey her, but still, she's doing all right. Oh, by the way I suppose you're wondering what her name is, it's Miss M . . . In Enquiry I think I've done well and I am satisfied with what I have done. At the beginning of the Enquiry work we went to Burgh Hill farm. Visiting the farm and looking round was very interesting and I enjoyed it very much, I can't say that much for the journey as I was sick, at least four times, twice going, twice coming back. All the other work we did is at the top of the page, it's not because I am to busy to right them down, I can just write about some of them as I go along.

This writing is very like written down speech, reflecting the ebb and flow of the writer's thoughts and feelings—and this is what expressive language (spoken or written) does. Speech is always on the move: it moves according to the demands of what it is for, what the listener wants to hear, and how the speaker's language resources allow him to meet these demands—his own and other people's. So expressive speech shuttles to and fro and expressive writing can be seen to move in a similar way.

Transactional: in which it is taken for granted that the writer means what he says and can be challenged for its truthfulness to public knowledge, and for its logicality; that it claims to be able to stand on its own and does not derive its validity from coming from a particular person. So it is the typical language of science and of intellectual inquiry, of technology, of trade, of planning, reporting, instructing, informing, advising, persuading, arguing and theorising. It is also the language most used in school writing.

> Greater London Council Ambulance Service was built in 1969. Before it was built for them there was a place called the Red Cross. The red Cross was made into a private service for all over the country. But even before that there was a place called Cadogan Iron Foundry. There is a peculiar pipe system in the building now, it is a heating system. The pipes come from the RAF runway which they used these pipes for burning lots of paraffin to clear the fog and so the planes can see the runway.
>
> (Nigel 12: writing for Local Studies)

Poetic: in which it is taken for granted that 'true or false?' is not a relevant question at the literal level. What is presented may or may not in fact be a representation of actual reality but the writer takes it for granted that his reader will *experience* what is presented rather in the way he experiences his own memories, and not use it like a guidebook or map in his dealings with the world. When Huck Finn said that all Tom Sawyer's stories were lies he was mistaking the function of stories (the poetic function) and operating the 'rules' of the other 'game'—the transactional. So a reader does different things with transactional and poetic writings: he *uses* transactional writing, or any part of it, but who can say what we do with a story or a poem that we read, or a play we watch? Perhaps we just share it with the writer; and not having to 'do' anything with it leaves us free to attend to its formal features— which are more implicit than explicit—the pattern of events in a narrative, the configuration of an idea, above all the pattern of feelings evoked: in attending in this noninstrumental way we experience feelings and values as part of what we are sharing. Writing in the poetic function shows a heightened awareness of symbolic, aural and even visual qualities—of *shaping* a verbal construct— as in this story by Eleanor, aged 6:

> *The prince and the princes*
> Once upon a time the was a prince and he whent for a ride on his horse, and he went past a castle and sore the most beautiful princess

in the whole wide woled and the prince said please will you mary me, but the princesses mummy wode not let her mary the prince so one day the priness saied I am going for a rid on my hores so of she went but realy she went to go and cellect the prince and thay went to another contre and gote mared and lived happily ever after.
The end.

Growth From the Expressive

The expressive is basic. Expressive speech is how we communicate with each other most of the time and expressive writing, being the form of writing nearest to speech, is crucial for trying out and coming to terms with new ideas. Because it is the kind of writing in which we most fully reveal ourselves to our reader—in a trusting relationship—it is instrumental in setting up a dialogue between writer and reader from which both can learn.

Expressive writing we think is the seed bed from which more specialised and differentiated kinds of writing can grow—towards the greater explicitness of the transactional or the more conscious shaping of the poetic.

Much effective writing seems to be on a continuum somewhere between the expressive and the transactional or somewhere between the expressive and the poetic. This applies to adult as well as children's writing. What is worrying is that in much school writing the pupil is expected to exclude expressive features and to present his work in an unexpressive transactional mode. The demand for impersonal, unexpressive writing can actively inhibit learning because it isolates what is to be learned from the vital learning process—that of making links between what is already known and the new information.

Believing, then, in the central importance of the expressive both in learning and in learning to write, it is hardly surprising that the writing research team were perturbed by the results of their analysis of the school writing which they had collected. The figures (percentages) were as follows:

Function By Year

	Year 1	Year 3	Year 5	Year 7
Transactional	54	57	62	84
Expressive	6	6	5	4
Poetic	17	23	24	7
Miscellaneous	23	14	9	5

Function By Subject

	English	History	Geography	RE	Science
Transactional	34	88	88	57	92
Expressive	11	0	0	11	0
Poetic	39	2	0	12	0
Miscellaneous	16	10	12	20	8

These figures suggest that most secondary school writing is *transactional* and that it becomes increasingly so as the pupils move up the school. If we put these figures beside those for 'sense of audience' quoted earlier, we have a picture of secondary school writing which begins as largely transactional, written for a teacher who is going to assess it, and that as pupils get older this becomes even more exclusively the way that they are required to write.

The expressive function, which the writing research team saw as so important, accounts for a mere 6% of school writing in Year 1, declining to 4% by Year 7.

But if the bulk of school writing is transactional, what sort of things are pupils writing? The informational subcategories of this function, which represent a scale of distance from an actual event, give an idea of the range of possibilities:

Transactional

Informational   Conative

1 Record: what is happening
2 Report: what happened   1 Regulative
3 Generalised narrative or description ⎫ what   2 Persuasive
4 Low level generalisation   ⎬ generally
5 Generalisation—classification   ⎭ happens
6 Speculation ⎫ what may
7 Theorising   ⎭ happen

However, up to the end of the fifth year almost all the transactional writing in the sample fell into the first five informational categories. Rarely was there any sense that they were taking part in a dialogue in which new ideas could be aired and explored. The writing, in most cases, was seen as an end product—an account of something that had already happened.

There was hardly any writing by pupils younger than sixteen which could be categorised as speculative, theoretical or persuasive. This was not because such pupils are incapable of writing in these ways but because they were not given opportunities to do so.

The research team commented: '. . . for whatever reason, curricular aims did not include the fostering of writing that reflects independent thinking: rather attention was directed towards classificatory writing which reflects information in the form in which both teacher and textbook traditionally present it.'

An example of the kind of speculative writing which was rare in the sample collected by the Research Project is this piece which is the last page of Nigel's CSE Project, 'Making alcohol from waste paper'. Nigel was not asked to present his project in any given way.

My project worked very well and I'm pleased because 1) I got alcohol from paper which I throught was never possible, 2) because I used some new equipment which I've never herd of let alone worked with. Another thing, I was pleased about was there was lots of experments and if there was anything I wanted to know there was book's at my finger tips so there wern't any time lost. If I had a lot more time what I would like to make is a lot more alcohol and do lots of flame tests because I only made about 1cm of pure alcohol. So I could not do much, I would allso like to find how much yeast is necessary to ferment it propley yet let the alcohol burn propley. I would also like to know if it was the yeast that stoped it burning. I would also like to learn how to control the heat when distilling because thats a mistake I made.

(Nigel 15)

Nigel is not only assessing for himself what he has achieved but he is also generating his own questions for further enquiry. His teacher commented: 'His enthusiasm and pleasure derived from the project is refreshing, but more important throughout there is evidence of clear scientific thinking in Nigel's own words.'

Genuine Communication

The trouble with most school writing is that it is not genuine communication. When adults write they are usually trying to tell someone something he doesn't already know; when children write in school they are usually writing for someone who, they are well aware, knows better than they do what they are trying to say and who is concerned to evaluate their attempt to say it. Even when they are writing a story, when the teacher does not know better than they do what they are saying, the response of the teacher is so often to the surface features of spelling, punctuation and handwriting. So once again the teacher is seen as an assessor and not as someone interested in being communicated with.

If the bulk of school writing is transactional (and of limited range from the transactional at that), and if much of what is not transactional is marked by the teacher for its technical accuracy, rather than responded to for its content, then only a small part of the possible range of writing purposes is fostered and there is limited opportunity for development.

The teacher's role is of great significance here. Pupils cannot operate a range of functions for a teacher who evaluates narrowly whatever is produced. Thus if an English teacher asks his pupils to write a letter to a local newspaper intending to give them the opportunity to write transactionally for a public audience and yet the pupils know that not only will the 'letters' go no further than the teacher but that he will correct their spelling etc, then this task is a bogus one and the pupils will be writing, yet again, to please the teacher. There are two ways out of this impasse. Either the teacher must find other audiences than himself for what the children write or he must agree to be communicated with as someone other than an assessor, or both. This means he must change his way of responding and this has social as well as pedagogic implications.

When we asked students to recall any of their school writing with which they had felt satisfied, it was clear that the sense of audience often played an important part in making the writing experience memorable—as in this example:

> The most satisfying piece of writing I have wrote was when I was reporting on the school's Rugby for the school magazine. Every week I wrote a small report on the Saturday match and worked out average points per match and how many games we had won and lost.
>
> At the end of the season a few of the match reports were put into the yearly magazine and also the facts and figures. I also gave each player (except myself) a mark out of ten for each match. In the end the best player to my way of thinking got an average of just over eight out of ten per match. The season was a successful one for our team, we won eighteen matches and lost only three, our average points per game were sixteen with only four against per match.
>
>   (Technical College student)

The enthusiasm for this writing can still be felt in the recollection of it and the student's desire to tell us the results of his calculations. And yet he didn't do this writing as a part of school 'work' but as an extra related to something he was obviously keen on—playing rugby. In addition, and equally important, he was writing for an audience who wanted to read what he wrote. So the student was writing a 'genuine communication' about something which interested him for a real audience who were also interested in what he wrote.

What happened to their writing was also very important to these students:

> The only other piece of writing I've done which sticks out in my memory was a poem I wrote at school. I can't remember now what it was about, but I do know it was printed in the school magazine.

> My most satisfying piece of work was a poem I wrote when I was about fourteen. When I had finished it, I felt extreemly satisfyed for some strange reason, mainly because it rymed well and had a meaning. It was also published in the school magazine which I thought was rather good.

> The pleasure of seeing one's name in print along with one's special story made up for all the worry of putting the story together.
>
>   (Technical College students)

Contrast those recollections with the comments below by intending teachers who were asked to write about whatever they could remember of the writing they did at school:

> In my fourth year mock 0 level Eng. Lang. I was penalised for writing an essay that was too long on a description of a building. The master told me that it was wrong to get too interested in a subject and said that I could do that after I left school; by then I didn't care anyway, I did the same thing in the exam and got a grade 1. I still have reams of poems at home that I never took to school because I

didn't think it was to do with school. In secondary school my English came under violent attack by a whole series of teachers. . . . The head thought I was dyslectic (never can spell even now). I think I just hated writting or rather I actually enjoyed writting untill work was returned to me with such red lines and a poor grade.

(College of Education students)

A first year girl in a comprehensive school makes a similar point:

Only thing is, the problem when you get it back there's a cross by it.

A fourth year boy was more explicit. He wrote:

When I get a piece of work back and I think its good and I get a bad mark I feel like frotiling the teacher.

When school writing in all subjects is marked chiefly for accuracy—either of content or form, or both—then pupils are constantly in a testing situation where they will take the minimum of risks. They don't want to make mistakes. So they will try to use the language which has been given to them—by the teacher or the textbook—and not their own language. They will be cautious and will try to disguise any lack of understanding if they are aware of it. But by not taking chances, by not trying things out in their own language, by not attempting to make connections between their own experience or knowledge and the new information that they are acquiring, they are being limited in their opportunities for growth.

Understanding new information means relating it to what we already 'know'—fitting it in to our view of how things are. So it will often mean not just giving an account of something but expressing a response to it—as in the following extract from a personal log book written by Kenneth, a 12 year old boy in a London comprehensive school. The log book is a kind of diary in which the pupils write their thoughts about their work and related subjects. The teacher reads it and writes back. He does not evaluate or 'correct' their writing:

This term I've learnt about the country side after are visit to burghill farm in sussex from which I learnt alot how the cows were milked and how it was transport it to the tanker. And enclosers which effected people's life. I learnt about iron, conditions of work, mines power and inventions. I fell that I have learnt a lot than I did in my primary school. I enjoy english and enquiry but some times it's hard to think like know because people are chattering away happily. I learn by listening to the teacher and reading books I think about it then write it in my own words. I think that the class should be split into half (the people who want to work and the people who don't). But I must be honest some time's me and robert stop working for a minute or two and have a chat after some hard work then we start work again. I am most interested in english when we do play's but I think that to many people write plays and every one starts shouting and arguring. I think that I work quite good as I enjoy my work. I think that the industrial revolation changed alot of peoples life's like Willaim Wilkins when his land was taken away from him by the squire and had it enclosed. He had to change the whole of his life style. He had to grow extra food to live on then he sold it to Nottingham the nearest town. I don't think it's fare to change the life style you alway's know just for the squire and a few rich farmers. The working conditions of 18th century life was terrible having to live in four rooms and going to a out sick (?), and children from the age of 5 having to go to work in factorys and mines.

Much of this is expressive, close to talk, but it also carries information, as well as the response to it. Kenneth speculates about how to improve his own working conditions by splitting the class in half—the people who want to work and the people who don't—and then realises that this division may not always be easy to recognise: 'But I must be honest some time's me and robert stop working for a minute or two and have a chat after some hard work then we start work again.' So through the writing Kenneth is working out his own view of things.

Another way of understanding information is to do something with it—as opposed to just recording or reporting it. David, another second year comprehensive school pupil, was invited by his history teacher to write the speech that a wealthy landowner might have made to persuade villagers to accept enclosures:

Lisiten to your trusted squire for if you lisiten your land will grow and your children will grow healthy. If your don't you will suffer badly and children will grow up to be unhealthy. I gather you have heard of enclosures. I reckon they are a very good idea, for if we have strips of land we waste time by going from one strip to another strips but if we have enclosures we save time and crops will grow bigger and the land will be bigger. Suddenly you will grow healthy and wealthy and your children will be so wealthy they will be able to stand in my position so will your trust me. When your have your harvest next year you will see that your crops grow bigger and better and you will even come and tell me. Thank you for lisitening. A roar comes from the poor landowners.

David is using the information he has been given about enclosures—what they were, that the wealthy benefited from them and that the poor did not— and has tried to show how a wealthy landowner might have presented this information to suit himself. The exaggerated promise 'you will grow healthy and wealthy' reminds us of advertising copy. David's final sentence, 'A roar comes from the poor landowners' is neatly ironic. The writing is for an imagined public audience but it is not the dead language so often found in textbooks.

To Sum Up

The writing research team asked two questions: Who is the writing for? What is it for? We think that these are important questions for teachers to ask themselves about any writing they expect their pupils to do. As a Development Project that is one of our main concerns—to offer teachers the way of looking at the writing process which the research project formulated. Arising from this we hope we can:

1 encourage teachers *of all subjects* to provide a variety of audiences for their pupils' writing so that they are not so often seen as the teacher-examiner who evaluates whatever the pupils write;
2 encourage teachers *of all subjects* to provide for their pupils a range of writing purposes (linked to a range of audiences) so that pupils are given more opportunity to express their thoughts on paper in a variety of ways—expressive, transactional and poetic;
3 encourage the use of written language as well as spoken for a wider range of thought processes: interpreting, reflecting, thinking creatively and speculatively, as well as recording, reporting, generalising and classifying;
4 encourage teachers of all subjects to discuss together how language (spoken and written) can most effectively help their pupils to learn.

References

Britton, J., Burgess, T., Martin, N., McLeod, A., Rosen, H. (1975) *The Development of Writing Abilities (11-18)* (Schools Council Research Studies) Macmillan Education.

How Well Does Writing Across the Curriculum Work?

by Toby Fulwiler

For over a year now my colleagues and I have been assessing the impact of Michigan Tech's six-year-old writing-across-the-curriculum program. We have surveyed, interviewed, and questioned both faculty and students, and we have measured, collected, and scored whatever and wherever possible. Some of these data, once analyzed, may confirm or deny with numbers that our program works. However, numerous unexpected problems and benefits are already apparent. It is these I wish to report on here.

This essay is my attempt to set down, as frankly as possible, some of the lessons I have learned from overseeing a writing-across-the-curriculum program and conducting faculty workshops for the past six years. The goals and objectives, the theories and the successes of writing-across-the-curriculum programs have been fully described elsewhere in books, periodicals, and conferences; this essay will try not to repeat those assertions and descriptions.[1] Suffice it to say that I believe the programs do work and that the interdisciplinary writing workshops are the very best way to introduce those programs to college and university faculties.

We attempted from the beginning to influence faculty first—through the writing workshops—and students second—through attending classes taught by faculty who had attended the workshops. We believed that to improve student writing we had to influence the entire academic community in which writing takes place, to make the faculty sensitive to the role of writing in learning as well as to the relationship of writing to other communication skills—reading, speaking, and listening. We began our program in 1977, based primarily on the ideas of James Britton and his colleagues (*The Development of Writing Abilities, 11-18* [London: Macmillan, 1975]), to introduce faculty from all disciplines to a variety of ideas and strategies for

---

Reprinted from *College Composition and Communication* (February 1984). Copyright 1984 by the National Council of Teachers of English. Reprinted with permission.

[1] For a description of the Michigan Tech Writing-Across-the-Curriculum program see: "Showing, Not Telling, at a Writing Workshop," *College English,* 43 (1981) 55-63; "Writing Across the Curriculum at Michigan Tech: Theory and Practice," *WPA: Writing Program Administration,* 4 (1981) 15-20; "Interdisciplinary Writing Workshops," *CEA Critic,* 43 (1981), 27-32; and *Language Connections: Writing and Reading Across the Curriculum,* ed. by Toby Fulwiler and Arthur Young (Urbana, Ill.: National Council of Teachers of English, 1982). Also see Randall Freisinger's "Cross-Disciplinary Writing Workshops: Theory and Practice," *CE,* 42 (1980), 154-156.

using more writing in whatever courses they teach. We conducted intensive, two- and four-day writing workshops off campus for fifteen to twenty-five faculty at a time to introduce them to these general concepts: 1) that writing can be used to promote learning as well as to measure it; 2) that the writing process can inform all assignments and evaluation; and 3) that students write poorly for a variety of reasons—including poor motivation, immaturity, inadequate rhetorical skills. To date, spring 1983, we have conducted twelve such workshops for approximately 200 faculty and staff at our university. In addition my colleagues and I have conducted similar workshops at numerous colleges and universities throughout the country.

Teaching writing in English classes or outside of English classes remains more art than science: we still know very little about what happens at the moment of insight, inspiration, or ideation. Nor do we know predictable routes of faithful translation from thought to language, from pen to paper. So in every attempt to "teach" others to teach writing more often and more thoughtfully in their classes, problems arise with translation, motivation, situation, assumptions, pedagogy, terminology, personality, and turf. At the same time we who started such programs hoping to amplify the lessons of freshman composition soon found that we had stumbled into fertile territory for pedagogical research, faculty development, institutional cohesion, and personal growth.

The following personal reflections address two central issues which may never yield answers solely in numbers: what didn't work that we thought would—and why didn't it; and what happened that we didn't expect, but liked when it happened.

Problems

In the course of conducting some forty workshops, both at Michigan Tech and elsewhere, I encountered numerous questions for which I didn't have good answers. Sometimes I used language that conjured up inappropriate images; other times I hazarded solutions to problems with which I had no direct experience. But I learned and I think my answers have become more accurate, qualified, and careful. While some of these problems are institutional, others are specific to the disciplines or personalities of workshop participants. All nonetheless need to be dealt with, one way or another, by people who plan and conduct writing-across-the-curriculum programs.

Terminology. From the start we designed our program around a particular unified set of ideas and hoped to stick to those ideas consistently from workshop to workshop. We did so hoping the entire academic community would soon share common assumptions about writing and terminology to describe those assumptions and perhaps assign and evaluate student writing with a good measure of consistency. In particular we introduced our colleagues to James Britton's scheme for explaining the functions of writing: "expressive" (personal, informal writing to yourself to find out what is on your mind); "transactional" (writing to inform, instruct, or persuade someone about something); and "poetic" (writing used as art, where form, structure, and style may be more important than content). We felt this schema made sense, was easy to explain, and pointed toward certain overlooked solutions to the underuse and misuse of writing throughout the curriculum; namely, that more expressive writing in all subject areas would help students both to learn better and to learn to write better.

Often, however, we had trouble explaining exactly what the term "expressive" writing meant: to many teachers "expressive" connoted a dangerous freedom of language that suggested all sorts of educational license. We could usually dispel these anxieties over the duration of a several-day workshop, but the problem kept surfacing when people who had attended workshops tried to explain the ideas to colleagues back at campus or when we made brief presentations using that term without having the time to explore it fully. As a colleague in the School of Business recounted later: "Toby and Art Young came over trying to sell the department on workshops and then we got involved in the expressive-transactional argument again. And I think that the whole department has gotten a negative attitude." No matter how hard and lucidly (we thought) we explained the crucial distinction and relationship between the two functions of language, a number of faculty would never accept the idea that informal writing to oneself had anything to do with formal communication to somebody else—teachers, for instance. My School of Business friend tried to explain his colleagues' misconceptions: "I think the attitude of the School of Business for the most part is that . . . transactional writing has been replaced by expressive writing, poor sentence structure and no concern for spelling."

This fundamental misunderstanding lasted for over three years until we finally arranged a special exam-week, two-day workshop for his whole department and cleared up the problem once and for all. Some of my co-directors substituted terms like "exploratory" or "speculative" writing to avoid some of this terminology problem; however, the concept of informal, personal, or journal writing is of questionable value to faculty outside the humanities and no matter what language you describe it in, you must be prepared for some unsettling questions. Ironically, I had fewer problems with this problem on campuses where I came in as an "outside consultant": my pedestal was higher and so my word less debatable.

Resistance. We learned right away that writing workshops cannot inspire or transform unmotivated, inflexible, or highly-suspicious faculty members. Participants must volunteer with an open mind and be willing to share ideas, rather than compete with them in order for the workshops to work. Some people seem to be constitutionally uncomfortable with workshop-style activities which require a lot of participant risks, such as reading aloud one's own writing to colleagues or generating consensus ideas or writing in a personal journal. These same teachers may never feel comfortable generating classroom dialogue, assigning journals, or trusting students to evaluate each other's writing. Such people often attend with good intentions, but cannot adapt the informal workshop style to their own learning and teaching styles. One person, for example, from mathematics could not identify with any

activity that encouraged multiple drafts as the route to good writing: he
always wrote well in one draft and could not understand why others could not
also. I believed that he spoke truly about his own writing process, but his
vocal resistance was such that many in the workshop found him difficult to
work with and I had a hard time being patient with his intolerance. The mode
of writing and learning we presented in our model did not match his model
at all.

Other participants who have been ordered by their department heads to
attend the workshops and who do so out of resentment rather than personal
interest often pose more serious problems. These professors most often block
things by negation, by what they won't do: they won't keep journals, they
won't try freewrites, they won't share writing with colleagues or revise or
participate in peer group exercises that would affirm the value of the workshop. While such participants have been few, I can vividly remember each
one of them. Their participation—or lack thereof—puts such a strong damper
on workshops that we think leaders should go to great lengths to insist that
participants attend voluntarily. Yet we realize that if only the already-
committed attend, we are not reaching out as widely as we would like.

Turf. People sometimes ask me, with a twinkle in their eyes, what
disciplinary group is the most difficult to work with at workshops, from
which disciplines do I expect trouble. I could generalize (dangerously) and
say that philosophers and English teachers, on whose language turf the workshops most obviously intrude, raise the most skeptical questions. "How do
you know Britton's theories are correct?" "What empirical evidence proves
that journal writing facilitates learning?" "The ideas of Quine and Chomsky
contradict what you are saying." Philosophers especially question every
assumption and argue fine points of terminology and language use. In the
process they have taught me to stay closer to ideas verifiable by personal
experience and to stay away from too much theory, which is always debatable
from one point of view or another anyway. English teachers, especially those
who view their proper domain as literature, often do not believe that their
colleagues in other disciplines can teach anything about writing; consequently
they often want to instruct them on how to do it—which gets dangerously
close to telling them how to teach—which raises severe problems in all sorts
of directions.

To be fair, I could also say that some of the most helpful people in
workshops have been astute philosophers and savvy English teachers. Critical
colleagues with open minds who raise questions of concern to all are the very
best people in a writing workshop; however, people out to celebrate their own
wit and wisdom cause problems and often incur the wrath of the other
participants who are confused by too much disagreement among experts. All
this is, of course, predictable; the remarkable fact is how well most of the
mixed discipline people get on most of the time.

Translation. A good workshop offers a smorgasbord of strategies, practices, and techniques to improve both writing and learning, and participants
are free to adopt those that suit their personality, pedagogy, or situation. But

it doesn't always happen the way we expect, predict, or prefer. As a group, mathematics teachers seem to have the hardest time figuring out how workshop ideas apply to their teaching. One mathematics teacher, for example, who seemed to understand theoretically most of what went on at the workshop, stated later that the only thing he could think to do, practically, was send all his 150 calculus students to tour the writing lab—under penalty of failing the course. He did, and they all went, but we believe such translations are as likely to make students resentful of the lab as to seek help in it. Another mathematics teacher who enthusiastically used writing in a small upper-division project-oriented course found it virtually impossible to include it in her several first-year calculus courses: "The course material itself is not very conducive to writing. You can have students read a story problem or maybe make up some of their own, but . . . they don't have the mathematical sophistication, because they're just starting out, to create story problems." So, while I may think writing workshop ideas translate to all disciplines, my colleagues often tell me differently, and I have learned to accept that.

Numbers. Professors who teach courses with enrollments larger than fifty or sixty, often several hundred, report major difficulties in including more writing in their classes, even though, in theory, there are ways to do this. I have stopped arguing with them. Large classes are lousy places in which to ask for writing, unless well-trained graduate assistants or "readers" are available to help out. A colleague who teaches electrical engineering technology, when interviewed a year after attending a workshop, described his situation this way: "Labs are part of our teaching load each term and generate approximately 80 labs [reports] a week. Correcting these labs makes it very difficult to be motivated to ask for additional writing assignments." A mathematics professor who teaches in a fixed three-term calculus course, one of many such sections offered by her department, explained that "not only is the class large, but our courses are so full of material that must be covered and because the students have to take these courses in sequence, the engineering departments tell us we have to cover a certain amount of material in a certain amount of time." In other words, general ideas only translate into specific practices when an instructor perceives the conditions are right and appropriate. Although there are a variety of non-graded writing assignments that do work for some instructors, large numbers of students in a class remain a problem.

Trust. Perhaps the most difficult practice for teachers across the curriculum to use is peer review, where students read (aloud or silently) and critique each other's papers in a draft stage and then revise them for the instructor's review. An otherwise successful forestry professor, after trying peer review in his class, called it "a lead balloon"—explaining that some good students "suffered because his peers didn't do a good review." Another colleague in civil engineering noted: "Some students take it kind of lightly and they don't do a very good job. And then the other student that's being reviewed, of course, resents that." He went on to say that even when students take it seriously, they do not like to hurt their classmates' feelings: "Most of the time they're afraid to be critical."

I fully understand that problem. Peer review only works for me when I trust both the process and the students enough to work them hard, that is, when I return to the process more than two or three times during the term in the same groups of four or five. Used less than that, students simply do not have the time to develop trust in each other or to develop that critical, skeptical eye so important to good revision. The teacher in content-area courses who tries this once or twice, with or without specific guidelines, will have a real problem making it work. The teacher who makes peer review work—and several of my cross-curricular colleagues do have good success stories here—modifies his or her course substantially to make enough time and room for it to happen.

Dabbling. I've come to believe that you can only teach a writing process approach to process-oriented people. This implies first, that some colleagues, already on our wavelengths, are already doing some of the things we suggest and use the workshops primarily for reinforcement. That's good. But it also implies that many others who attend have a rather product-oriented approach to the whole teaching business: students must learn that what counts in the real world is the final report, the finished letter, the completed project—not the evidence of effort as one struggles to get there. (My own bias shows strongly here.) For these teachers, no matter how much we stress techniques and strategies to *generate* good final products (journal writes, freewrites, multiple drafts, etc.), the workshop produces only superficial change in their attitudes or practices. (Six months after she attended a workshop and told us how much it meant to her, a professor who teaches in forestry said that the main things she looks for on papers are "spelling, style, and neatness." While we don't dismiss these items, her answer dismays us.)

On the one hand, we are not surprised when product-oriented teachers leave the workshop with one or two ideas, but no real commitment to process-oriented education. On the other hand, we are surprised when the process-oriented teacher can't get a good process-idea to work. And this problem haunts a lot of really good committed teachers. If we only try peer reviews a few times they will fail; if we don't keep a journal ourselves the journals will seem like busywork; if we don't carefully plan papers to come in at different draft stages, they'll all come in at once at the end of the term. The point is that lots of good ideas fail because we don't fully commit ourselves to make them work; we don't or can't spend the requisite time to make them work. Large classes, or too many classes, or research and publication pressure—whatever the reason, teachers need to be awfully dedicated to make a new idea a regular part of their pedagogical repertoire. We don't mean to, but we often do, dabble rather than commit ourselves.

Location. On a related note, it is instructive to examine the colleges where writing-across-the-curriculum seems to work best. It doesn't get too far at large, research-oriented universities where teaching is not a high priority. Or if it does, the program is shaped like that at the University of Michigan, where one upper-level writing course and one committed teacher per discipline is the solution; no attempt is made to make most teachers pay attention to writing. Nor is writing across the curriculum needed at certain places—at well-endowed small liberal arts colleges with high SAT students and low teacher-student ratios—because writing has been an integral part of instruction all along: teaching was always valued and writing remained a natural way to teach well. The places where such writing-across-the-curriculum programs seem most likely to be needed and have a chance of success are the public schools where faculty have fairly high teaching loads and medium to low research and publication pressure. But these same institutions, like my own, work their teachers hard, and good ideas therefore need to be awfully practical and good teachers awfully dedicated to get writing back into the curriculum.

Overselling. I learned that when I strongly endorse one idea which works well for me, I can set up other teachers for failure: no idea will work for absolutely everyone every time. This has happened several times with journals, for example, an idea which I probably oversold at earlier workshops. A business teacher who tried to use journals found herself feeling silly asking classes of 100 students to "take out your journals"; it's a phrase you actually need to practice to feel comfortable saying out loud. Another colleague in metallurgy collected student journals from all of his three sections at the same time and was overheard cursing me out loud in his office, 180 journals piled high on his desk: he overdid what I oversold and the result was not good. To teach journals well, teachers need to keep one themselves and learn how it works first hand. The same is true for multiple-draft assignments: teachers need to watch their own writing process to know how to assign and evaluate best. And while a workshop of several days allows some opportunity for teachers to learn what it takes to write and read certain kinds of assignments, it's never really enough unless a teacher is sympathetic to begin with. This last point is crucial: the teachers who take the most away from a workshop are always those who were already doing some of the things we talked about. Perhaps the greatest value of the workshops is reinforcing one's current predispositions and practices. But even those sympathetic to a good idea know better than I when an idea *won't* work in their classes. One teacher explained that journals had no place in her course because "In mathematics, at least at the stage we're talking about, something's either right or wrong—there's seldom an in-between. You don't offer opinions about it in the same way you would discussing D. H. Lawrence, Hemingway, or Shakespeare."

Follow up. Short-term attitude changes do not guarantee long-term pedagogical changes. We already know that ideas which seemed bright and shiny in the workshop light have dimmed considerably after a year and two in our long, dark Michigan winter, due to increased teaching loads, large classes, administrative responsibilities, lack of collegial support, pressures to research, publish, write grants, and the like. We would be naive to believe we could maintain workshop-level intensity throughout the academic year. As my co-director Cynthia Selfe put it: "Of course they write and think about writing in the pine-scented wilderness that surrounds Alberta [where we do our summer workshops]. What else is there to do?" So while some teachers change their syllabi to reflect a new awareness of the role of process in assignment making, others do not. While some teachers immediately try out journals, others do not—and some who optimistically assigned journals one term find them too much trouble to assign the next.

But just as many follow-up problems can be traced to those of us who lead the workshops. Some years we have had alumni reunions, winter workshops, guest speakers, discipline-specific seminars with individual departments and informational mailings—one year we even published a monthly newsletter. Other years we, who were supposed to keep the writing spirit alive on campus, initiated nothing at all, for whatever reasons, because we were careless, overworked, lazy, or forgetful. In fact, it is hard to assess "blame" here; universities are busy places with lots going on, pulling all of us in multiple and different directions. We don't believe a writing-across-the-disciplines program can maintain white heat (or even red) throughout its term of operation. At the same time we remain convinced that these programs only work when they are long-term; that is, follow-up activities must continue no matter how difficult it becomes to find something new to do or how discouraging when no one shows up. As Art Young, the co-founder of our Tech program, puts it: "Ours is a model that will need continual care and thought—even after the five-year period [of external funding]—because it is primarily a faculty program rather than curricular." In other words, the teacher-centered model depends on teacher energy and informed pedagogy to work and keep working.

Carrots. At the very time we initiated our writing-across-the-curriculum program, with the strong encouragement of our deans and academic vice president, these very same administrators were encouraging higher standards for tenure and promotion, asking for more research, more publications, and the generation of more external money. Over the past six years these competing movements have actually pushed faculty at our university in opposing directions, suggesting that they spend more time assigning and evaluating student writing, on the one hand, while asking them to research and publish more of their own work on the other. Mixed messages. One colleague in mechanical engineering wearily described himself in a double bind: the better his teaching, which included using lots of workshop ideas, the further behind he fell with his own research, and the less recognition he received from his department or profession. This, again, may be a faultless position, one of the many double binds that serious teacher-researchers face all the time. I have no doubt that the pressure to be a publishing professional modifies, to some extent, the energy available to be an innovative teacher—which doesn't mean that the two roles cannot be kept in some sort of positive balance. But it isn't easy. A colleague in anthropology confided: "I have been, as you know, an enthusiastic supporter of student writing assignments, but to be honest, I'm souring. It's taken a lot of time and I feel it's not rewarded. Hence I have decided that next year I won't spend so much time 'teaching'; I am going to spend those 30 hours of student conference time doing my own writing. I agree it was valuable for them . . . it's just not so for me."

Unexpected Benefits

When we initiated our writing-across-the-curriculum program, we articulated our central concern as "improving students' writing ability." We soon learned—as we should have expected—that "writing ability" was related to all sorts of social, intellectual, and emotional domains which involved the entire campus community. As soon as the business of teaching writing, as well as the act of writing itself, was placed in this larger context, and as soon as we decided to offer our workshops as "explorations" rather than "conclusions" about the teaching of writing, we opened a much larger door than we ever anticipated. This part of the essay describes some lessons we didn't expect to learn and testifies to the power of an open-ended model to continue to stimulate and inform all involved.

Community of scholars. We all learned, after the very first workshop, how wonderful it was to join with one's colleagues to discuss substantive issues of mutual concern without the everyday distractions of phone calls, mail, meetings, and memos. Prior to the writing workshops no such mechanism for promoting collegial interactions existed in a regular way on campus: neither department, senate, and committee meetings nor special-topic seminars provided the focused time for social and intellectual stimulation across disciplinary lines. As one colleague put it: "The support of colleagues has been magnificent. I appreciated the opportunity to become better acquainted with my colleagues, the opportunity to form friendships." Another said: "Many faculty members who did not know each other or did not understand each other's discipline now feel a common bond. I think this will be useful and valuable to the college in a number of ways . . . committee assignments, interdepartmental projects, advice, etc." The chance for such interaction, even more than the reason for the interaction in the first place, has proved the most powerful reason for the program's success. The workshops actually remind some people why they became college teachers in the first place—before they retreated to separate buildings, isolated offices, and competitive research.

Environment. There has been a noticeable, but difficult to measure, shift in the general campus atmosphere about writing. It crops up in lunchroom talks, when colleagues joke that they'd better get out their journals for a quick entry now that I've arrived. But the jokes suggest to me an increased and not unpleasant consciousness about writing that did not exist before. In a conversation I had with the president of our university, Dale Stein, who had helped initiate the program in 1977, he said that recruiters had been telling him recently that MTU graduates were better at both writing and speaking than in former years. I mentally raised my eyebrows in disbelief, not willing to accept that such a generalization, nice though it was to hear, could possibly be true. But President Stein added that he firmly believed that an attitude shift had occurred which elevated writing to serious business in the campus community and that this was reflected in the communication skills of graduating seniors. I want, of course, to believe in such an improvement—but it remains difficult to prove. Informal clues like this tell us that something is at work here that may never show up in one or two concrete assessments of teacher attitudes or student writing abilities.

Teacher writing. By being asked to write themselves, many participants gained confidence in their own writing ability, or at least an awareness of why they were nervous about it. As one participant wrote: "I was quite apprehensive about attending this workshop when I found out that we would be writing a lot. . . . Writing has not always been my strength. . . . But I found that the apprehension was unwarranted; I found I could write OK, even my colleagues in the English Department said so. This was a pleasant surprise and morale/ego booster." Another wrote: "I now see that much of my hesitancy and anxiety about writing comes from a fear of censure from . . . my professional peers. I've assumed that all my writing must be witty, intelligent, elegant, etc., so that composing takes on crisis dimensions. This is something I will have to grapple with." What this teacher sees is how unwitty and inelegant his colleagues can be too. Such insights are, I believe, crucial for progress in one's own composing skills as well as for increased empathy for student writers.

Sometimes those of us who teach English, who enjoy using language and do not fear writing, forget how many of our colleagues have had unpleasant experiences themselves at the hands of English teachers in high school or freshman composition classes. Sadly enough, our profession has become better known for its concern with conventionality and correctness than for its celebration of joy and risk-taking in writing. Not only do current students fear our "red pencils," so do all our past generations of students who are now PhD's and who now teach biology, history, geography, and business in many university departments. Some of them too, along with carpenters and shopkeepers, exclaim when they meet us: "Better watch my grammar." It's not enough to come back with a flip, "It ain't so." The John Simons and Edwin Newmans have terrified us all.

One of the really nice things that happens at these workshops, sometimes, is that our colleagues gain confidence in their writing which extends to their professional work. A participant from political science who attended our first workshop later credited that session with giving him the confidence to write a book—which was published two years later. And my colleague, Art Young, received a letter from a workshop participant who wrote: "You probably don't need at this point further proof that your workshop processes work, but I thought I'd write and tell you that my essay that I wrote during the 1st August College workshop . . . "The Poor Man's Word Processor" was just accepted by [a professional business journal]. And I did it with almost no further revision other than that suggested by you and the other readers in my group. . . ."

Teaching methods. Some teachers learned that they could still learn something about teaching. We suspect that, at the college level in particular, teachers often assume they are talking to adults and that all they need to do is impart knowledge in some matter-of-fact way and it will be learned. And of course no college teacher worth his or her salt will ever admit to having taken an "education course" during college—whatever the merit of such courses. As a consequence, the model of the faculty workshop, which is inquiry based, and in which problems are posed for group solution and answers generated by participant interaction, offers a process view of teaching quite different from the traditional lecture and discussion format to which many teachers are accustomed. One geography professor told me a year later that ideas from the workshop ("WAC ideas") changed the learning atmosphere in his class: "When I have used WAC ideas, I have found my courses, especially the larger enrollment courses, are less stiff, formal, and dependent on lectures. Especially the use of freewrites has been a great help in stimulating discussion and class participation. I have been more likely to *plan* a class so that discussion will occur." Such translations occur when sensitive teachers watch how they themselves enjoy learning and in turn pass those "lessons" on to their students.

We interviewed a forestry professor six months after he attended an August workshop and found that he had already tried out a lot of specific workshop ideas in his fall classes: some worked well, like the "field-trip journals" he required in place of field notebooks, and "audience-specific assignments" in which his students wrote reports for multiple audiences in the forest management industries. But more than applying any specific practice, the instructor reported modifying his basic pedagogical approach because of the overall learning model introduced at the workshops. In his own words he began moving "away from the evaluation approach and more toward the process. I feel more attuned to teaching thought processes." Along with Dewey, Piaget, Bruner, and Britton, we believe strongly in the power and authenticity of discovery learning and are pleased when this larger translation occurs, but we do not expect it.

Tenure and promotion. One administrator told us that the workshops should improve overall faculty performance: "I am frankly most impressed by the potential for *faculty development* that stems from this program. Granted the students will benefit, but I will be much surprised if the individuals who have completed the experience do not perform better as researchers and in their service activities, as well as in the classroom." We know this is true in cases where the workshops give teachers more confidence about their writing ability, but I would also propose that the workshops have been stimuli for new pedagogical research questions in a variety of disciplines. In our own department there has been a documentable rise in faculty publications since the project began, most of which stem from the project work itself. In particular, a number of collaborative research-in-writing projects have developed involving an English instructor and someone from a different discipline. Of the projects I know about personally, here are some of the more interesting ones.

Biology: two of my colleagues have been working with three biologists to find out which of several teaching techniques—modeling, revision, or guidelines—helps students learn to write more careful and comprehensive laboratory reports; results of this experiment were delivered at the 1982 NCTE convention in Washington, D.C.

Civil Engineering: one colleague and a civil engineer have been experimenting with the effect of asking students in a junior-level engineering class to keep "project journals"; an article based on this experiment has been accepted for publication by *Engineering Education*.

Electrical Engineering: another colleague working with an electrical engineer and two graduate assistants is running a controlled experiment to find out which of two techniques—quiz and discussion or frequent expressive writing—prepares students better for a final examination.

Psychology: an English teacher and a psychology teacher are experimenting with the effects of asking students to write poetry and fiction in an Introduction to Psychology class. They want to find out if such "creative" writing assignments have a measurable effect on how well students learn certain concepts; results of this experiment were reported at the 1982 Conference on College Composition and Communication in Detroit

Philosophy/Geography/English: I am collaborating with two colleagues to find out how well students learn material in these different disciplines when their sole writing and testing assignment is to keep an intensive "dialogue journal" which they share regularly with their teachers. My geography colleague described this as a "term-long interactive essay examination."

Mathematics: two different English teachers have been working with a mathematics teacher in two different sections of a calculus course, looking at the differences in student learning generated by journal-writing assignments which place higher and those which place lower cognitive demands on the writer.

While these experiments are in different stages of development, their net effect has been increased social and intellectual inquiry among our faculty.

Cohesion. Neither Art Young nor I entered the project with the idea of writing a book, nor could we have predicted that the department, as it was formulated in 1977 when we began the project, could author a book. But that is what happened. As we recruited new faculty for our department, who had varying specialties from "technical writing" and "reading" to "problem-solving" and "conferencing," we realized that we did, in fact, have the material for writing a book aimed at workshop participants from all disciplines. Consequently, the process of planning, writing, and editing this book, *Language Connections: Writing and Reading across the Curriculum* (Urbana, Ill.: National Council of Teachers of English, 1982), helped unite a dozen teachers on our staff in a collaborative effort providing both intellectual and social cohesion among the participating writers. Constructing this book gave us a common concern, apart from teaching and conducting workshops; in some cases, it actually provided colleagues with their first substantial professional publication. And it gave us a goal to shoot for: finishing the manuscript.

The collaborative book became a symbol of the collaborative activity and research which this project inspired from the beginning. The workshops are always conducted by teams from our department, which rotate from year to year. Other department members make guest appearances to present special workshops on "reading" or "speaking" or "the language laboratory" within the larger workshop. New teams were created to visit different departments and publicize and recruit for the workshops. Through it all we met off and on, as a group, planning what to do next to make things work. The net professional effect of this cooperative effort were numerous joint teaching experiments, collaborative grant proposals, and co-authored articles: for example, I have co-authored articles with eight different colleagues in the department over the past five years.

I think that, in general, the scientific and technical fields do more cooperative research and scholarship than those in the humanities, though there are notable and admirable exceptions, usually promoted by NEH. This project taught us well about the fruits of working together on funding, teaching, researching, and writing to effect positive changes in both our university and the profession at large.

So we did not know when we started our program in 1977 that what began as an effort to improve student writing skills would develop into a comprehensive long-term program to develop more fully all the interrelated learning and communication skills of the whole campus community. Nor did we realize in how many different directions research and evaluation questions would take us, nor the degree of local cooperation and national publicity we would receive. Nor did I know, personally, that this project would become the substance of my professional life for the better part of a decade.

As a department we will continue to monitor and nurture the program which now possesses a life of its own. Remember, there are two hundred or so of our colleagues out there doing all sorts of stuff in the name of "writing across the curriculum." I believe that most of it is beneficial to students and teachers alike. The empirical measures that are sought by my statistically trained colleagues may eventually demonstrate conclusively that the program is a howling success—or they may not. As I said at the outset, the program we have conducted is amorphous, hard to pin down, and impossible to keep total track of. As my dissertation advisor, Merton Sealts, used to say when I wanted to try something off-beat or experimental: "What works, works." To which I add, "But not all the time, nor for everyone, and sometimes better than we guessed."

Writing Across the Curriculum

by James L. Kinneavy

The phrase "writing across the curriculum" is relatively new, as far as I am aware. I want to examine its underlying meaning, its various administrative forms, and its implications for the faculties of colleges and of high schools to look at the theory, the practice, and occasionally the history of the notion.

Despite its novelty, the practice of writing across the curriculum, in one form or another, has spread rapidly. Prestige institutions like Harvard and Yale; large state institutions like Michigan, Maryland, and Texas; large private institutions like Brigham Young; small liberal arts institutions like Beaver College in Philadelphia or St. Mary's College in California; community colleges in many states; and high school systems (even a whole state like Michigan) have considered or are considering adopting some version of the practice. I know of scores of institutions that are implementing the notion. In a short time (much less than it took Piaget, for instance), writing across the curriculum has been entered in the list of descriptors for bibliographic searches for the ERIC system (Educational Retrieval Information Centers).

The central idea behind the various practices seems to embody a resurrected sense of the responsibility of entire faculties and administrative bodies for the literacy competence of the graduates of our high schools and colleges. Almost twenty years of declining SAT, ECT, ACT, and GRE scores, registered regressions in writing skills reported by the National Assessment of Educational Progress, continual complaints from industry and government, and the daily intuitive reactions of thousands of teachers have all made us realize that we can no longer deny the hard facts—for whatever reasons, writing and reading skills of students in this decade are not what they were twenty years ago.

Writing across the curriculum is one response of the academic world to this chorus of concern. Some of the others include higher entrance requirements in admission tests for colleges, more required courses in English composition at the high school and college levels, competency tests in some thirty-five states, competency tests for students in the junior year in college, tougher tests for prospective teachers, and in-house courses and workshops for persons in business and industry.

Reprinted from *ADE Bulletin* 76 (1983): 14-21. Reprinted with permission.

Writing across the curriculum may become the most important and far-reaching of these responses to what has been called the literacy crisis. The reason is that the others are Band-Aid provisions affecting only some aspects of a massive concern, whereas writing across the curriculum can, if properly interpreted, be a total immersion, horizontally in all departments and vertically at all levels of high school and college.

Writing across the curriculum may be seen as reasserting the centrality of rhetoric to the humanities tradition, a position it has not occupied since the middle of the eighteenth or the beginning of the nineteenth century. In fact, the ability to write intelligent prose has been the hallmark of the educated person from antiquity to the present. The student of the *ephebia,* the two-year college training for citizenship, was mainly taught to write speeches for the political assembly or for the courts, speeches that he then memorized and delivered The *ephebia* was the core educational experience for hundreds of city-states in the Mediterranean area for nearly eight hundred years. The cleric in the Middle Ages was, before anything else, a man who could read and write. And if there is anything in common to the university experiences in England, the Continent, South America, Asia, and the United States, and to the community colleges of this country, the *gymnasium* in Germany, the *lyceo* in Italy, or the *lycée* in France, it is the ability to write intelligent prose. When the college student no longer has this ability, the central achievement of higher education has been missed.

To support the importance I attach to the notion of writing across the curriculum, I want to define the term more carefully.

Ordinarily two different meanings are given the phrase. Perhaps most frequently, the phrase is used to mean that the business of writing is taken over by the various departments, such as government, physics, history, and music. Typical of this approach is the program at the University of Michigan, where, in the College of Letters, Arts, and Sciences, each department proposes specific writing courses to the English Composition Board of the college. The courses, after being approved by the board, are carried out by the teachers of the various subjects, usually with the help of a teaching assistant from that department who has been given some training in the teaching of composition by teachers designated by the board. This fall over one hundred and forty such courses were offered. Members of the board have also got in touch with all the high schools of the state and advocated the adoption of a similar program in the secondary level. Let me call this the individual subject approach to writing across the curriculum.

A second, rather different approach can be seen in programs at the University of Maryland, Brigham Young, and others. These schools retain the notion that all students should write prose about the concerns of their disciplines, but they centralize the responsibility of training students in individual writing departments, usually English or rhetoric. At Maryland and at Brigham Young, for example, the English department offers courses in four different areas: the natural sciences and technology, the social sciences, the humanities, and business (at Brigham Young, however, the business courses are taught by teachers in that discipline). But the generic offerings by college are not further differentiated into subject courses. Let me call this second approach the centralized generic system. It clearly differs in important respects from the individual subject approach.

Both approaches can be called horizontal, giving this metaphor the meaning of extending across the various subjects and disciplines of a college or high school viewed as a static structure.

Another issue concerns the developmental sequence of a student's college experience. Studies at Harvard and Bradley have shown that it is possible to train freshmen to a certain level of skill in writing ability but that such a skill, if not used, can deteriorate during a student's college career. The Harvard study of 1978 showed that, because of a lack of sustained practice, seniors in the natural sciences wrote worse prose than did their freshman counterparts who had just finished a course in freshman composition (Bok). By contrast, seniors in the humanities wrote better than their freshman counterparts. The Harvard experience and a research study at Bradley, as well as the common experience of many teachers of advanced courses of composition for juniors and seniors, have caused many writing-across-the-curriculum programs to incorporate a vertical dimension into their system (Snider). Part of the writing experience should occur in the upper-class years of the student. The faculty of the University of Texas, for example, has approved a program with a freshman course in writing, a sophomore course in literature with required writing components, and a junior course in writing across the curriculum (offered in four generic areas, like the Maryland and Brigham Young programs); and a fourth course in the senior year specifically located in the particular subject department (like the Michigan program). Such a program would monitor students' writing at every year of their college careers. This is another dimension of writing across the curriculum.

Let us now look in some detail at the two major types of writing across the curriculum, the single subject approach and the centralized writing department approach.

Single Subject Approach

In recent times the two examples of a subject specialization in writing across the curriculum are the earlier textbooks on technical writing and programs like the one at Michigan. In both, the particular department is in charge of the writing in that discipline. In effect, European universities function the same way.

Some theoretical and many practical results follow from what seems simply an administrative decision to adopt the single subject approach. The most obvious feature of such a program is that the teacher is an expert in the field in which the writing is being done; he or she knows the subject, its vocabulary, and the methods of reasoning and the major genres of the field. Outsiders are often looked on as aliens, persons incapable of following the jargon and arguments of the specialist. The more specialized and advanced the discipline, the more pronounced this attitude becomes. In fact, as Percy Tannenbaum reported in *Science*, "J. Robert Oppenheimer stated the dilemma of science communication succinctly when he said some years ago that science is defined in words and phrases which are almost impossible to translate into conventional lay language" (581). Since the specialist teacher is the immediate audience for the student's writing in these programs, students can be as technical as they want, and the accuracy of their statements can be checked by an expert. There are obvious pedagogical advantages to this relationship.

In such circumstances, students tend to write in the genres of the specialist, use the vocabulary of the technician, and make commendable efforts to address and imitate peers or even superiors. The situation approximates the actual career circumstances where experts write for their equals. The logic and methodology of the specialist are exploited to the full. The resulting themes are comprehensible to the insider, sophisticated, and technical—much like the writing of the scholarly journals of the department. They are, indeed, a far cry from "What I Did Last Summer."

But these advantages bring with them correlative disadvantages. Students do not learn to address a popular audience, they use the jargon of the trade, and they make no concession to the university at large. The department is isolated, fragmented, and increasingly withdrawn from a common intellectual ferment. Even more important, the specialist does not attempt to go beyond the university community and speak to the populace at large. Students write esoteric prose, often incomprehensible even to their university comrades, a fortiori to the great unwashed.

Certainly this picture is not far removed from the current situation. Most of the writing of the academic world is light years away from the ordinary citizen and some years away from the rest of the university community. This holds true for disciplines as far apart as physics and physical education or engineering and English. Indeed, it is probably true that the latest piece in the journals of literary criticism is as unintelligible to the general reader as the latest article in the publications of petroleum engineering. Neither would seem terribly relevant to the average citizen of the polis, who, if forced to a choice, would probably take the engineering article.

A further disadvantage can be seen in the subject matter decentralization. Precisely because the programs are decentralized and operate on the unexamined assumption that disciplinary products are accessible only to the initiated, they often resist a centralized scrutiny. Dan Fader, in charge of the program at Michigan, expressly takes this stand; his overseer board approves of programs that are suggested almost solely on the basis of quantitative norms (actual pages of writing). He does not look into the actual themes written in the classes. In the past such an attitude has permitted carelessness and neglect in some programs of this type, leading occasionally to their demise.

The drawback cited most frequently by the teachers in the classes is that they are not trained to teach students to write. It is true, as Fader and others point out, that most of the teachers are writers themselves and therefore know, in an intuitive way, something about writing. But to assume that they can thereby teach writing is a position that could reduce almost any discipline to the level of the dabbling amateur. We all know something about the English language since we use it every day, but that does not make us linguists or speech teachers. We all think, but that does not make us logicians.

The systematic analysis of the processes and products of writing constitutes a particular discipline of long historical standing. And if all of us are to become writing teachers, it would benefit us to learn something about the discipline. Otherwise it might be said that the university assigns one of its most important functions to amateurs, unskilled and bungling, while it subjects other concerns to all the careful disciplinary methodologies that modern science and art can muster. Perhaps this very disparity has caused our present crisis.

One final drawback must be mentioned. At my university, it was clear that many departments did not want to take on the responsibilities of teaching writing because of the time it takes to correct, grade, and assess compositions. Busy assistant professors or even professors do not feel that such a commitment of their time would be rewarded by the university's promotion and merit system. Promotions and merit follow on scholarship, teaching, and service—usually in that order. And assigning and correcting themes do not fit neatly into any of these categories without extensive readjustments. This objection, a serious one, probably obtains more in the institutions that insist on a "publish or perish" reward system. I don't see it in small liberal arts institutions.

Of all these objections, only the lack of training in rhetoric is necessarily inherent in the single subject approach.

The Centralized Writing Department Approach

The centralized writing department is a peculiarly American phenomenon in the university. American English departments, like their British counterparts, are a relatively late development in university organizational structures. And their function as almost sole guardians of literacy is generally unparalleled in university history.

When professors with some backgrounds in classical and modern rhetoric and composition move into writing-across-the-curriculum courses, what sorts of things happen in the classes? Let me take as prototypes of these programs the courses offered at Brigham Young University, the University of Maryland, and the University of Texas, since I have followed each of them with some interest.

The Brigham Young program grew out of the success of the university's technical writing classes, organized under the direction of John S. Harris. He extended the technical writing classes to courses in writing for all the science and engineering students. This success was repeated in the social science classes and then in the humanities. The departments of business offered their own courses. But the first three sets of courses were offered by members of the English department.

Harris' approach represents that of most modern authors in technical writing. Building on programs pioneered by Mills and Walter at Texas, these authors of college texts have moved away from the early emphasis on individual subjects to considerations of rhetorical principles that transcend departments—such as careful description, explanation and proof, and problems of definition and classification—and to some considerations of style and audience.

With a knowledge of these basic concerns, which might be called logical or rhetorical, anyone can train writers in various disciplines as long as the subject matter does not get too esoteric. These have been the assumptions made by most of the successful texts and teachers of technical writing over the past twenty years. And most of the courses have been offered through English departments—as they are at Brigham Young. When such a mentality is extended to all the undergraduate schools of a university system, as it is at Brigham Young and Maryland and Texas (each offering four college-generic courses), a different kind of approach to writing across the curriculum results.

Let us describe this approach and, in the process, contrast it to the single subject approach considered earlier. Most likely, the teacher is from the English department and hence an expert only in that discipline, usually in literature but sometimes also in rhetoric. Since the teacher is only generally knowledgeable in such areas as chemistry, physics, economics, and petroleum engineering, the student writer cannot assume the sophistication about the discipline that the single subject approach takes for granted. Consequently, the assumed audience in such programs becomes the generally educated reader. The task of the writer is to make clear to a generalist, who knows less than the writer, the intricacies of a discipline that he or she has been learning for two or three years (assuming that these courses are given in the junior or senior year, as they are at all three of these schools).

The rhetorical effects of such a task are massive. The writer must eschew the usual genres of the career specialist, translate technical vocabulary into language the generalist can understand, and sacrifice subtlety in argumentation and methodology. All these constraints are distinct losses. And, if one argues that specific disciplines really do have their own logics, then the unique logic of a discipline is adjusted to the general logic of the educated reader—assuming there is such a thing.

The gains of such a program are substantial, however. First, the university does not have to train the entire faculty to be expert teachers of writing; such a role can be left to specialists. And if the specialists are trained to their métier, they ought to be better at it than just anyone. Such a concept gives dignity to the career and to the concept of the writing teacher and to the importance of teaching writing.

Second, the centralized writing department, by forcing all students of the college to speak about their specialties to the uninformed generalist, imposes a common language on the university community. It reunites the fragmented "pluraversity" of the twentieth century into a linguistic *uni*versity. This would be a major achievement by itself. It has happened, I believe, at Beaver College, in Pennsylvania, as a result of the school's program in writing across the curriculum. At the college's summer seminars, organized under the auspices of the English department and led by rhetoricians of some note, the faculty members discovered that they could talk to one another about their particular interests without getting lost in occult obscurities. The college became a collegium, a unified intellectual community.

The purpose of the writing tasks in this situation also changes. Whereas the single subject approach tends to the demonstrative or the exploratory, the audience change in the centralized approach requires the writer to move in the direction of the explanatory or informative. These movements have organizational and stylistic corollaries.

It seems that this approach is radically different from the first one. And an institution that commits itself to one or the other is committing itself to different kinds of writing in audience, in purposes, in genres, in style, and even in organizational patterns (though I haven't stressed them in this article).

It also seems that what the single subject approach gains in depth it sacrifices in breadth, what it gains in audience specificity it loses in intellectual community, what it gains in subtlety it loses in clarity, what it gains in demonstrative power it loses in informative reach, what it gains in precision it loses in lucidity, what it gains in freedom it loses in accountability, and what it gains in scientific rigor it loses in rhetorical appeal.

A Suggestion: The Best of Both Worlds

These two options are not incompatible. And in my opinion, both are desirable. But no program has successfully combined the two in a workable sequence, as far as I know. Maryland, Texas, and Brigham Young have a semester of freshman English not committed to any particular subject and then a semester of junior English of the centralized type. Michigan and Beaver College have a similar semester of freshman English and a specialist-type course in the junior year.

Part of the reticence to adopt the full set of options is governed by administrative units of semester sequences and hours of courses allotted to departments. Each institution has to face up to its own student body and implement the theoretical and practical program it needs. Some prestige institutions with elite entrance requirements may not need the large beginning freshman composition courses that institutions like Maryland, Texas, Brigham Young, and even Michigan feel are necessary. Maybe it will eventually be possible to use this first-year experience in conjunction with some writing-across-the-curriculum subjects. A few community college experiments in this direction teach us something about what is possible at the under-class level. But I am not too optimistic: both options seem to call for the sophistication and maturity of the upper-class student.

Whatever administrative structure the final program takes, I believe that it must meet certain theoretical and practical criteria. First, there must be some sort of vertical sequence; the Harvard experience demonstrates this necessity even for the very gifted. Second, there ought to be some training for the teachers of writing, whether specialists or generalists. Third, there ought to be a period in which the mature student explains his or her discipline to the general reader in a common university dialect; this requisite should entail persuasive in addition to explanatory and informative purposes. I shall return to this point later. Fourth, there ought to be a period in which students can write as subtly and as esoterically as they wish in the genres of their careers to an audience of peers or superiors. Fifth, there ought to be recognition that literacy is the concern of the entire faculty since it is the cornerstone of a higher education. Finally, there ought to be a system of accountability at all levels of a vertical continuum.

I do not wish to propose any single system for different colleges and universities. But, to illustrate these different criteria, let me describe the program we are in the process of constructing at Texas. If adopted, it will meet most, though not all, of the criteria I have outlined.

We find that about three fourths of our freshmen need a first course in composition that emphasizes basic rhetorical principles, the fundamentals of reading, and a review of mechanics with a handbook. At this level we use general topics generated by a reading anthology or, in a few sections, some literary readings.

The second course in our sequence is required because of its literary content and only secondarily because of its composition component. Although it is basically an introduction to either British, American, or world literature, there are four required themes. This course is offered at the sophomore level, mainly for logistic reasons—the English department could not handle a heavy infiltration of sophomores into the freshman sequence. The course does, by design, continue the literary component of the liberal arts tradition.

The third course, offered in the junior year, is a course in writing across the curriculum modeled on either the Michigan or the Maryland variation. The departments in the university that wish to offer their own classes may do so. So far, there has not been a mad rush to accept this responsibility. Generally, most students choose the sort of course offered in the Maryland version—one with the subject matter drawn from their own discipline but taught by a member of the English department. It meets the criteria of addressing informative and persuasive writing to the general reader and of being taught by teachers trained in rhetoric.

The fourth course is in the specific subject with a heavy writing component. It meets the criterion of demonstrative and exploratory prose addressed to an expert in the field and written in the career genres of the specific major. And, of course, since it is a university-wide requirement, it places the final responsibility for the student's literacy in the hands of the entire faculty. In essence, it is a course like that offered upperclassmen at Michigan. Ideally, as at Michigan, graduate students in the particular departments will be trained to help professors with the grading and holding of conferences in this fourth course also. This will help the program meet the criterion of trained teachers, assuming that the English department trains its own members to be rhetorically knowledgeable.

Let me say a word about the desirability of writing persuasive papers addressed to the general reader. This kind of writing serves two purposes. First, it continues the rhetorical component of the liberal arts tradition, just as the literature course at the sophomore level continues the "grammar" component of the tradition and just as the demonstrative and exploratory writing at the fourth level continues the logic and dialect components of the tradition.

The continuation of the liberal arts tradition is not merely an exercise in meaningless antiquarianism. The liberal arts tradition is valid today because it represents a care for three quite different kinds of thinking—scientific (in logic and dialectic), persuasive (in rhetoric), and aesthetic (in the study of literature, the grammar of the tradition). In my opinion—and I can only state it dogmatically, given the current circumstances—these are the three types of thinking that it is the duty of the university to get each student to engage in for a full mental life. Without any of the three, a person's intellectual health is impaired. In effect, he or she is missing a mental limb.

Most of the university courses giving some attention to writing emphasize the logical and the exploratory. Some pay attention to the aesthetic (literature, art, music, drama). But few consciously focus on the persuasive. This alienation of rhetoric from the university's explicit goals has had some unfortunate corollaries. First, it has broken the major connection between the humanities and the daily life of the average citizen of the state. Rhetoric, more than literature and more than science (the grammar and logic of the tradition), was the linking bridge of the humanities to the ordinary person. Without this bridge the university has lost its major relevance contact with real life, in the view of the populace. This partly explains the university rebellions in this century in France, Germany, and this country. The academic can become, well, academic.

Second, the alienation of rhetoric from the university has produced a new exemplar of the teacher since the Renaissance. The reduction of the training of the student writer to an expertise in expository writing (demonstrative, exploratory, informative prose) has narrowed the writer's conceived audience down to peers or superiors and has separated ethical and moral responsibilities from scientific concerns. Once the scientist-teacher no longer feels a duty to address the populace in rhetorical genres and can pursue scholarly interests untrammeled by the intervention of religious or moral beliefs, he or she can perform amorally in the laboratory and in the classroom *as* a scientist-teacher. Scientist-teachers can pass on to intermediaries—political or journalistic or marketing—the responsibility of using the objects of their scientific research, since they are no longer responsible to the populace directly.

Yet it does seem immoral for a discipline as a whole to disavow the responsibility for its creations. Computer scientists, chemists, philosophers, journalists, novelists, and engineers, as social groups, have a responsibility for the abuses to which society puts their products, just as they have a right to the plaudits that follow on their successes. The chemist and the computer scientist can most accurately foresee the beneficial and harmful uses to which their inventions may be put. Each profession has a rhetorical obligation to alert society to new benefits and also to new dangers.

This informative and rhetorical function should be taught to the practitioners of the professions. In practice this means that the politics, the ethics, and the rhetoric of a profession ought to be a part of the curriculum of any discipline. And the rhetoric of the discipline means the ability to address the populace in persuasive language that, to be listened to, will often have to be intensive, even impassioned, audience-biased, and stylistically appropriate to a segment of the populace. We don't teach our majors to write this kind of prose.

Consequently, it is not enough to teach the practitioners of a given craft how to communicate with one another in the jargon of their department. They must also be taught the common language of humanity in its full rhetorical scales. This means that all disciplines must offer training in the persuasive techniques of rhetoric. Thus at least some physicists, chemists, pharmacists, journalists, political theorists, and so on should engage in the impassioned and simple prose that affects the multitude. Training these future professionals to write only expository prose is training them to ignore their political and ethical responsibilities.

The wholesomeness of the teacher exemplar who was scholar and rhetorician and also aesthete is a wholesomeness we cannot dispense with. Fragmented scholars are irresponsible scholars, as capable of turning out iniquitous monsters as beneficent marvels.

Rhetoric, consequently, should be incorporated into the curriculum of all college students. Its exile has been costly.

Some Problems That Remain

The distinction between writing for a general audience and writing for a specialist audience, however, does not answer some of the questions raised by the problems of general audiences trying to read translated messages from the individual disciplines. In fact, a wholesale attempt to translate these messages may bring to light hitherto hidden issues having to do with the particular logical patterns of each discipline. The issues occur in at least three different stages of the scientific method of the various sciences. I use the word "science" in a tolerant and pluralistic sense for the kinds of evidence that each discipline accepts in its textbooks and professional literature. In addition, these "logics" will require some major readjustments of the centralized reading and teaching departments (usually English). Let us consider a few examples of these logics and then turn briefly to a sketch of the administrative changes they entail.

Anthropologists frequently talk about the ethno-science of a culture, that is, the material accepted by that culture as scientific, regardless of how it may be viewed by other cultures. Using this distinction, I have talked in *A Theory of Discourse* about the ethnologic of scientific proof, the kind of logic accepted as valid within an academic subculture. Thus "even within the matrix of Western civilization, the German view of *science* can tolerate a brand of metaphysics and a *Literaturwissenschaft* which much Anglo-Saxon thought would term speculation at best" (128).

But we don't have to go as far as Germany to find such cultural differences in ethnoscience and ethnologic.

> Indeed one does not have to go beyond the province of a single major university in this country. Many physicists, sociologists, even educators, would not label much dissertation work by literary critics *scientific* at all. Similarly, many English professors would consider the endless survey and statistical techniques of educators trivial and inconsequential. Even within the individual English departments, the time is not too removed when historical critics would not speak to "new critics" or "descriptive" to prescriptive" linguists.
>
> (Kinneavy 128)

I have personally been involved in some of these cross fires. And the general reader of courses in different disciplines had better be prepared for such cross fire, even within the narrower limitations of, say, Writing in the Humanities, as opposed to Writing in the Natural Sciences.

These differences, as far as I can see, occur more in the sciences that use deductive methods than in those that use inductive and statistical techniques. The reason is simple: the various disciplines start off from different axiomatic beginnings. The axioms of the law student are the constitutional foundations, the legislative additions, and the judicial precedents and interpretations given the first two. Obviously these axioms differ from country to country, often from state to state. By contrast, the axioms of the theologians within a given church may frequently be international (at least to the extent that the church is), but they certainly differ from those of other churches of the same generic persuasion (such as Christianity) and even more from those of other churches of different general creeds.

Such axiomatic differentiations seem obvious enough in law and theology. But they are not so obvious in politics or literary theory or even mathematics. Indeed, they are frequently not neatly stated in unambiguous formulas but hidden in premises and reasoning methodologies. They may not even be articulated by the users of the subculture. Many of us, for example, used some now questionable axioms in our study of literature under the auspices of New Criticism without being aware of their existence in any explicit promulgation.

These differences are just now beginning to be studied. Chaim Perelman and L. Olbrechts-Tyteca, in *The New Rhetoric: A Treatise on Argumentation,* have begun to work on these problems, as well as on the possibility of something like a universal audience. Some German scholars have revived the notion of rhetorical topic analysis as an analysis of the different ethnologics of various disciplines. Otto Pöggeler, the disciple of Heidegger, has applied the notion of topic analysis to philosophy, and Theodor Viehweg has applied it to jurisprudence. A number of scholars have applied the notion to literature ever since Robert Curtius used it in *European Literature and the Latin Middle Ages*. Sometimes, however, the topics of literary analysis can simply degenerate into subject matter or theme analysis—and I am not talking about this notion of topic. In any case, there is room for many fertile dissertations and research monographs in the field of the differing axiomatics of different disciplines and their rhetorical applications to the classroom of the writing-across-the-curriculum movement.

There is also some room for the analysis of the varying treatments given inductive generalizations in various disciplines. The general acceptance of the methods of inductive probability and of statistical methods from education to physics indicates much less divergence in induction from discipline to discipline than in deduction. Members of English departments, however, if they are to become general readers for these logics, will have to capitulate to this widespread "ethnologic" and teach something about induction and statistical methodology. Such an innovation should have some beneficial by-products in literary and rhetorical and maybe even linguistic scholarship.

In this article I am going to pass over such ethnologic issues as the differing exploratory methods of different sciences and even the differing persuasive techniques operating particularly in grant proposals—that curious hybrid of exploration and persuasion. There are, however, a few major divergences in the way the various disciplines use what I call the modes (narration, description, classification, and evaluation). As far as I am aware, these differences have never been seriously studied.

Let me give a few illustrations. In English literary studies, we are accustomed to a fairly narrow range of types of definition. Most of those we use are of the genus-species kind, often called the "logical" definition by logicians. Frequently these logical definitions are used in a purposive or teleological framework. Aristotle's definition of tragedy in *On Poetics* ends with such a purposive statement:

> A tragedy, then, is the imitation of an action that is serious and also, as having magnitude, complete in itself; in language with pleasurable accessories, each kind brought in separately in the parts of the work; in a dramatic, not in a narrative form; with incidents arousing pity and fear, wherewith to accomplish its catharsis of such emotions.
>
> (1449b.24-27)

Many definitions in the arts, whether fine or useful, are of this type: a watch, for instance, is defined as a small instrument (genus) for telling time (species, denoting purpose).

But if English teachers are to become general readers, they will have to become accustomed to recursive definitions (in mathematics and linguistics), environmental or slot definitions (linguistics), operational definitions (many of the physical sciences), nominal definitions (those with no pretense to real objects exemplifying them), and so forth. Even the translated messages of the sciences will embody these types of definitions.

One additional example from the modes: Evaluation is a mode that is theoretically proscribed by many disciplines, at least in some circumstances. Value judgments, as they are often called, are taboo in some formal kinds of media and academic discourse. I was once told at a dissertation oral examination for a student in English education that my value judgments were showing. I replied that I hoped that they were and that the colleague who was upbraiding me for such a value display was himself engaging in value judging by repudiating value judgments. In a sense, however, my response was unfair. Some disciplines find it much more necessary than others to distinguish between descriptive and evaluative judgments. In fact, another good study would be for someone to make a comparative study of this matter; it would entail distinguishing between the valid value judgments, though sometimes implicit, and the invalid value judgments of such disciplines and describing the circumstances in which they are invalid.

We in English departments have also to learn to extend our knowledge of plot narrative to expository narrative, in which cause and effect are the determining issues. Case histories in psychology and medicine, physical forces in geology and meteorology, social forces in history all embody a notion of narrative that we have largely neglected in our literary studies.

We are going to have to learn too about some media and genres that we have not encountered or analyzed. Lab reports, case histories, field studies, and other subgenres are only a few examples; the textbook by the five members of the Beaver College staff, Elaine Maimon and others, is a pioneer in this direction.

Preparing English teachers for this kind of reading and teaching will require administrative changes. At such institutions as Brigham Young, Maryland, and Texas, where the centralized department teaches the writing-across-the-curriculum courses at the junior level and asks the students to write for the generally educated reader, some sort of faculty preparation ought to be made for optimal results. Ideally, I would propose that faculty choose one of the three major areas—empirical sciences, humanities, and business—and make some general study of the methodologies, definitions, criteria of evidence, general axiomatic systems, and views of value judgments. Also ideally, these faculty members should meet with the members of the target disciplines and acquaint themselves with the expectations of these faculties. Reading lists and different types of professional writings, textbooks, and student themes should be collected to give incoming teachers realistic ideas of what the students are dealing with in the various disciplines. The teaching assistants who help the members of the separate disciplines in the writing-emphasis courses should be trained by teachers with the same sort of generic and general background knowledge of the field.

Extending the functions of an English department in this way could have miraculous results. I know "miraculous" sounds pretentious and exaggerated, but for me the word describes the effect I observed at Beaver College the first time I acted as consultant to the writing-across-the-curriculum program there. All the faculty from different departments were speaking the same academic dialect, the dialect of the educated reader, to the members of the English department. The college was a collegium, a unified body of academics, speaking the same language about the problems of the various disciplines.

All the fragmented disciplines of the usual pluraversity can become a university with such a dual movement. The English department must learn to speak the generic logics of the other departments of the university, and the isolated and insulated departments can make the other step toward a unifying language, the dialect of the generally educated reader. Thus the writing-across-the-curriculum movement could, if properly pursued, place the English department at the center of the entire university community. But the price of this enviable and appealing prospect is for the English department to enlarge its interests from literary discourse to all discourse. English should be the study not just of literary artifacts and their production but of all language artifacts written in English, and especially of scientific and rhetorical artifacts. The department can then rightfully assume the title it usually takes; the Department of English. Such a department accepts as its province the scientific, the literary, the rhetorically persuasive, and the expressive texts of the language.

Works Cited

Aristotle. *Aristotle.* Trans. Ingram Bywater. Ed. Robert Maynard Hutchins. Chicago: Encyclopaedia Britannica, 1952.

Bok, Derek. "Report to the Board of Overseers." *Harvard Gazette,* 17 March 1978, 1-12.

Curtius, Ernst R. *European Literature and the Latin Middle Ages.* Trans. Willard R. Trask. Princeton: Princeton Univ. Press, 1973.

Kinneavy, James L. *A Theory of Discourse.* New York: Norton, 1980.

Maimon, Elaine, et al. *Writing in the Arts and Sciences.* Cambridge: Winthrop, 1981.

Perelman, Chaim, and L. Olbrechts-Tyteca. *The New Rhetoric: A Treatise on Argumentation.* Trans. John Wilkinson and Purcell Weaver. Notre Dame, Ind.: Univ. of Notre Dame Press, 1969.

Pöggeler, Otto. "Dialektik und Topik." In *Hermeneutik und Dialektik.* Ed. R. Bubner et al. 2nd ed. Tübingen: Mohr, 1970, 273-310.

____. "Metaphysik und Seinstopik bei Heidegger." *Philosophisches Jahrbuch* 70 (1962): 118-37.

Snider, June. *An Experimental Composition Program for Prospective Secondary School English Teachers.* Washington, D.C.: U.S. Office of Education, 1968. USOE project no. HE-145.

Tannenbaum, Percy H. "Communication of Scientific Information." *Science,* 10 May 1963, 579-84.

Viehweg, Theodor. *Topik und Jurisprudenz.* 5th ed. Munchen: C. H. Beck, 1974.

Writing Across the Curriculum: The Second Stage, and Beyond

by Susan H. McLeod

The writing-across-the-curriculum movement has entered a new stage. Now that the idea is no longer new, now that faculty workshops are commonplace, now that articles on using writing in mathematics, management, and chemistry appear regularly in journals in those disciplines, those of us involved in writing programs need to think about and plan for what happens after the first workshop glow has faded. We need to try to answer the question C.W. Griffin asked in "Programs for Writing Across the Curriculum": "the first act is now over; what do we do for the second?" *(CCC* 36 [Dec. 1985]: 403).

First, let me clarify what I mean by the second act or "second stage," since, quite clearly, many WAC programs are still in the first or beginning stage. For instance, about half of those who attended the meetings of the National Network of Writing Across the Curriculum Programs held at 4 C's in the last three years came because they wanted to start a program and needed advice; the other half came because they knew they were beyond the beginning, and needed advice on how to continue. It is these continuing programs—and the nationwide WAC movement itself—that are in what I term the "second stage."

As a member of the Board of Consultants for the National Network of WAC programs, I decided three years ago that I needed to know more about this second stage. I wanted answers to such questions as: How many of these second-stage programs are there nationwide? What sorts of problems are they facing? How have they changed as they have matured? I decided that a survey would give me more accurate information than the anecdotal evidence gathered at conferences; in 1987-88, with funding from the Jerard Trust of Washington State's English Department, I sent one out. One purpose of this survey was to gather data for an annotated list of WAC programs which Susan Shirley and I prepared (see *Strengthening Programs for Writing Across the Curriculum*, Ed. Susan McLeod, Jossey-Bass, 1988, 103-30). But the second purpose was to examine the extent and nature of continuing programs, so that

Reprinted from *College Composition and Communication*, Vol. 40, No. 3, October 1989, 337-343. Copyright 1989 by the National Council of Teachers of English. Used with permission.

I could paint a larger picture of the WAC movement in the late 1980s.

Earlier surveys of WAC programs only sampled American colleges. For example, Laurance Peters' "Writing Across the Curriculum: Across the U.S." (*Writing to Learn*, Ed. Christopher Thaiss, Kendall-Hunt, 1983) surveyed just 122 post-secondary institutions; there were 36 replies. Griffin's 1984 survey was sent to 404 schools, 194 of which replied. But since the first purpose of my survey was to generate a comprehensive list of programs, I sent questionnaires to all 2735 post-secondary institutions in the United States and Canada. Of those, 1113 (40%) replied.

Of the institutions that responded, 695 (62%) had no WAC programs, but 73 of those indicated that their institutions were in the planning/discussion stage and hoped to set up such a program soon, and 40 others asked for more information, saying that they were interested in starting one up. Only five of the 695 respondents in the "no program" category indicated that their institutions had once had a WAC program which had become defunct, a figure which indicates the resiliency and staying power of WAC programs. The remaining 418 respondents (38% of the total) reported that their institutions did have a WAC program. This seems a remarkable number, considering that just a decade ago only a handful of such programs existed. Writing across the curriculum is clearly alive and well, and just as clearly, is still growing as a movement.

The 418 institutions with WAC programs divide almost evenly into two distinct groups (as do the people who come to the WAC National Network meetings mentioned earlier). The first consists of new or first-stage programs: 42% indicated that they were just starting, or had programs less than two years old. This boomlet of new WAC programs (182 total) is all the more interesting given the fact that federal granting agencies like NEH and FIPSE are no longer funding WAC programs as such. Unlike many of the older WAC programs which started off with large outside grants, these new programs are relying on comparably small amounts of internal funding, or are getting their external funding from Title III grants (challenge grants to institutions with a certain percentage of minority or disadvantaged students), from state monies (such as California Lottery funds or state departments of higher education), or from private foundations (such as Ford, Lilly, Pew, Mellon, and Glenmede). The new programs have been developed at institutions of all stripes: small private colleges like St. Mary's (CA); two-year institutions like Pike's Peak Community College; specialized institutions like Caltech, the Maine Maritime Academy, and the U.S. Air Force Academy; and research institutions like Carnegie Mellon University.

More than half of the institutions responding to the survey (56%—235 total) have continuing programs, ones which have been in existence for three years or more. These second-stage programs have gone beyond the "first workshop" stage, beyond the first blush of enthusiasm, and are moving towards permanence in their institutions. In the rest of this essay I will describe how these successful programs have survived and changed with the years, and I will speculate about the future of the WAC movement as indicated by the direction of these continuing programs.

Basic Survival

A crucial point for some of the 235 mature programs in the survey is the time when funding from outside granting agencies comes to an end. This is a time when directors must find new sources of funding, adapt their programs to run on less generous internal funding, or let the programs die. The very successful WAC program at Dawson College (Quebec), for example, is threatened with extinction soon if continued funding is not found; numerous WAC programs in Minnesota, funded originally by generous grants from the Bush Foundation, are now facing the end of that funding and casting about for other resources. Programs that have successfully negotiated the funding rapids report that key administrators are usually responsible for making sure that essential funding (in the form of released time for a director of the WAC program and monies for faculty development) is provided internally. Program directors report scaling down workshops (from one week to two days) and reducing the reward system for participating faculty (from stipends to free lunches), while still maintaining the integrity of the program and the interest of the faculty. It remains true that college-level faculty have had little training in how to teach, and spend little time discussing pedagogy with their peers; WAC programs which began with faculty development as their primary focus are able to continue despite decreased funds, because they are fueled by the interest of faculty who want to better themselves in their chosen profession. WAC programs cannot be run on that interest alone, but many continuing programs are finding that with a history of successful faculty seminars and strong administrative moral support, they can get along on less money than they once had. A few, however, will probably not survive; of the five now-defunct programs, four reported lack of financial and administrative support as the reason for their demise.

But most of the continuing programs in the survey report internal funding from the beginning of the program. Many writing-across-the-curriculum programs began as "quick fix" projects aimed at improving student writing, responses by administrators and faculty to a perceived literacy crisis. Now, however, WAC seems to be seen as a more or less permanent fixture by institutions that have programs, part of the writing program (like the writing lab) or part of faculty development (as a good way of revitalizing middle-aged faculty approaching burn-out). The perceived benefits of successful programs are such that administrators seem willing to provide funding on an ongoing basis.

Changes: Faculty Development

Most WAC programs begin with a faculty workshop, often led by an outside expert, on using specific classroom strategies to improve student writing. Once this "first workshop" stage has passed, it is clear that successful programs do more than repeat the same workshop for newcomers—they also have to provide for the veterans. One response is to offer workshops for different levels of faculty expertise. La Salle University, for example, offers two- to three-hour departmental workshops, longer intersession meetings, and an eight-day summer workshop. Faculty can enter the program at any level; about half of those who agree to attend the summer workshop and work with the coordinator of the program have become interested because of previous workshops they have attended. At the University of Vermont, there is a two-day intensive summer workshop for newcomers to WAC, and then a series of follow-up meetings aimed at training workshop participants to be faculty writing consultants in their own departments and disciplines. Another response is to involve other members of the university community in WAC efforts. Radford University is developing a program to invite not only the faculty but also members of the administration and student leaders to consider the use of writing to accomplish institutional purposes; William Patterson College has held workshops for Chairpersons and Deans.

Many schools report moving to an emphasis on writing and critical thinking in faculty workshops. Beaver College, one of the earliest institutions to establish a WAC program, was also one of the earliest to incorporate critical thinking in WAC workshops; Spelman College now offers workshops in which faculty look at ways of using writing not only as a mode of learning, but also as a way to encourage analytical modes of thinking; Missouri Western State College holds a six-month seminar called Teaching Critical Thinking. Others, like LaGuardia Community College, report faculty seminars that examine language development skills—emphasizing reading, speaking, and listening as well as writing across the curriculum. Some schools, like Fitchburg State College, Towson State, St. Cloud State University, and Ferris State College, have begun faculty writing seminars, where faculty get together to share their writing with peers and get helpful feedback before they submit it for publication. Some, like Hostos Community College/CUNY, El Paso Community College, and the University of Texas-El Paso, are concentrating faculty efforts on the needs of students with ESL backgrounds. Finally, some institutions are moving towards what I consider the most interesting development theoretically: an exploration of the social construction of knowledge in discourse communities, based on the work of researchers like Kenneth Bruffee, and again spearheaded by Beaver College. St. Olaf College, for example, is exploring in its WAC seminars the relationship between rhetoric and ways of knowing and thinking in disciplinary communities. At the University of Wisconsin, Stevens Point, faculty are working on descriptions of the specialized writing conventions of each discipline, and at the College of the Holy Cross, Patricia Bizzell (who is well known for her research on the topic) conducts departmental workshops on the discipline-specific uses of language.

Institutions have not limited themselves to designing different kinds of workshops. Faculty are also involved in various awareness and outreach programs involving the campus, the community, and even national audiences.

There are special events, like one described as a "local talent show" at Monroe Community College—where four teachers from Biology, Business Administration, Nursing, and Sociology described for attending colleagues how they used writing in their classrooms—or the public debate on WAC at Missouri Western State College which was sparked by an opinion piece in the May 1985 issue of the *Journal of Chemical Education* stating that WAC threatened quality instruction in the sciences (because writing in the disciplines means less coverage of class content, a common misunderstanding of WAC principles). SUNY at Fredonia sponsored a state-wide conference for SUNY faculty (Oct. 1986), and Old Dominion University produced a two-hour national teleconference on WAC programs in general and in Virginia in particular (Spring 1987). Many schools (William Patterson, Houston Community College system, Wittenberg University) are working with faculty to develop links to local school districts; others, like New Mexico State, are developing ties to industry.

And there are written products everywhere as a result of WAC faculty development efforts. Some programs, like the ones at Loyola College (Baltimore), Cal. Poly. Pomona, Queensborough Community College, and Miami Dade Community College, have published impressive handbooks for faculty to help them with assigning and evaluating writing in their classes; most of these handbooks have been developed with materials from faculty workshops or have been written in cooperation with faculty in the disciplines. Some institutions, like the New Jersey Institute of Technology, have faculty submit student papers for publication in an anthology of student writing; some, like the University of Maine at Farmington, have published faculty essays on writing. There is a crop of WAC newsletters, like *Crosscut*, from California State-San Bernardino, *Word Works* from Boise State University, and *Writing Across the Curriculum* from Southern College of Technology, and even videotapes used to publicize WAC programs (Borough of Manhattan Community College and Stevenson College, University of California-Santa Cruz). And of course, many WAC programs have resulted in research projects and scholarly articles too numerous to mention, as well as a tide of new composition textbooks.

Changes: Curriculum and Administration

As the faculty change, so does the curriculum. The earliest efforts in curricular reform connected with WAC focused on advanced writing courses at the junior level, the now-familiar "writing intensive" courses, where writing in a particular subject-matter area is the center of the class. The most well-known of these programs is the Junior Composition program at the University of Maryland. (George Miller has published useful descriptions of these advanced writing courses at various institutions in the Fall 1987 issue of *Teaching Writing*.) The effects of WAC at the freshman level, mentioned by Griffin in his article, seem to be spreading; there are now a number of freshman WAC seminars, like the team-taught interdisciplinary freshman seminar at Colby College, the freshman seminars at Pomona College, and the one-week freshman workshops at Simon's Rock of Bard College and the University of Puget Sound taught by faculty in all disciplines. There are also regular freshman composition courses taught by non-English Department faculty; SUNY Brockport, for example, uses faculty from 20 different departments across the curriculum to teach introductory composition. (A cross-section of WAC undergraduate courses is described in Toby Fulwiler and Art Young's new book, *Writing Across the Curriculum: Programs, Practices, Problems* (Heinemann-Boynton/Cook, forthcoming).

It appears, however, that the number of required "writing intensive" courses seems to be moving beyond the usual pattern of freshman composition plus one "WI." West Chester University, for example, now requires students to take three writing intensive courses; Wittenberg University now requires students to take nine such courses; Gustavus Adolphus reports writing intensive courses offered not just at the junior level but at all levels in the curriculum. Several institutions (Brainerd Community College, Post College, Brookdale Community College, and Medgar Evers College) report requiring writing in all classes, "even in Math," as one respondent proudly announced. Requiring something and actually executing that requirement can of course be two different matters, but the existence of such a requirement at a number of institutions certainly seems to indicate a trend.

Reform of general education requirements and the formation of new "core" courses in higher education continue at a rate important enough to make headlines; most schools making such changes are emphasizing writing in their new general education programs. Some, like Washington State University and DePaul University, have developed freshman-level core courses with a special linked composition course. Others are adding other cross-curricular components. George Mason University's innovative Plan for Alternative General Education (PAGE) extends the term "literacy" beyond reading and writing skills to include analytical thinking and the use of computers; the University of Louisville's general education program now emphasizes not only writing but also oral communication skills. Colorado College, Essex County College, Pima Community College, and St. John's University and The College of St. Benedict (the last two have one shared program) now include what they call "speaking across the curriculum" (SAC, perhaps?) in their WAC programs. And faculty interest in the connection between writing and critical thinking, mentioned above, is reflected in the number of schools linking writing and critical thinking in their new general education requirements; the continuing popularity of the University of Chicago's series of conferences on writing and higher-order reasoning tells us that this is a direction toward which WAC efforts will continue to move.

Not only are WAC concerns in the mainstream of the present surge of curricular reforms, but there are also administrative structures in place to help carry out newly designed writing curricula; fully one-third of those answering the survey reported that the program was operated under the auspices of some larger administrative entity. Some of the structures are old ones that have taken WAC under their roof (learning resource centers, general education commissions, offices of academic deans or vice provosts for instruction); but some are new. The earliest of the new structures was the English Composition Board at the University of Michigan; now there are a number of others, such as the Campus Writing Program at the University of Missouri, Columbia; the Writing Across the Disciplines program at Cal. State, Chico; the Center for Writing and Thinking at the School of the Ozarks; the Writing Center at the University of Minnesota, Minneapolis; and the Writing Center at Mary Washington College. The precise structure of these programs varies (as does, I am sure, their power), but the fact that there are such structures at all bodes well for the WAC movement. As David Russell has pointed out in "Writing Across the Curriculum and the Communications Movement" (*CCC* 38 [May 1987]: 184-94), it seems clear that in order for genuine curricular change to take place, some central administrative set-up is needed to monitor and nurture the changes: approving courses for writing-intensive status, making sure faculty and TA's are properly prepared for teaching such courses, sometimes overseeing writing placement and writing proficiency exams, sometimes monitoring program evaluation efforts. In many institutions, WAC is now part of the administrative structure of the institution, either housed in English departments or included elsewhere in the administrative structure.

Future Directions: The Third Stage?

It is this institutionalization of WAC that is its most outstanding success. Writing across the curriculum programs began much as Freshman English began, as a response to a perceived problem. The benefits of successful programs are such that administrators seem willing to make WAC as permanent as Freshman Composition. A reform movement which began little more than a decade ago (a microsecond in institutional terms) seems well on its way to becoming part of the established order. The ratio of half new programs and half continuing programs will certainly change in the next decade; I foresee a third stage in which most existing programs are continuing ones.

But, as is the case with any reform movement, there are problems which can arise once the idea is accepted into the mainstream, once most institutions have decided that they need something called WAC. Institutionalization of an idea implies success, but also can imply a certain rigidity which comes with administrative structures and lines of authority. In some cases it could result in a homogenization, a blandness—taking a vital new idea and making it into something more like familiar structures and programs, and therefore less free for experimentation, less interesting, perhaps less effective.

I have no evidence that this has happened to particular programs on particular campuses; but how the WAC idea might be misapplied was certainly illustrated in the surveys I received. About a dozen of those responding described programs that were not WAC programs at all in the sense that the term is usually understood—i.e., cognitively based (on the idea of writing as a mode of learning) or rhetorically based (on the idea of introducing students to the discourse communities of various disciplines). Instead of detailing faculty workshops or curriculum changes based on such ideas, these respondents simply attached catalogue descriptions of existing writing courses which are newly required but which have no discernible WAC orientation, or described newly-established proficiency examinations for students in ways that suggested gatekeeping devices. It seemed clear that these respondents knew of WAC only as a catchy new name for something they already had, not as a concept which would change the existing order of things.

This cavalier use of the term "writing across the curriculum" indicates to me that we need, as we move towards WAC as a permanent fixture in higher education, to define our terms carefully for our administrative colleagues, so that they understand that the term does not mean a program that is merely additive—more term papers, more courses, more proficiency tests—but one that is closely tied with thinking and learning, one that will bring about changes in teaching as well as in student writing. We also need to establish quite clearly that WAC programs certainly do not exclude examinations and more coursework in writing as a means of establishing proficiency, but that WAC is not to be identified solely with writing proficiency.

Finally, there is an issue not dealt with directly by my survey, but which has come up in anecdotal comments at the meetings of the National Network of Writing Across the Curriculum Programs and which deserves further study—the matter of change and faculty resistance to it. The idea and the practice of writing to learn goes against the predominant paradigm of education in the university, which valorizes the teacher-centered lecture class. In this paradigm, students are passive rather than active learners; they learn from the expert, not from each other. WAC programs challenge this notion of education, and those of us involved in such programs like to point to the successes we have had in changing faculty attitudes towards writing and learning (See Robert Weiss and Michael Peich, "Faculty Attitude Change in a Cross-Disciplinary Writing Program," *CCC* 31 [Feb. 1980]: 33-41). But changing attitudes and changing actual classroom practice may be two different things. Faculty resistance to change can be profound, as Deborah Swanson-Owens found in "Identifying Natural Sources of Resistance" (*Research in the Teaching of English* 20 [Feb. 1986]: 69-97). Such resistance could, over a number of years, gradually wear away even the most firmly established institutional program.

But I do not want to end on a negative note. While we need to be aware of the dangers that face the WAC movement in general and second-stage programs in particular, the survey results indicate cause for some cautious celebration. WAC as a movement is strong and is continuing to grow. It is up to all of us involved in such programs to be alert to the dangers, but also to be pleased that we have come this far.

Section 3:
What Happens in the
Disciplinary Classroom?

Writing as a Mode of Learning

by Janet Emig

Writing represents a unique mode of learning—not merely valuable, not merely special, but unique. That will be my contention in this paper. The thesis is straightforward. Writing serves learning uniquely because writing as process-and-product possesses a cluster of attributes that correspond uniquely to certain powerful learning strategies.

Although the notion is clearly debatable, it is scarcely a private belief. Some of the most distinguished contemporary psychologists have at least implied such a role for writing as heuristic. Lev Vygotsky, A. R. Luria, and Jerome Bruner, for example, have all pointed out that higher cognitive functions, such as analysis and synthesis, seem to develop most fully only with the support system of verbal language—particularly, it seems, of written language.[1] Some of their arguments and evidence will be incorporated here.

Here I have a prior purpose: to describe as tellingly as possible *how* writing uniquely corresponds to certain powerful learning strategies. Making such a case for the uniqueness of writing should logically and theoretically involve establishing many contrasts, distinctions between (1) writing and all other verbal languaging processes—listening, reading, and especially talking; (2) writing and all other forms of composing, such as composing a painting, a symphony, a dance, a film, a building; and (3) composing in words and composing in the two other major graphic symbol systems of mathematical equations and scientific formulae. For the purposes of this paper, the task is simpler, since most students are not permitted by most curricula to discover the values of composing, say, in dance, or even in film; and most students are not sophisticated enough to create, to originate formulations, using the highly abstruse symbol system of equations and formulae. Verbal language represents the most *available* medium for composing; in fact, the significance of sheer availability in its selection as a mode for learning can probably not be overstressed. But the uniqueness of writing among the verbal languaging processes does need to be established and supported if only because so many

Reprinted from *College Composition and Communication* 28 (May 1977): 122-28. Copyright 1977 by the National Council of Teachers of English. Reprinted with permission.

[1] Lev S. Vygotsky, *Thought and Language*, trans. Eugenia Hanfmann and Gertrude Vakar (Cambridge: The M.I.T. Press, 1962); A. R. Luria and F. Ia. Yudovich, *Speech and the Development of Mental Processes in the Child*, ed. Joan Simon (Baltimore: Penguin, 1971); Jerome S. Bruner, *The Relevance of Education* (New York: W. W. Norton and Co., 1971).

curricula and courses in English still consist almost exclusively of reading and listening.

Writing as a Unique Languaging Process

Traditionally, the four languaging processes of listening, talking, reading, and writing are paired in either of two ways. The more informative seems to be the division many linguists make between first-order and second-order processes, with talking and listening characterized as first-order processes; reading and writing, as second-order. First-order processes are acquired without formal or systematic instruction; the second-order processes of reading and writing tend to be learned initially only with the aid of formal and systematic instruction.

The less useful distinction is that between listening and reading as receptive functions and talking and writing as productive functions. Critics of these terms like Louise Rosenblatt rightfully point out that the connotation of passivity too often accompanies the notion of receptivity when reading, like listening, is a vital, construing act.

An additional distinction, so simple it may have been previously overlooked, resides in two criteria: the matters of origination and of graphic recording. Writing is originating and creating a unique verbal construct that is graphically recorded. Reading is creating or re-creating *but not* originating a verbal construct that is graphically recorded. Listening is creating or re-creating but not originating a verbal construct that is *not* graphically recorded. Talking is creating *and* originating a verbal construct that is *not* graphically recorded (except for the circuitous routing of a transcribed tape). Note that a distinction is being made between creating and originating, separable processes.

For talking, the nearest languaging process, additional distinctions should probably be made. (What follows is not a denigration of talk as a valuable mode of learning.) A silent classroom or one filled only with the teacher's voice is anathema to learning. For evidence of the cognitive value of talk, one can look to some of the persuasive monographs coming from the London Schools Council project on writing: *From Information to Understanding* by Nancy Martin or *From Talking to Writing* by Peter Medway.[2] We also know that for some of us, talking is a valuable, even necessary, form of pre-writing. In his curriculum, James Moffett makes the value of such talk quite explicit.

But to say that talking is a valuable form of pre-writing is not to say that writing is talk recorded, an inaccuracy appearing in far too many composition texts. Rather, a number of contemporary trans-disciplinary sources suggest that talking and writing may emanate from different organic sources and represent quite different, possibly distinct, language functions. In *Thought and Language*, Vygotsky notes that "written speech is a separate linguistic

---

[2] Nancy Martin, *From Information to Understanding* (London: Schools Council Project Writing Across the Curriculum, 11-13, 1973); Peter Medway, *From Talking to Writing* (London: Schools Council Project Writing Across the Curriculum, 11-13, 1973).

function, differing from oral speech in both structure and mode of functioning."[3] The sociolinguist Dell Hymes, in a valuable issue of *Daedalus*, "Language as a Human Problem," makes a comparable point: "That speech and writing are not simply interchangeable, and have developed historically in ways at least partly autonomous, is obvious."[4] At the first session of the Buffalo Conference on Researching Composition (4-5 October 1975), the first point of unanimity among the participant-speakers with interests in developmental psychology, media, dreams and aphasia was that talking and writing were markedly different functions.[5] Some of us who work rather steadily with writing research agree. We also believe that there are hazards, conceptually and pedagogically, in creating too complete an analogy between talking and writing, in blurring the very real differences between the two.

What Are These Differences?

(1) Writing is learned behavior; talking is natural, even irrepressible, behavior.
(2) Writing then is an artificial process; talking is not.
(3) Writing is a technological device—not the wheel, but early enough to qualify as primary technology; talking is organic, natural, earlier.
(4) Most writing is slower than most talking.
(5) Writing is stark, barren, even naked as a medium; talking is rich, luxuriant, inherently redundant.
(6) Talk leans on the environment; writing must provide its own context.
(7) With writing, the audience is usually absent; with talking, the listener is usually present.
(8) Writing usually results in a visible graphic product; talking usually does not.
(9) Perhaps because there is a product involved, writing tends to be a more responsible and committed act than talking.
(10) It can even be said that throughout history, an aura, an ambience, a mystique has usually encircled the written word; the spoken word has for the most part proved ephemeral and treated mundanely (ignore, please, our recent national history).
(11) Because writing is often our representation of the world made visible, embodying both process and product, writing is more readily a form and source of learning than talking.

Unique Correspondences Between
Learning and Writing

What then are some *unique* correspondences between learning and writing? To begin with some definitions: Learning can be defined in many

---

[3] Vygotsky, p. 98.
[4] Dell Hymes, "On the Origins and Foundations of Inequality Among Speakers," *Daedalus*, 102 (Summer, 1973), 69.
[5] Participant-speakers were Loren Barrett, University of Michigan; Gerald O'Grady, SUNY/Buffalo; Hollis Frampton, SUNY/Buffalo; and Janet Emig, Rutgers.

ways, according to one's predilections and training, with all statements about learning of course hypothetical. Definitions range from the chemo-physiological ("Learning is changed patterns of protein synthesis in relevant portions of the cortex")[6] to transactive views drawn from both philosophy and psychology (John Dewey, Jean Piaget) that learning is the re-organization or confirmation of a cognitive scheme in light of an experience.[7] What the speculations seem to share is consensus about certain features and strategies that characterize successful learning. These include the importance of the classic attributes of re-inforcement and feedback. In most hypotheses, successful learning is also connective and selective. Additionally, it makes use of propositions, hypotheses, and other elegant summarizers. Finally, it is active, engaged, personal—more specifically, self-rhythmed—in nature.

Jerome Bruner, like Jean Piaget, through a comparable set of categories, posits three major ways in which we represent and deal with actuality: (1) enactive—we learn "by doing"; (2) iconic—we learn "by depiction in an image"; and (3) representational or symbolic—we learn "by restatement in words."[8] To overstate the matter, in enactive learning, the hand predominates; in iconic, the eye; and in symbolic, the brain.

What is striking about writing as a process is that, by its very nature, all three ways of dealing with actuality are simultaneously or almost simultaneously deployed. That is, the symbolic transformation of experience through the specific symbol system of verbal language is shaped into an icon (the graphic product) by the enactive hand. If the most efficacious learning occurs when learning is re-inforced, then writing through its inherent re-inforcing cycle involving hand, eye, and brain marks a uniquely powerful multi-representational mode for learning.

Writing is also integrative in perhaps the most basic possible sense: the organic, the functional. Writing involves the fullest possible functioning of the brain, which entails the active participation in the process of both the left and the right hemispheres. Writing is markedly bi-spheral, although in some popular accounts, writing is inaccurately presented as a chiefly left-hemisphere activity, perhaps because the linear written product is somehow regarded as analogue for the process that created it; and the left hemisphere seems to process material linearly.

The right hemisphere, however, seems to make at least three, perhaps four, major contributions to the writing process—probably, to the creative process generically. First, several researchers, such as Geschwind and Snyder of Harvard and Zaidal of Cal Tech, through markedly different experiments, have very tentatively suggested that the right hemisphere is the sphere, even

---

[6] George Steiner, *After Babel: Aspects of Language and Translation* (New York: Oxford University Press, 1975), p. 287.
[7] John Dewey, *Experience and Education* (New York: Macmillan, 1938); Jean Piaget, *Biology and Knowledge: An Essay on the Relations between Organic Regulations and Cognitive Processes* (Chicago: University of Chicago Press, 1971).
[8] Bruner, pp. 7-8.

the *seat*, of emotions.[9] Second—or perhaps as an illustration of the first—Howard Gardner, in his important study of the brain-damaged, notes that our sense of emotional appropriateness in discourse may reside in the right sphere:

> Emotional appropriateness, in sum—being related not only to *what* is said, but to how it is said and to what is *not* said, as well—is crucially dependent on right hemisphere intactness.[10]

Third, the right hemisphere seems to be the source of intuition, of sudden gestalts, of flashes of images, of abstractions occurring as visual or spatial wholes, as the initiating metaphors in the creative process. A familiar example: William Faulkner noted in his *Paris Review* interview that *The Sound and the Fury* began as the image of a little girl's muddy drawers as she sat in a tree watching her grandmother's funeral.[11]

Also, a unique form of feedback, as well as reinforcement, exists with writing, because information from the *process* is immediately and visibly available as that portion of the *product* already written. The importance for learning of a product in a familiar and available medium for immediate, literal (that is, visual) re-scanning and review cannot perhaps be overstated. In his remarkable study of purportedly blind sculptors, Géza Révész found that without sight, persons cannot move beyond a literal transcription of elements into any manner of symbolic transformation—by definition, the central requirement for re-formulation and re-interpretation, i.e., revision, that most aptly named process.[12]

As noted in the second paragraph, Vygotsky and Luria, like Bruner, have written importantly about the connections between learning and writing. In his essay "The Psychobiology of Psychology," Bruner lists as one of six axioms regarding learning: "We are connective."[13] Another correspondence then between learning and writing: in *Thought and Language*, Vygotsky notes that writing makes a unique demand in that the writer must engage in "deliberate semantics"—in Vygotsky's elegant phrase, "deliberate structuring of the web of meaning."[14] Such structuring is required because, for Vygotsky, writing centrally represents an expansion of inner speech, that mode whereby we talk to ourselves, which is "maximally compact" and "almost entirely predicative"; written speech is a mode which is "maximally detailed" and which requires explicitly supplied subjects and topics. The medium then of written verbal language requires the establishment of systematic connections and

[9] Boyce Rensberger, "Language Ability Found in Right Side of Brain," *New York Times*, 1 August 1975, p. 14.

[10] Howard Gardner, *The Shattered Mind: The Person After Brain Damage* (New York: Alfred A. Knopf, 1975), p. 372.

[11] William Faulkner, *Writers at Work: The Paris Review Interviews*, ed. Malcolm Cowley (New York: The Viking Press, 1959), p. 130.

[12] Géza Révész, *Psychology and Art of the Blind*, trans. H. A. Wolff (London: Longmans-Green, 1950).

[13] Bruner, p. 126.

[14] Vygotsky, p. 100.

relationships. Clear writing by definition is that writing which signals without ambiguity the nature of conceptual relationships, whether they be coordinate, subordinate, superordinate, causal, or something other.

Successful learning is also engaged, committed, personal learning. Indeed, impersonal learning may be an anomalous concept, like the very notion of objectivism itself. As Michael Polanyi states simply at the beginning of *Personal Knowledge*: "the ideal of strict objectivism is absurd." (How many courses and curricula in English, science, and all else does that one sentence reduce to rubble?) Indeed, the theme of *Personal Knowledge* is that

> into every act of knowing there enters a passionate contribution of the person knowing what is being known, . . . this coefficient is no mere imperfection but a vital component of his knowledge.[15]

In *Zen and the Art of Motorcycle Maintenance*, Robert Pirsig states a comparable theme:

> The Quality which creates the world emerges as *a relationship* between man and his experience. He is a *participant* in the creation of all things.[16]

Finally, the psychologist George Kelly has as the central notion in his subtle and compelling theory of personal constructs man as a scientist steadily and actively engaged in making and re-making his hypotheses about the nature of the universe.[17]

We are acquiring as well some empirical confirmation about the importance of engagement in, as well as self-selection of, a subject for the student learning to write and writing to learn. The recent Sanders and Littlefield study, reported in *Research in the Teaching of English*, is persuasive evidence on this point, as well as being a model for a certain type of research.[18]

As Luria implies in the quotation above, writing is self-rhythmed. One writes best as one learns best, at one's own pace. Or to connect the two processes, writing can sponsor learning because it can match its pace. Support for the importance of self-pacing to learning can be found in Benjamin Bloom's important study "Time and Learning."[19] Evidence for the significance of self-pacing to writing can be found in the reason Jean-Paul Sartre gave last summer for not using the tape-recorder when he announced that blindness in his second eye had forced him to give up writing:

---

[15]Michael Polanyi, *Personal Knowledge: Toward a Post-Critical Philosophy* (Chicago: University of Chicago Press, 1958), p. viii.

[16]Robert Pirsig, *Zen and the Art of Motorcycle Maintenance* (New York: William Morrow and Co., Inc., 1974), p. 212.

[17]George Kelly, *A Theory of Personality: The Psychology of Personal Constructs* (New York: W. W. Norton and Co., 1963).

[18]Sara E. Sanders and John H. Littlefield, "Perhaps Test Essays Can Reflect Significant Improvement in Freshman Composition: Report on a Successful Attempt," *RTE*, 9 (Fall, 1975), 145-153.

[19]Benjamin Bloom, "Time and Learning," *American Psychologist*, 29 (September 1974), 682-688.

I think there is an enormous difference between speaking and writing. One re-reads what one rewrites. But one can read slowly or quickly: in other words, you do not know how long you will have to take deliberating over a sentence. . . . If I listen to a tape recorder, the listening speed is determined by the speed at which the tape turns and not by my own needs. Therefore I will always be either lagging behind or running ahead of the machine.[20]

Writing is connective as a process in a more subtle and perhaps more significant way, as Luria points out in what may be the most powerful paragraph of rationale ever supplied for writing as heuristic:

Written speech is bound up with the inhibition of immediate syn-practical connections. It assumes a much slower, repeated mediating process of analysis and synthesis, which makes it possible not only to develop the required thought, but even to revert to its earlier stages, thus transforming the sequential chain of connections in a simultaneous, self-reviewing structure. Written speech thus represents a new and powerful instrument of thought.[21]

But first to explicate: writing inhibits "immediate synpractical connections." Luria defines *synpraxis* as "concrete-active" situations in which language does not exist independently but as a "fragment" of an ongoing action "outside of which it is incomprehensible."[22] In *Language and Learning*, James Britton defines it succinctly as "speech-cum-action."[23] Writing, unlike talking, restrains dependence upon the actual situation. Writing as a mode is inherently more self-reliant than speaking. Moreover, as Bruner states in explicating Vygotsky, "Writing virtually forces a remoteness of reference on the language user."[24]

Luria notes what has already been noted above: that writing, typically, is a "much slower" process than talking. But then he points out the relation of this slower pace to learning: this slower pace allows for—indeed, encourages—the shuttling among past, present, and future. Writing, in other words, connects the three major tenses of our experience to make meaning. And the two major modes by which these three aspects are united are the processes of analysis and synthesis: analysis, the breaking of entities into their constituent parts; and synthesis, combining or fusing these, often into fresh arrangements or amalgams.

Finally, writing is epigenetic, with the complex evolutionary development of thought steadily and graphically visible and available throughout as a record of the journey, from jottings and notes to full discursive formulations.

---

[20]Jean-Paul Sartre, "Sartre at Seventy: An Interview," with Michel Contat, *New York Review of Books*, 7 August 1975.
[21]Luria, p. 118.
[22]Luria, p. 50.
[23]James Britton, *Language and Learning* (Baltimore: Penguin, 1971), pp. 10-11.
[24]Bruner, p. 47.

For a summary of the correspondences stressed here between certain learning strategies and certain attributes of writing see Figure 1.

This essay represents a first effort to make a certain kind of case for writing—specifically, to show its unique value for learning. It is at once over-elaborate and under specific. Too much of the formulation is in the off-putting jargon of the learning theorist, when my own predilection would have been to emulate George Kelly and to avoid terms like *re-inforcement* and *feedback* since their use implies that I live inside a certain paradigm about learning I don't truly inhabit. Yet I hope that the essay will start a crucial line of inquiry; for unless the losses to learners of not writing are compellingly described and substantiated by experimental and speculative research, writing itself as a central academic process may not long endure.

Figure 1

Unique Cluster of Correspondences between
Certain Learning Strategies and Certain Attributes of Writing

Selected Characteristics of Successful Learning Strategies	Selected Attributes of Writing, Process and Product
(1) Profits from multi-representational and integrative reinforcement	(1) Represents process uniquely multi-representational and integrative
(2) Seeks self-provided feedback:	(2) Represents powerful instance of self-provided feedback:
(a) immediate	(a) provides product uniquely available for *immediate* feedback (review and re-evaluation)
(b) long-term	(b) provides record of evolution of thought since writing is epigenetic as process-and-product
(3) Is connective:	(3) Provides connections:
(a) makes generative conceptual groupings, synthetic and analytic	(a) establishes explicit and systematic conceptual groupings through lexical, syntactic, and rhetorical devices
(b) proceeds from propositions, hypotheses, and other elegant summarizers	(b) represents most available means (verbal language) for economic recording of abstract formulations
(4) Is active, engaged, personal— notably, self-rhythmed	(4) Is active, engaged, personal— notably, self-rhythmed

Writing in Academic Settings: A Study of the Contexts for Writing in Two College Chemical Engineering Courses

by Anne J. Herrington

Abstract. This study investigated the context for writing in two college chemical engineering classes, viewing each as a disciplinary community. The study used a combination of quantitative and qualitative methods: a survey of all students and professors participating in these classes, open-ended and discourse-based interviews with ten students and two teachers, observation of classes, and analysis of claims and warrants used in students' written reports. The findings indicate that these two courses represented distinct communities where different issues were addressed, different lines of reasoning used, different writer and audience roles assumed, and different social purposes served by writing. These findings show the function that writing can serve in introducing students not only to the intellectual activities of a discipline, but also to the social roles and purposes of various disciplinary communities. The findings also show some of the problems that arose in specific classroom contexts when professors gave students mixed messages as to the audience for writing and when no issue was perceived for writing.

This study investigates the context for writing in two college chemical engineering courses. Although it is limited in scope to these two courses, the study addresses two broader questions that underlie much of the practical and theoretical scholarship on writing-across-the-curriculum: 1) What function does writing serve in a course in a given academic discipline? More specifically, how do writing assignments introduce students to the intellectual activities, social roles, and purposes for writing that are important within a given discipline? and 2) How can teachers create contexts conducive to using

Reprinted from *Research in the Teaching of English* (December 1985). Copyright 1985 by the National Council of Teachers of English. Reprinted with permission.

I wish to thank the faculty and students from the Chemical Engineering Department at Rensselaer Polytechnic Institute, Troy, NY, who participated in this study. I am particularly indebted to three professors: Michael Abbott, A. H. Johannes, and P. K. Lashmet. Considerable thanks are also due to three professors from the Department of Language, Literature, and Communication who offered me guidance throughout the study: Lee Odell, Michael Halloran, and Teri Harrison.

writing to achieve their objectives in a given course?

Odell (1980) argues that to answer the first question we have to address such questions as "What does it mean to learn history? What does one have to do in order to think and write like a biologist?" Odell frames the question in terms of process and suggests that we will answer those questions by identifying the "conceptual activities" entailed by writing assignments in a given discipline. Other theorists who address the same questions (Bazerman, 1982; Bizzell, 1982) shift the focus from process to context and argue that in order to answer such questions we need to consider both the intellectual and the social conventions of a given disciplinary community. These conventions, which are assumed to vary from one community to another, include the kinds of issues the discipline tries to address, the lines of reasoning used to resolve those issues, and shared assumptions about the audience's role, the writer's *ethos*, and the social purposes for communicating (e.g., Bazerman, 1981; Bizzell, 1982; Toulmin, 1972; Toulmin, Rieke & Janik, 1979). Bazerman (1981) and Roland (1982) speculate that these conventions differentiate not only one discipline from another, but also subcommunities within a given discipline.

This theoretical work has not yet been complemented by empirical studies exploring how a given disciplinary community might be manifest within a classroom or how students' writing might vary as conventions vary from one disciplinary subcommunity (what I will call a forum) to another. This theoretical work invites such studies, however, giving us reason to believe that as we understand more about the differences within communities, we understand more about the role writing can play in learning the social and intellectual conventions of a community—in other words, the role writing can play in learning to think and act like a member of, for instance, a community of chemical engineers.

The second question arises implicitly from the first. How do faculty create classroom contexts where writing might serve as one means of introducing students to the conventions of a given disciplinary community? To begin to answer this question, we need to study particular classrooms directly. Such studies seem particularly important since much of the writing-across-the-curriculum scholarship depicts classroom contexts as problematic in one way or another. Some scholars (e.g., Kinneavy, 1971) depict these contexts as quite artificial because students are expected to write informative discourse to an audience already fully informed about the subject of that discourse. Other scholars (e.g., Fulwiler & Young, 1982) characterize classroom contexts as rather homogeneous, teaching students to write for only one purpose, to inform, to one type of audience, a teacher-as-examiner. Still others (e.g., Odell, Goswami, & Quick, 1981; Mathes & Stevenson, 1976) claim that classroom contexts are quite unlike nonacademic contexts. Finally, some (e.g., Odell et al., 1981; Flower & Hayes, 1977; Knoblauch & Brannon, 1983) claim that the "circumstances" for writing in classrooms do not lead students to be concerned with questions "that would lead them to think critically" (Odell et al., p. 95).

This scholarship is useful in that it makes us realize that the posited problems may not be inherent in academic writing assignments themselves, but may instead be rooted in the social contexts that are created for that writing: students are often asked to write for limited purposes, to no other audience than the teacher-as-examiner or expert, and in circumstances that do not lead them to think critically. If these general conclusions are valid, then composition scholars and teachers should seek ways to change these contexts to make them more conducive for writing and learning. Before we accept these claims, however, and presume to advocate changes, we need to understand more about the nature of these classroom contexts. Are they as undifferentiated as the scholarship just reviewed characterizes them to be? Would studies that examined specific classroom contexts directly find more diversity in the contexts and the writing done in those contexts?

Another group of research studies which do study classroom contexts directly gives us reason to believe that these contexts are more diverse than is suggested by the scholarship noted above (Graves, 1978; Calkins, 1980; Kamler, 1980; Florio & Clark, 1982; Applebee, Auten, & Lehr, 1981; Kantor, 1984). Further, they demonstrate the central role of the teacher, as initiator and audience for most student writing, in controlling the functions writing will serve.

Although these studies are of elementary and secondary classrooms, they suggest what we might learn from similar naturalistic studies of college classrooms. Specifically, they show that by uncovering diversity, we see not only some of the problems that arise in specific classroom contexts, but also some of the possibilities—that is, ways teachers can create contexts conducive for using writing to achieve various objectives in a given course. In studies of college classrooms, it is important to view writing in relation not only to a school community but also to the intellectual and social conventions of professional forums within a given discipline, considering the issues addressed, the lines of reasoning used, writer and audience roles, and social purposes for writing.

Characteristics of the Study

Both the theoretical assumptions and research approach of the study are grounded in sociolinguistic and rhetorical theories. The underlying theoretical assumption is that each classroom represents a community in its own right, situated at once in two larger communities: a school and a disciplinary community. As a community, a classroom is constituted by a group of people who share common understandings of, among other things, the social aims they are trying to accomplish, roles they assume in specific situations, values, and ways of using language to accomplish their social aims (Hymes, 1972b; Halliday, 1978). These common understandings (i.e., conventions or, to use Bauman and Sherzer's terms, "shared ground rules and principles of speaking," 1975, p. 113) enable members to communicate with one another and to accomplish their social aims because they can assume that they are acting on the same ground rules. When members do not share a common understanding, their aims may not be achieved, they may misinterpret each other, or, at the least, they may become confused or frustrated in their attempts to communicate (Hymes, 1972a, 1972c).

The research approach is naturalistic. I chose not to devise special writing tasks for the study, but rather to study writing assignments as they were typically done as part of the regular activities of the two classes studied. Further, to understand the context for this writing and the relation of this writing to that context, I studied not only features of the writing, but also students' and teachers' perceptions of that writing and the issues, purposes, roles, and lines of reasoning associated with it.

The study uses a combination of research methods, including both quantitative and qualitative approaches and such specific methods as text analysis, close-ended surveys, interviews with writers and readers, and participant observation. Such a triangulated approach (Denzin, 1970) has two major advantages: First, it can enable an assessment of convergent validation (Albrecht & Ropp, 1982; LeCompte & Goetz, 1982). Second, a triangulated approach enables a researcher to obtain the advantages of various procedures, using one to compensate for the limitations of another. The most obvious balance is between a structured, quantitative survey and a more open-ended, qualitative interview.

Method

Courses Studied

This study focused on two courses required of all seniors majoring in Chemical Engineering at Rensselaer Polytechnic Institute, Troy, NY. One of the courses, Chemical Engineering Laboratory (Lab), is a two-semester course for which students, working in groups of three or four, do six experiments and write six lab reports, each for a different professor. While doing each lab, each student work group meets once with the professor supervising that lab. That meeting, called an Interim, is a one-half to one-hour conference during which the professor helps students interpret data from the actual experiment.

Chemical Process Design (Design) is a one-semester course taken during the second semester of the senior year. During the semester, each design group is to solve two design problems. While working on each problem, the groups write weekly progress memos; once the problem is solved, they write a formal report. The course is team-taught by two professors. It meets twice weekly, once as a lecture conducted by one of the professors and again as a consultation period during which each design group may meet separately with one of the professors.

After a preliminary study, I chose these two courses for the full study because they seemed to provide an opportunity to reassess the monolithic view of classroom contexts presented in other writing-across-the-curriculum scholarship. More specifically, the preliminary study indicated the following:

1) These courses appear to represent different forums within the same broad disciplinary community: apparently, students write to resolve different issues, assume different writer roles, address different audiences, and write for different purposes. 2) The same students and faculty participate in each course. This would let me assume that any differences would reflect differences in the courses and not differences in the students and faculty.

Participants

The participants in the study included a sample of students and faculty who completed a structured response survey about both courses and a sub-set of this larger sample who participated in extensive interviews.

For the survey, the large sample included 71 students who completed the survey for Lab (total enrollment = 103) and 63 for Design (total enrollment = 91). It also included eight professors for Lab: two senior faculty who had previously taught the course and the six for whom the students in the study were doing their six labs. Two of these six, Professors Michael Abbott and A.H. Johannes, also team-taught Process Design. The three professors surveyed for Design include Abbott and Johannes and P.K. Lashmet, one of the senior professors who had previously taught that course.

The participants in the interviews represented a sub-set of the larger sample. The two professors included were Abbott and Johannes since they were the ones teaching both a Lab and Process Design. Abbott, who had taught both courses a number of times and has a particular interest in writing, became my principal consultant throughout the study.

The student participants in the interviews were members of three work groups, totalling 11 students in Lab and 10 students in Design. These groups were chosen on the basis of Abbott's judgment that the students in them were average to superior students who would be willing to participate in the study. My aim was to interview three work groups whose membership would remain the same for both Lab and Design; however, the membership of two did change somewhat from first semester, when I interviewed them about Lab, to second semester, when I interviewed them about Design: Group A dropped from four to three students. Group C was entirely reconstituted: for Lab, it had four students; for Design, it included the one student originally in Group A and two new members not interviewed about Lab. Group B, with four members, remained unchanged.

Instrumentation

Contexts for Writing

To examine the contexts for writing in the two courses, I relied on three procedures: my own observations of these two courses; a Writing Profile Survey administered to the larger sample of students and faculty; and more extensive interviews with the three student work groups and two professors.

Observation. The purpose of my observation was to gain an insider's knowledge of each class as a background for interpreting writers' and readers' perceptions. My specific observational activities for Lab included the following:

1. observing and audio-taping one lab group over a three-week period as they did their first lab experiment and wrote their report;
2. observing and taking field notes at the introductory lecture of Lab, at Abbott's Interims with each of three groups, and at Johannes' Interim meeting with three groups combined; and
3. collecting and analyzing course documents (e.g., the Lab Manual, all assignments).

For Design, my observations included the following:

1. observing and taking field notes at all class lectures and consultation sessions (one of each per week for the full semester);
2. collecting and analyzing course documents; and
3. participating as a Writing Consultant for the course: this role entailed advising one half of the student groups on their writing. Of the student groups included in the study, I advised Group C, but not Groups A or B.

Writing Profile Survey. A survey using closed-ended questions was administered to the larger sample of students and faculty to obtain their perceptions of the audiences and purposes for both Lab and Design reports. More specifically, the survey asked respondents to 1) distinguish primary and secondary audiences; 2) rate the audience's knowledge of technical detail, theory, and technical terms; and 3) identify their purposes for writing each type of report. In all instances, respondents were given a list of possibilities and asked to rate each on an ordinal response continuum. The specific survey items are indicated in Tables 2, 3, and 4. During the fall semester, the students completed the survey for Lab immediately after completing their first lab report; during spring semester, they completed the survey for Design immediately after completing the first Design report.

Discourse-Based Interviews. These interviews which focused on specific stylistic and substantive features of each work group's reports were conducted to elicit students' and professors' perceptions of the rhetorical context for each type of report (Odell & Goswami, 1982; Odell, Goswami, & Herrington, 1983). Using this procedure, I was able to ask all three work groups about the same types of features of the reports each group had written. The interviews were restricted to the Discussion and Conclusion sections of two Lab and two Design reports written by each group. One of each type of report had been written for each of the principal faculty, Abbott and Johannes. The types of stylistic and substantive features asked about included the following:

Form of Reference to Self: These included sentences in the active voice with "we" as the subject and sentences in the passive voice which could be recast in active voice with "we" as the subject.

Statements of Elaboration: These include parenthetical phrases, nonrestrictive clauses, phrases or clauses beginning with "for example" or "that is," and sentences defining or elaborating in more concrete terms an idea stated more generally in the preceding sentence.

Statements of Justification or Rationale: These included phrases or clauses beginning with "in order to" or "since" and other verbal phrases stating a rationale.

Statements of Conclusion: These included phrases, clauses, or sentences containing such words as "thus" and "therefore" as well as ones containing evaluative words and making a summative judgment.

To prepare for the interviews, I bracketed specific occurrences of each type of feature in each report, bracketing a total of 9 features in each report. I then interviewed each student separately about the reports his or her group had written. I also interviewed Abbott and Johannes separately about the reports submitted to each of them from Groups A and B. In the interviews, I would ask whether the interviewee would be willing to delete the introductory clause from the sentence "[Since all the flow rates were adjusted manually,] this source of error prevailed throughout the experiment." I explained that I was not in any way implying that the bracketed section should be altered or deleted and that I was most interested in the reasons interviewees gave for whatever decision they made. By interviewing each member of a group and the professor about the same features of the group's report, I obtained the independent perceptions of writers and their readers about the same features of text.

The interviews about Lab reports were conducted during the final week of first semester; those about Design reports, during the final week of second semester. In all, I conducted 21 student interviews and 4 faculty interviews, each lasting approximately one hour. These interviews were then transcribed for subsequent analysis.

Open-Ended Portion of the Interview. Each interview concluded with a set of less structured questions focusing on students' and professors' perceptions of the purposes for writing the reports, the issues each report addressed, and writer and audience roles. Some of these questions were derived from comments the professors made in Interim meetings or lectures. The final portion of the last interview included a discussion of my provisional conclusions, asking the participants whether they thought these conclusions are valid.

Lines of Reasoning Evident in the Writing

To examine the lines of reasoning used in the texts written by these students, I analyzed the claims and warrants appearing in the Discussion and Conclusion sections of the two Lab and two Design reports discussed with each group in the interviews. Claims were identified as conclusions, "assertions put forth with the implication that there are underlying 'good reasons' that could show them to be 'well founded'" (Toulmin et al., 1979 p. 29). Using that definition, I identified specific claim statements on the basis of explicit cues in the texts (Herrington, 1983). These cues included the following:

> *Logical connectives indicating conclusions*: e.g., so, therefore
> *Modal qualifiers*: e.g., perhaps, apparently
> *Modal auxiliaries*: may, might, should, would
> *Adjectives of evaluation*: e.g., good, incongruous
> *Sentence leads introducing a conclusion*: e.g., We conclude that . . .

> Sentences with two propositions where one proposition states a reason to justify the other proposition as well-founded.

> Otherwise unmarked sentences that begin a paragraph and are followed by a sentence or more giving reasons to justify the claim in the opening sentence.

In identifying these cues, I was guided by the work of Gardner (1977) and Toulmin (1958; Toulmin et al., 1979). Using these cues, I identified specific claim sentences and excerpted them from the texts for subsequent analysis.

Warrants were defined as "rules, principles, inference-licenses" that "authorize claim statements" (Toulmin, 1958). In Aristotelian terms, they are called variously lines of argument, enthymemes, and special topics. Using this definition, I identified warrants by my own critical analysis of the reports, focusing on those used to authorize the previously identified claim statements. The warrants identified included chemical laws, theories, and analytic procedures (e.g., "flat plate boundary theory," "a second law analysis"), as well as more general, often implicit warrants. For example, in Design reports, the following general deliberative warrant was often used: of two things, the one which produces the greater good (in this case, saves money) is the preferred one. (See Aristotle's *Rhetoric*, Book 1, Chapter 7.)

Scoring

Survey

The Writing Profile Surveys were used to make comparisons both between the two courses and within each course. For the comparison between Lab and Design, the data were analyzed using descriptive statistics (e.g., means, standard deviations, and variance). Within each course, data were analyzed using a *t*-test to compare students' responses with those of their professors.

Discourse-Based Interviews

The interview transcripts were first analyzed using a classification scheme (Herrington, 1983) to categorize the types of reasons writers and readers gave for their decisions about specific features of text. The classification scheme, an adaptation of the one developed by Odell et al. (1983), has four rhetorical categories (audience-based, writer-based, subject-based, and text-based) plus a category for arhetorical reasons. (See Table 1 for a listing of the categories and subcategories.)

This classification scheme was then used by two readers and me to analyze the interview transcripts. Two of us independently read and analyzed each transcript, classifying each of the reasons given to explain a decision about a feature of text. When more than one reason was given, all reasons were coded, unless an audience-based reason was coded, in which case a subject-based reason was not.

For these independent readings, we achieved an overall agreement of 82 percent for the students' transcripts and 84 percent for the professors'. In any cases where the original two readers did not agree, the three of us discussed the response and reached a consensus on how to classify it. The agreed scores were then included in the analysis.

Open-Ended Interviews

In analyzing the open-ended portions of the interviews, I read all of the student and faculty responses to a given question, looked for patterns in these responses, and excerpted specific interview responses to illustrate each generalization.

Claims

Claim statements were analyzed using a procedure similar to that used to analyze the discourse-based interviews: First, a categorization scheme was devised and then, using this scheme, two judges classified each claim statement (Herrington, 1983). The categorization scheme is based on Aristotle's classification of the divisions of rhetoric (*Rhetoric*, Book I, Chapter 3 and Book III, Chapter 17) and the nature of scientific reasoning (*Posterior Analytics*, Book II, Chapter 1). The divisions appropriate to this study are forensic (Was some past act justified?), deliberative (Is a proposed action expedient?), and scientific (Of what nature is some phenomenon?).

While developing the scheme, I reviewed it with Abbott and pilot-tested it with two doctoral students in Rhetoric. When the final categorization scheme was formulated, a second pair of readers and I used it to classify the specific claim statements in the reports written by Lab Groups A, B, and C, and Design Groups A, B, and C. The claim statements had been excerpted from the reports, and readers did not know which group's reports they were reading or for which class they had been written.

The overall percentage of agreement in categorizing claims was 87 percent. In those instances where the original two readers did not agree, the third reader read and rated the claim also. The claim was then categorized on the basis of agreement by two of the three readers.

Warrants

To characterize the type of warrants used and identify patterns in the way

they were used, I relied on two sources: Toulmin et al.'s (1979) character-
izations of the warrants typical of science and management and Aristotle's
characterization of the special *topoi* of forensic and deliberative rhetoric
(*Rhetoric*, Book 1, Chapter 7 and Book II, Chapter 23.20).

Results

The information obtained from all sources supports three general
conclusions, two relating to the context for writing in the two classes, and the
third to the lines of reasoning used in the texts the students wrote. First, these
two courses did represent different classroom contexts or forums: different
issues were addressed, different writer and reader roles assumed, and different
social purposes served by writing. These differences were evident not only
from the differences in the assignments, writing profile surveys, and open-
ended interviews, but also in the discourse-based interviews with students
where the reasons students cited to explain features of Lab reports differed
from those they cited to explain Design reports. (See Table 1.)

Second, in both Lab and Design, members of each community did not
always agree on the conventions appropriate to that forum. More particularly,
the professors' perceptions of the conventions sometimes differed from those
of the students. In Lab, these differences seem to reflect the conflicting
signals faculty gave to students of the issue, audience and writer roles, and
social purposes for writing. In Design, these differences seem to reflect the
newness of this forum for students. There, while students and faculty did
agree on the issue, purpose, and writer and audience roles, they did not, in all
instances, share a common perception of the audience's knowledge and
expectations, the *ethos* the writer should project, and appropriate lines of
reasoning. When they did not agree, students' perceptions were often those
more appropriate to Lab. This finding suggests that students might have been
carrying over into Design the conventions they had learned in the Lab course
and other courses.

Third, corresponding to the differences in context, the lines of reasoning
used in Lab and Design reports differed as well.

These general conclusions are elaborated in the following sections that
report findings first about the classroom contexts (issues, audiences, writer
roles, and purposes) and then about lines of reasoning.

The Context for Writing in Lab and Design

Issues

The dominant issues at stake in the Lab and Design courses differed in
two ways. First, they differed in the specific conceptual issue posed by the
assignments in each course, reflecting two different types of issues addressed
by chemical engineers. Second, they differed in the social issue that the
writers felt was at stake for them with their audience in each course. This
difference reflects the complexity of Lab and also the degree to which Lab

Table 1

Types of Reasons Given by Students in Discourse-Based Interviews About Laboratory and Design Reports

	Percent of Reasons	
	Lab Reports (n = 388 reasons)	Design Reports (n = 340 reasons)
Type of reason		
I. Audience-focused		
A. To explain something to readers they need to know	21.9	22.9
B. To explain something to readers they expect you to know	2.3	.6
C. To persuade or convince readers	.8	2.9
D. To make the text easier for readers to read	1.0	2.6
E. Reference to actual prior dealings with this audience	5.4	2.6
F. Reference to personal preferences of the audience	3.1	.9
II. Writer-focused		
A. To clarify something for oneself	.8	.9
B. To show that one is knowledgeable	3.6	.6
C. To project an *ethos*, other than as knowledgeable	1.0	4.4
D. Reference to experiences of the group	5.4	10.3
E. Reference solely to personal preference	2.6	3.8
F. Reference to own prior training or experience	.8	.9
G. Reference to own role	.3	.9
III. Subject-focused		
A. To explain something about the subject	20.1	16.8
B. To justify a conclusion about the subject	2.1	3.5
C. Reference to importance of the subject	9.0	6.8
IV. Text-focused (e.g., conventions of a genre, general grammatical rule or style principle)	15.9	15.6
V. Arhetorical	3.8	3.0

was still very much perceived to represent a classroom forum, not a hypothetical professional forum. These conclusions are based on three sources of information: my analysis of the assignments for each course, the writing profile survey, and the discourse-based and open-ended interview responses.

My analysis of the assignments showed that the conceptual issues do differ. In Lab, the issue was more of a scientific/technical issue, answering a question about the nature of some chemical process (e.g., ion exchange, absorption of a gas by a liquid) as it took place in a given piece of equipment (e.g., how does the "performance of a helical flow tubular reactor" compare "with that expected from idealized flow tubular reactors for the hydrolysis of crystal violet dye . . ."). (See Appendix A for an example of a typical assignment.) According to the faculty interviewed, this type of issue would be similar to that addressed in industry when a company wants, say, to assess the performance of a pilot plant or to determine the properties of a certain chemical. The task for the engineers would be to run an experiment, collect and interpret experimental data, and report the results. In contrast, the issue posed by assignments for Design shifted the focus from interpreting "what is" to making a judgment about "what should be." That is, the issue for Design was more deliberative, asking engineers to design a process that was both technically feasible and economically expedient and make a recommendation to management. For example, one Design problem asked students to determine whether distillation to the required purity (99.8%) made economic sense. (See Appendix B for the full problem statement.) According to the faculty interviewed, this is the type of issue that might typically be addressed in the Process Engineering section of a company when the company is deciding, say, whether to build a facility to produce a new product that might be profitable for them.

The courses differed not only in the conceptual issue posed by the assignments, but also in the social issues the writers perceived were at stake as they wrote in each forum. For Lab, the discourse-based interview responses indicted that students perceived as equally dominant two types of issues that, taken together, seem more characteristic of the classroom than a professional forum. The first issue was forensic: can one's own actions be justified? As one student commented, "you're showing you did it the right way." Another said, "it's like a test." These comments reflect the second type of issue, epideictic: can one show one's own actions worthy of praise? As another student commented, "we wanted to put together a really good report to impress him that we knew what we were doing." In other words, the issue at stake for students was to demonstrate to an audience who would evaluate them that their actions were not only justified but also praiseworthy.

Obviously, both forensic and epideictic issues are at stake for students in most classrooms, Lab and Design being no exceptions. Still, they seemed a less dominant concern in Design than in Lab. Instead, in Design, students seemed to be more conscious of a deliberative issue. That is, they were anticipating future actions and trying to provide the kind of information that they perceived the audience would need to make a decision about the substantive issue posed by the assignment. For instance, one student commented that one report had to include a specific conclusion about a design's feasibility because "only if it's feasible will they go back and design the reformer to do it."

That comment suggests that in the Design course, students perceived a plausible substantive issue for the audience, an issue that went well beyond the classroom issue of judging their performance. This difference in perception reflected an important difference in the Lab and Design courses. In Lab, both students and faculty were all too aware that the conceptual issue posed in the assignments was *not* an issue for the audience, whereas it was perceived as one in Design.

This difference came out repeatedly in the open-ended interview responses when I asked both faculty and students to compare the courses. As Professor Abbott explained, "these labs have been around for so long that most of the new things are old things." In contrast, for Design, he said, "we don't know when we put these design problems together what reasonable answers are. That makes it a fun course to teach, much more fun than Lab." Students' perceptions that the Lab experiments did not present an issue for their professors seemed to make it less of an issue for them as well. As one explained in a remark representative of other students' perceptions, "Lab is a prefabricated situation and has been done 100 times and when you go in to do a Lab you just go in and say 'Okay, the professor has read 800 of these. We're just doing the same thing again. Let's just do it, write it up, and get it done. . . .' But, in Design, the professors are going to read 30 different designs. So the Discussion has a lot more meaning. It's your original work."

Audiences: Roles, Knowledge, and Expectations

Roles. Audience roles also differed in Lab and Design. The survey and interview results also indicate that in Lab, students' and professors' perceptions of the audience often conflicted. This conflict in perception seemed to reflect the problematic nature of the context of Lab.

The assignments themselves were part of this problem in Lab. While four of the six faculty for whom students wrote labs said that the boss was to be the audience, the assignments they gave out did not create a plausible context for this role. The assignments did not come from the boss, and no mention was made of a specific company or issue for that company. The only reference to a context was in Johannes' assignment which advised students that they should use "a format appropriate for presentation, say, by a pilot plant team to a supervisor" (Appendix A). In contrast, the assignments in Design did create a plausible context for the hypothetical audience. These assignments were presented on a hypothetical company's letterhead as a memo from management to the project chief, who then forwarded it to the design team (Appendix B). Students were also asked to write weekly progress memos to their project chief and address their final report to management, setting it in the specific situational context created by the assignment memo.

The writing profile survey indicated both the difference in student and faculty perceptions of the audience and the mixed messages that faculty gave as to the audience for Lab reports. For both the Lab and Design courses, most faculty perceived the audience to be the writers' "boss" in some hypothetical industry. Lab was complicated, however, because no uniform audience was presented for all six labs: not only did the specific professor change for each lab, but also the audience role they stipulated for assignments. Three of the six said the audience role would be that of the "boss," a manager who might not be an engineer; the fourth said other students; the fifth said the "boss," other students, and a professor; and the sixth, Abbott, said it would be himself as professor. In contrast, in Design, the primary audience was consistently presented as the writers' project design chief (a person with engineering training) and secondarily higher management. As Table 2 indicates, students' perceptions differed somewhat from the faculty's. For Lab, regardless of which professor they were writing their report for, students perceived the professor as the only primary audience. In contrast, for Design, they were more likely to share the professors' perceptions that the "boss" was also a primary audience.

These differences reflected the degree to which Lab remained more of a classroom forum than a hypothetical professional forum, even though most faculty, by naming the "boss" as the audience, seemed to want it to be perceived as a professional forum.

Knowledge. The results of the writing profile survey indicated that students' and professors' perceptions of the audience's knowledge differed as well (Table 3). Specifically, for Lab, the students perceived their audience as quite knowledgeable of detail, theory, and technical terms while the faculty perceived the audience as less knowledgeable, particularly of details and

Table 2
Students' Perceptions of Their Primary Audience for Laboratory and Design Reports

	Laboratory Reports (n = 71)		Design Reports (n = 63)	
Potential audience	*M*	*SD*	*M*	*SD*
Professor	1.0	.12	1.2	.42
Teaching assistant/Writing consultant[a]	2.8	.45	2.3	.59
Other students	2.8	.39	2.7	.50
Boss in industry (hypothetical)	2.5	.77	1.7	.83
Self	2.3	.72	2.2	.84

Note. Means are based on a scale of 1 (primary audience) to 3 (not an audience for this report at all). Data from Writing Profile Survey.
[a] The Teaching Assistant is a potential audience for Laboratory Reports, the Writing Consultant for Design Reports; *n* for Design Reports on this item equals 62.

Table 3
Perceptions of Audience Knowledge

	Students			Professors			t
	M	SD	n	M	SD	n	
Knowledge of detail							
Lab	5.2	1.30	71	3.4	1.30	8	3.66*
Design	4.6	1.48	63	4.5	1.50	3	.09
Knowledge of theory							
Lab	5.3	1.12	71	3.4	1.45	8	4.21*
Design	5.1	1.36	63	5.8	.29	3	− .96
Knowledge of technical terms							
Lab	5.2	1.09	71	4.6	1.51	8	1.43
Design	5.1	1.37	63	5.8	.29	3	− .86

Note. Means are based on a scale of 1 (not knowledgeable) to 6 (very knowledgeable). Data from Writing Profile Survey.
*$p < .001$

theory. In contrast, for Design, students and faculty shared the perception that the audience was relatively knowledgeable.

The discourse-based interview responses suggested that students' perception of their audience for lab was more complex than the Survey results indicated. On the one hand, students were well aware that their real audience was the professor, who, as one student explained, "is the book that you can't look at. He knows the answers." On the other hand, when explaining why they included explanations of basic terms and theories, students fictionalized some vaguely-defined, less knowledgeable person. For example, one student justified including one statement of elaboration, saying "I know we're writing to the professor, but I always feel we're writing to someone who is intelligent but someone who doesn't exactly know what ion exchange is." This other audience seemed to be a convention appropriate to the school-centered purpose of the Lab report. As Abbott commented in one interview, "In the Laboratory [course], at least for almost all the people I know who work with it, it's acceptable to and in many cases encouraged to lead the reader through the material as though he didn't really know what was going on technically. . . . Here they're still learning." His comment implied that the intended purpose of the explanations was as much for the student as for the teacher-reader. As one student commented, explaining why she included a definition of a basic chemical law, "it's for my own knowing."

Trying to write for these multiple audiences for the Lab reports in some instances led to confusion. As one student explained, "we weren't sure who we were writing to. That was the problem we had through the whole lab. We didn't know how detailed to be." As a consequence, in some instances, students included explanations of technical terms, like linear function, that the audience did not need to have explained. When I asked Johannes about a report where "linear function" was defined, he said that the definition was not necessary, commenting "I can't say that I really fault them [the students] for it."

In Design, while the Survey results indicated that students and faculty shared a perception that the audience was relatively knowledgeable, the discourse-based interviews indicated that students within each Design work group were less in agreement with the professors and among themselves about what explanations were necessary for that audience. I base this conclusion, in part, on six of the interview questions that focused on phrases or clauses that defined basic terms. When I asked Abbott, Johannes, and Lashmet whether they would delete these definitions, they said yes, saying, for example, "it's not really required for a technical audience." Not all students, however, agreed with this judgment. Obviously, when they wrote the reports, they thought it necessary to include these passages of definition. Further, when interviewed about the completed reports, half of the students said the passages should remain because "some people might not know what you mean"; the other half said delete the phrases because "You'd have to assume that the person you're doing this for would have the same technical knowledge as we do."

Audience Expectations. The discourse-based interviews about Lab and Design reports written for Abbott and Johannes indicated that the same students and professors perceived a different set of audience expectations for these reports—even though they were written to the same two professors in each course. These differences corresponded to differences in the perceived issues, audience roles, and social purposes for each report.

For Lab reports, both students and faculty perceived that the audience wanted results interpreted and the students' own procedures and assumptions justified. These perceptions were consistent with the perceived forensic and epideictic issues for the Lab reports:

- Why did something happen?
  ("AJ wants to know why things happen.")
- How reasonable are your results?
  ("He [Abbott] wanted something that shows how good our data is.")
- How can your results be explained, specifically in relation to theory or possible experimental errors?
  ("Let's say Abbott were reading through this and looked and said, 'Geeze, they have weird heat transfer coefficients. I wonder why?' That explains it.")
- How can your procedures and assumptions be justified?
  ("I was trying to show that 'Hey, this is no good!' If he wants to question why it's no good, I'd just tell him, we couldn't get more information.")

For Design reports, both students and faculty perceived that the reader expected answers to a quite different set of questions:

- What major design decisions did you make and can they be justified as technically or economically advantageous?
  ("If we didn't say this, the reader might wonder why it's economically attractive.")
- What do you conclude? Is the design technically feasible and economically advantageous?
  ("The whole idea of this report is that later it goes to the Economics section for someone else to do. So that's sort of a lead-in for them to take over." [This comment is in reference to a conclusion about costs.])

These questions were consistent with the deliberative issue for the Design reports. As these questions suggest, the audience still wanted a justification of a past act, the decisions the engineers made, but they wanted those decisions justified as a means to some future pragmatic end for the company. The excerpts cited from the student interviews also indicated that although students were still writing to Abbott and Johannes, they made fewer specific reference to them than they did when interviewed about the Lab reports. Instead, they referred to the general hypothetical audience (superiors in some fictitious company) and what they would expect.

Writer: Role and *Ethos*

Students' and professors' perceptions of the writer's role paralleled their perceptions of the audience's role. In Lab, students' and professors' perceptions differed. That is, in the open-ended interviews, six of the eight faculty who supervised the Labs said that they perceived of students in the role of engineers. Johannes was one of these professors. The other two faculty, including Abbott, said they perceived the students' role as that of students. As Abbott explained, in Lab "it's more of a student-professor relationship; whereas in the Design course, it's more like an employee-boss relationship. And that really implies a more equal relationship than the student-professor one."

Abbott's comment summarized the students' perceptions as well. Of the ten students interviewed, nine of them agreed with the one student who said, "definitely students. We were still writing for the professor, and we have to show him we did the experiment." Two students also commented that they weren't even conscious of having an identity for the Lab reports. One said, "It was almost without any identity. It was just kind of reporting something." The other reported, "in Lab, I didn't even think about that. In Lab, I just wrote. In Design, you've got to, you know, we're intelligent engineers, and we know what we're doing." Both students and faculty shared this perception that the students' role for Design was that of practicing engineers. As one of the professors commented, "suddenly, they're experts."

The perception of a student versus a professional role was evident as well in the writers' perceptions of the *ethos* they were to project. As the discourse-based interview responses indicated, in general, writing the Lab reports, students perceived that they were to project themselves as ones who were knowledgeable of theory and experimental procedures. For example, one student explained that she wanted to keep in a justification because "it sort of shows our understanding of theory." It appeared that projecting this *ethos* was consistent with faculty expectations as well. In discussing the same passage, Professor Abbott agreed it should remain even though he said "it would be pretty obvious for an application like this." He went on to say that "it's critical for them to know that!" This concern to show that one is knowledgeable was cited fourteen times in students' discourse-based interviews about Lab reports and only twice in their interviews about Design reports. (See Table 1. Category II. B.)

In Design, both professors and students perceived the appropriate *ethos* to be that of "experts." As "experts," these writers no longer needed to demonstrate their knowledge of basic engineering practice and theory. As Abbott said, "the boss would just assume they're comfortable with all this stuff." While this basic knowledge was assumed, these engineers were still concerned with projecting themselves as competent and confident. One student perceived that you evoke an *ethos* of one who is technically competent by showing that you anticipated and designed a process to avoid future design problems. As he said explaining why he wanted a justification left in a report, "A technical guy might read it and say, 'Oh, these guys are cool. They think ahead.'" In another instance, a student said he wanted to state a design decision in active voice using "we" as the subject instead of in the passive voice "because it sounds more authoritative this way."

In some instances, however, some students were not quite sure how to project that type of image, particularly when their Design turned out not to be feasible or money-making. For example, in one report, a group tried to deal with the failure of their design to meet the design objectives by writing "We tried to find a feasible plan to recover 20% of our investment." In the discourse-based interviews, one student explained that statement saying, "We were trying to couch as well as we could the fact that we were losing over $3,000,000 and we didn't know why. . . . You know, we really tried hard." In the discourse-based interview about that same passage, Professor Lashmet said, "This sounds like they're not confident in what they can do. They may not be, but you certainly don't want to emphasize it." Commenting on the same passage, Abbott agreed, going on to say, "This is something they have to learn to do."

Purposes

As the survey results reported in Table 4 indicate, both students and faculty perceived "demonstrating the writer's knowledge" to be the dominant purpose for writing the Lab reports (student mean = 5.1, faculty mean = 4.8.; $t(75) = .64$, n.s.). This perception was consistent with the perceived forensic and epideictic issues for these reports. Faculty, however, also saw a learner-centered purpose as dominant for the Lab reports: "exploring and shaping the writers' own ideas." The faculty's perception is reflected in Abbott's comment that writing the Lab reports "is an academic exercise in the good sense in that, as with Design, it's a chance to get some concepts straight." Students did not share this perception (Table 4). One of the obstacles to doing so seemed to be the obvious non-issue that students perceived both for the professors and often for themselves. One student summed it up as follows: "In Lab, basically, you know what you have to do. It doesn't—well, it requires some thinking, but not that much. I think of it as something tedious, and that the professors know what type of answer they want."

In contrast, in Design, both students and professors perceived that the professors as audience did not know exactly what the solution was. Not surprisingly, then, students perceived two audience-centered purposes to be as important as "demonstrating their knowledge." These two purposes were

Table 4
Perceived Purposes for Laboratory and Design Reports

	Students			Professors			t
Perceived purpose	M	SD	n	M	SD	n	
Demonstrating knowledge							
Lab	5.1	1.09	69	4.8	1.85	8	.64
Design	4.4	1.25	62	4.3	1.53	3	.15
Exploring own ideas							
Lab	3.6	1.21	69	5.2	1.73	8	−3.30**
Design	3.5	1.29	62	4.0	1.00	3	−0.60
Directing someone							
Lab	2.5	1.56	69	1.6	1.05	8	1.65
Design	2.5	1.39	62	1.0	0.00	3	−1.87
Convincing someone							
Lab	2.6	1.64	69	2.7	1.71	8	−0.19
Design	4.3	1.53	62	5.7	.58	3	−1.49
Instructing someone							
Lab	2.7	3.69	69	3.7	1.58	8	−1.76
Design	3.4	1.51	60	4.0	1.00	3	−0.69
Informing someone							
Lab	4.2	1.48	69	5.7	.70	8	−2.82*
Design	5.3	.75	62	6.0	.00	3	−1.68
Proving a point							
Lab	3.8	1.52	69	3.2	2.30	8	−1.71
Design	4.2	1.20	62	4.0	2.65	3	−1.40

Note. Means are based on a scale of 1 (not a purpose at all) to 6 (very much a purpose). Data from Writing Profile Survey.
*$p < .01$
**$p < .001$

"informing someone" and "convincing someone." This concern with convincing someone was reflected in the discourse-based interviews about Design reports. Here, students often justified decisions because they wanted to persuade or convince readers and to justify a conclusion about a subject. (See Table 1. Categories I. C and III. B.)

For Lab reports, while students perceived "informing someone" to be a less dominant purpose, the faculty perceived it to be a dominant purpose. This discrepancy may be explained by the different perceptions students and faculty had of the audience for these reports and the issue for this audience. Recall that students perceived this audience, the professor, as someone for whom the Lab presented no conceptual issue and who had already read hundreds of reports just like theirs.

Lines of Reasoning: Claims and Warrants

The analyses of claim statements and warrants indicated that the lines of reasoning used in the Lab reports differed from those used in the Design reports. Relevant results follow.

Claims

As Table 5 shows, the claims made in reports written for Lab differed from those written for Design. The claims made most frequently in the Lab reports were Forensic claims identifying sources of error or wrong-doing (e.g., "The spectrophotometer was another likely source of error") and justifying the group's past actions, primarily on the basis of theory or experimental procedure (e.g., "The criteria that apply to the Dittus-Boelter relationship are satisfied by our experiment. [Therefore,] we decided to employ the correlation in a modified form."). The Lab reports also contained some Scientific claims making a generalization about the nature of some phenomenon (e.g., "The helical flow is more closely represented by the plug flow reactor"). Of the Deliberative claims made in the lab reports, 50 percent were technical recommendations of ways to improve the laboratory procedures.

Table 5
Types of Claims Made in Laboratory and Design Reports

	Percent of Claims	
	Lab Reports (n = 123 claims)	Design Reports (n = 92 claims)
Type of Claim		
Forensic	71	48
Deliberative	15	52
Scientific	15	0

In contrast to the Lab reports, the Design reports primarily made Deliberative claims, specifically ones evaluating the expediency of a proposed course of action or recommending that action. They were most frequently claims stating a finding about feasibility and expediency (e.g., "The methanol/synthesis process presented here is economically and thermodynamically feasible") and claims making a recommendation on the basis of expediency (e.g., "We therefore recommend the multi-effect distillation scheme. Although the initial investment is substantial, the long term savings from energy conservation will be worthwhile."). The Design reports also contained a number of Forensic claims although most of them were of a different type from those in the Lab reports. That is, 54 percent of the Forensic claims in Design reports were justifications of design decisions on the basis of expediency. In contrast, only 2 percent of the Forensic claims in Lab reports cited expediency as the basis for decisions. Instead, they cited theory or experimental procedures.

Warrants

The types of warrants used to support the claims corresponded to the types of claims. The most frequently cited warrants in the Lab reports were of three general types: 1) theories, established correlating equations, or other research reported in refereed journals; 2) error analysis; and 3) plots of the students' own Lab results. For example, in one report, the students claimed "From the results obtained one can see that the correlation yields excellent values, thus further supporting the validity of the functional dependence of the heat transfer coefficient on the Reynolds and Prandtl numbers." In this instance, their warrant was the high correlation between their own experimental results and an established correlation.

In contrast to the Lab reports, the Design reports rarely cited scientific/technical theories or error analysis to support claims. Instead, the claims made in Design reports were supported by warrants more common to deliberative rhetoric: that is, the "accepted notions" of industry as to what will serve the "good" of that company, profit. For example, in one report, the writers included the following claim and warrant: "Electric motors were chosen over steam turbines to drive the compressors because the operating costs are less for electric motors than for steam turbines."

These differences in the lines of reasoning used in the Lab and Design reports might appear quite obvious. Certainly one could say that the students were answering different questions, so of course the lines of reasoning would differ. This difference was not so obvious, however, to all the work groups writing Design reports. As Table 6 indicates, in the Design reports, Group C made proportionately more Forensic claims appropriate to the Lab reports than did Groups A and B. Also, although Group B made more Deliberative than Forensic claims, the specific nature of these Deliberative claims in their first Design reports was more appropriate to Lab reports: that is, 3 of these claims gave technical accuracy as the rationale and only 1 gave expediency as the rationale. In their second Design report, this distribution shifted to 2 based

Table 6

Types of Claims Made by Each Student Work Group
in Laboratory and Design Reports

| | Frequency of Claims | | | | | |
| | Lab Reports Work Groups | | | Design Reports Work Groups | | |
Type of Claim	A	B	C	A	B	C
Forensic	31	27	29	12	14	18
Deliberative	8	6	4	14	21	13
Scientific	11	4	3	0	0	0
Total	50	37	36	26	35	31

on technical accuracy and 5 based on expediency.

The professors' perceptions of the inappropriateness of these claims was evident in their interview responses. For example, in one Design report, Group C made the following claim about the reasonableness of their results: "A value of 0.02 (which sounds too low) was estimated." When asked whether this parenthetical claim should be deleted, Professor Lashmet said certainly it should because "All it does, is—it creates—it says that they did something wrong. 'Maybe we goofed somewhere.'" In this instance, it seems that the claim reflected negatively on the engineers, who ended up projecting an *ethos* of uncertainty and, even worse, incompetence for failing to double-check a calculated value they felt was erroneous.

Just as the Design groups differed in the claims they made, they differed in the warrants used to support those claims. Specifically, Groups B and C in some instances cited theoretical warrants more appropriate to the Lab than to Design and a proportionately lower number of warrants of expediency. They also cited warrants of expediency that were not "good reasons" for this forum, at least not as judged by the faculty. They were not good reasons because they focused on what was expedient for the engineers themselves, not the company they worked for. For example, in one Design report, Group B stated the following claim and supporting warrant: "In the base case it was decided to preheat the feed stream to ensure a saturated liquid entered the column. This simplified the graphical calculation of minimum reflux ratio." When Professor Johannes was asked about the warrant, he commented "that is not a good reason. . . . If they had said we did this for minimization of the utilities or something like that, that would be good engineering. This is just because it made their calculations easier. . . . That's not professional." In this instance, then, using a warrant that the audience did not consider a sound one for justifying an engineering decision in turn reflected poorly on the engineers.

Discussion

The findings from this study lead us to rethink some of our assumptions about the monolithic nature of writing in academic settings. The study shows that even within one discipline, chemical engineering, different courses may represent distinct forums where different issues are addressed, different lines of reasoning used, different writer and audience roles assumed, and different social purposes served by writing. These differences were apparent not only in students' and professors' perceptions of these courses, but also in the reports students wrote for each course.

These findings shed some light on the two broader questions posed at the outset of this article: What function does writing serve? and How can teachers create classroom contexts conducive to using writing?

This study shows that the function of writing can be to introduce students not only to the "conceptual activities" central to a given discipline (Odell, 1980) and to expected structures and styles of professional writing (Mathes & Stevenson, 1976), but also to the social roles and purposes for writing within a given disciplinary forum. In other words, writing can function as a way of introducing students to what it means to think and act in various disciplinary forums. For example, from this study, it appears that learning Chemical Engineering means learning to think and act both in a scientific/technical forum and in a deliberative forum. Each is constituted by a characteristic configuration of issues, lines of reasoning, roles, and purposes for reasoning and writing. Lab and Design, to different degrees, recreated these forums.

As the results indicate, the differences in these forums are significant for those who would reason and write in them. As students' experiences in Design demonstrated, learning to participate in a new forum means learning the ways of that forum: learning, for example, the kind of knowledge claims it is appropriate to make and what count as good reasons to support those knowledge claims. It also means learning accepted writer and reader roles as well as the social purposes that are to be served by writing. Such learning takes time and practice. The Design course, in particular, represented an attempt to create a classroom forum for such learning.

This study also suggests that learning the conventions of a professional forum may be all the more difficult if one is shifting from a context where the social conventions of a school community are dominant to a context where those of a professional community are dominant. Lab represented such a school-dominated context, although it was problematic because, given the mixed messages the faculty gave to students, it represented a confused mix of both school and professional community conventions.

Despite these problems, the Lab course did suggest some of the possibilities of a classroom as a viable school forum in its own right. Abbott's lab, in particular, was presented implicitly as situated within a school community without trying to recreate a professional setting. Here, the purposes were more strictly learner-centered: "to explore and shape one's own ideas" and "demonstrate one's knowledge." In such a forum, writing could provide the occasion for students to learn the basic concepts of a discipline by using them to resolve issues typically addressed within that discipline and to justify their interpretation to their teachers.

Given these purposes, it was appropriate for students to decide what to include in their Lab reports on the basis of different expectations than was appropriate for Design reports. That is, in Lab, as a school forum, it seemed to be appropriate for students to decide what to include based on what was new to them, that is, to put into words what they were learning, even if that was old information to the professor. As one student said, explaining why she included an explanation of a basic concept, "Writing is my way of putting things together. That's one of the reasons I like Lab a lot." Referring to the distillation lab she had done, she explained, "A lot of things I didn't quite understand about distillation, I really put distillation together when I wrote that Lab." Her comment echoes Polanyi's claim that by using the language of a particular intellectual community, we "assimilate" what he calls the interpretative framework" of that community (1962).

Such explanations were appropriate in Lab but not so in Design, the professional forum, as was evidenced by the different expectations of Abbott, the audience for reports in both courses. According to him, in Lab, "they're still learning, so if they want to tell me what a breakthrough curve is, that's fine, but in Design, we don't want to be hit again with all the basics."

My point is that there is an educational value to the purposes and writer-audience roles of the school community, purposes and roles that may be inconsistent with those of a professional forum, at least one like Design. Further, we may be working at cross purposes when we unconsciously try to create both forums in the same classrooms, particularly if we give mixed signals to students about our own role. In some instances, the aims of a course might be better realized if we try to create a viable school forum instead of a hypothetical professional one.

This discussion of functions of writing assumes that teachers *can* create different forums in their classrooms. The findings from this study support that assumption: teachers do have a good deal of influence over the nature of the community that is created in a given class. One of the ways they exercise this influence is through the role they assume and expectations they project as audience. In this study, the findings show that students' perceptions of their own role as writers, the purposes for writing, and lines of reasoning they should use varied with their perceptions of their audience's role and expectations. That students perceived these differences—even between the two labs and the Design course, all taught by Abbott and Johannes—was in part because in each course, during class and consultation sessions, Abbott and Johannes assumed different roles and posed questions that reflected the kinds of lines of reasoning valued in each forum. By doing so, they were focusing students' attention on the particular questions and warrants that would guide students in investigating and resolving the particular issue posed in that class. This finding about differences is contrary to the finding of the Odell et al. study (1981) that students perceived the same "circumstances" for writing regardless of the course they were writing for. I attribute these different findings to differences in the research methods.

The study also shows that faculty and students together create a community through their on-going interactions. One of the problems with Lab was that there was little opportunity for these interactions: each lab was done for a different professor and, while doing each lab, student and professor met only once. Not surprisingly, then, students and faculty did not share a common sense of roles and purposes, and many students found writing the Lab reports quite frustrating. As one commented, "I don't think it's profitable because you're constantly trying to second guess, 'what does he want? what was he trying to say?'" In Design, where students and professors remained the same for the entire course and where they had frequent interaction in class and through the writings, they were more in agreement as to roles and purposes, and students had a more positive attitude toward the writing.

This study also shows the importance of integrating assignments into the total context of a course. Lab was problematic because in many instances there was a disjunction between the written assignment and the roles faculty assumed in their meetings with students and the purposes they perceived for writing. In contrast, in Design, the writing assignments were consistent with the context that was *enacted* in the classroom, in this case a hypothetical professional forum: a fictitious company was created; design problems were posed as specific problems the company needed to solve for a particular reason; both students and teachers assumed roles in this company and these roles remained the same throughout the course. All of this combined to create what one student called "a different environment," different that is, from Lab.

Finally, this study shows how writing can be used both to create a community and to learn the intellectual and social conventions of a disciplinary forum. In Design, in particular, the professors' written assignments and the students' weekly memos and final reports helped create the community because in them professors and students enacted the roles appropriate to the community (i.e., section chiefs and engineers in a hypothetical company). The weekly memos helped to achieve another important aim of the classroom community. As both students and faculty commented, these memos serve as a way of carrying-out an on-going interchange as students worked on each design project. Finally, in both courses, as I have already discussed, writing provided the occasion for learning a particular line of reasoning by *using* it and for learning a particular social role by inhabiting it.

References

Albrecht, T., & Ropp, V. (1982). The study of network structuring in organizations through the use of method triangulation. *The Western Journal of Speech Communication, 46*, 162-178.

Applebee, A., Auten, A., & Lehr, F. (1981). *Writing in the secondary school: English and the content areas* (Research Report No. 21). Urbana, IL: National Council of Teachers of English.

Aristotle (1955). *Posterior analytics* (W. D. Ross, Ed. and A.J. Jenkinson, Trans.). London: Oxford University Press.

Aristotle (1954). *Rhetoric*. In *The rhetoric and the poetics of Aristotle* (W. Rhys Roberts, Ed. and Trans.). New York: Modern Library.

Bauman, R., & Sherzer, J. (1975). The ethnography of speaking. *Annual Review of Anthropology, 4*, 95-119.

Bazerman, C. (1981). What written knowledge does: Three examples of academic prose. *Philosophy of the Social Sciences, 11*, 361-387.

Bazerman, C. (1982, December). *Discourse paths of different disciplines*. Paper presented at the annual meeting of the Modern Language Association, Los Angeles.

Bizzell, P. (1982). Cognition, convention, and certainty: What we need to know about writing. *PRE/ TEXT, 31*(3), 213-243.

Calkins, L. (1980). Research update: When children want to punctuate: Basic skills belong in context. *Language Arts, 57*, 567-573.

Denzin, N. (1970). *The research act*. Chicago: Aldine.

Florio, S., & Clark, C. (1982). The functions of writing in an elementary classroom. *Research in the Teaching of English, 16*(2), 115-130.

Flower, L., & Hayes, J. R. (1977). Problem-solving strategies and the writing process. *College English, 39*(4), 449-461.

Fulwiler, T., & Young, A. (Eds.). (1982). *Language connections: Writing and reading across the curriculum*. Urbana, IL: National Council of Teachers of English.

Gardner, P. L. (1977). *Logical connectives in science*. (A Report to the Education Research and Development Committee, Commonwealth Government). Melbourne, Australia: Monash University.

Graves, D. (1978). *Balance the basics: Let them write: A report to the Ford Foundation*. New York: Ford Foundation.

Halliday, M. A. K. (1978). *Language as social semiotic: The social interpretation of language and meaning*. Baltimore: University Park Press.

Herrington, A. J. (1983). Writing in academic settings: A study of the rhetorical contexts for writing in two college chemical engineering courses. (Doctoral dissertation, Rensselaer Polytechnic Institute).

Hymes, D. (1972a). Introduction. In C. N. Cazden, V. John, & D. Hymes (Eds.). *Functions of language in the classroom*. New York: Teachers College Press.

Hymes, D. (1972b). Models of the interaction of language and social life. In J. J. Gumperz & D. Hymes (Eds.). *Directions in Sociolinguistics*. New York: Holt, Rinehart, & Winston.

Hymes, D. (1972c). On communicative competence. In J. B. Pride & J. Holmes (Eds.). *Sociolinguistics: Selected readings*. Baltimore: Penguin Books.

Kamler, B. (1980). One child, one teacher, one classroom: The story of one piece of writing. *Language Arts, 57*, 680-683.

Kantor, K. (1984). Classroom contexts and the development of writing intuitions: An ethnographic case study. In R. Beach and L. S. Bridwell (Eds.). *New directions in composition research*. New York: Guilford.

Kinneavy, J. (1971). *A theory of discourse*. New York: W. W. Norton.

Knoblauch, C. H., & Brannon, L. (1983). Writing as learning through the curriculum. *College English, 45*(5), 465-474.

LeCompte, N. D., & Goetz, J. P. (1982). Problems of reliability and validity in ethnographic research. *Review of Educational Research, 52*, 31-60.

Mathes, J. C., & Stevenson, D. W. (1976). Completing the bridge: Report writing in 'real life' engineering courses. *Engineering Education, 67*, 154-158.

Odell, L. (1980). The process of writing and the process of learning. *College Composition and Communication, 31*, 42-50.

Odell, L., & Goswami, D. (1982). Writing in a non-academic setting. *Research in the Teaching of English, 16*(3), 201-224.

Odell, L., Goswami, D., & Herrington, A. (1983). The discourse-based interview: A procedure for exploring the tacit knowledge of writers in nonacademic settings. In P. Mosenthal, L. Tomor, and S. Walmsley (Eds.). *Research on writing: Principles and methods*. New York: Longman.

Odell, L., Goswami, D., & Quick, D. (1981). Writing outside the English composition classroom. In *Writing in non-academic settings* (Final Report NIE-G-0224). Troy, NY: Rensselaer Polytechnic Institute, Dept. of Language, Literature, and Communication.

Polanyi, M. (1962). *Personal knowledge: Towards a post-critical philosophy* (corrected ed.). Chicago:

University of Chicago Press.

Roland, R. C. (1982). The influence of purpose on fields of argument. *Journal of the American Forensic Association, 18*, 228-244.

Toulmin, S. (1972). *Human understanding*. Princeton, NJ: Princeton University Press.

Toulmin, S. (1958). *The use of argument*. New York: Cambridge University Press.

Toulmin, S., Rieke, R., & Janik, A. (1979). *An Introduction to reasoning*. New York: Macmillan.

Appendix A
Sample Laboratory Assignment

Chemical Reaction Engineering Experiment

Object. To compare the performance of a helical flow tubular reactor with that expected from idealized flow tubular reactors for the hydrolysis of crystal violet dye with an excess of sodium hydroxide in aqueous solution

$$(C_6H_4 N (CH_3)_2)_3 C Cl + NaOH \rightarrow (C_6H_4 N (CH_3)_2)_3 COH + NaCl \qquad (1)$$

Procedure. Reaction (1) is to be carried out in the flow system provided at (at least) three different constant temperatures and for (at least) three different flow rates of reactants at each temperature. After the bath temperature has reached the desired value, the reactant flow rates are adjusted and the clock is started. Outlet samples are analyzed colorimetrically for the concentration of dye at various times until a steady state conversion is reached. (How can you tell that a steady state is reached?) Inlet samples are also analyzed. Flow rates of reactants are then changed, keeping the ratio of reactant flow rates the same, and the procedure is repeated. After several steady state conversions have been obtained at the same temperature, the bath temperature is raised and the process is repeated.

The concentration of dye in the inlet and outlet streams of the flow reactor is obtained indirectly by measuring the absorbance of 590 nm wavelength light in a given amount of the sample using the Spectrophotometer. Data for obtaining dye concentrations from the absorbance measurements are provided in Table 1.

The rotameters for regulating and monitoring the flow rate of NaOH and dye solutions have nominal ranges of 0-1500 ml/min and 0-50 ml/min respectively. The flow reactor is 20 m long and has an internal diameter of 3/8 inch. Data from a batch reaction of dye and NaOH in aqueous solution at various temperatures are given in Table II. Use this information to plan your experiments.

Report Format. In preparing your final report, please observe the following guidelines:

Your report should be an *intelligent presentation* of your work in a format appropriate for presentation, say, by a pilot plant team to a supervisor. SI units should be used. Repetition of knowledge available in reference texts is generally not required. However, reference to this information and presentation of the basic equations that you use is necessary. When you finish your report, *read it at least one more time*. Note that language and neatness of the report affect your grade considerably.

Appendix B
Sample Design Assignment

Ephemeral Chemical Corporation
"Profectus Fugit"

To: A. N. Sweeney, Section Head, Process Engineering
From: M. R. Appollinax, Division Chief, Process Engineering
Subject: Porcene Purification Process

A market has recently developed for high-purity porcene, currently produced as an undesirable byproduct at our East Coker Chemical Complex. Unfortunately, it is present in a waste stream with nearly equal amounts of cycloporcane, which has no appreciable market value. Since the two compounds have almost identical boiling points, simple separation by distillation appears infeasible. Instead, we are contemplating extraction with β-miasmone (which is highly selective for porcene), followed by distillation of the extract to produce high-purity porcene. There appears to be no problem with the extraction: with available technology, we should be able to obtain an extract containing about 21 mol % porcene, at high levels of recovery. The real question is whether distillation to the required purity (99.8 mol %) makes economic sense.

I'd like your engineers to do preliminary designs for the distillation facility. Please have them consider at least two cases:

A) Conventional distillation, at 65 psia.
B) Multieffect distillation, at appropriate pressure levels.

Case (A) will be a base case, employing steam or cooling water for heat-exchange operations. For case (B), the idea is to minimize utility requirements relative to the base case.

A design basis is given in the first attachment. Please size all units, including accumulators, heat exchangers, and pumps. Also, perform a thermodynamic second-law analysis for each case, to pinpoint major sources and relative magnitudes of process inefficiencies. Costing need not be done by your people: Tom Macavity's engineers will handle the economics.

Dr. Channing-Cheetah, from Engineering Technology, notes that porcene and β-miasmone form nonideal liquid mixtures. He suggests that you treat liquid-phase activity coefficients as functions of composition only, with infinite-dilution values $\delta_1 = 1.4$ and $\delta_2 = 1.9$, and that you represent their composition dependence with the two-parameter Margules equation. (Here, $1 \equiv$ porcene and $2 \equiv$ β-miasmone.) C. C. has also provided us with physical-property information, summarized in the second attachment.

We require a final report by Wednesday 23 February 1983.

A Stranger in Strange Lands: A College Student Writing Across the Curriculum

by Lucille Parkinson McCarthy

Abstract. This study asks questions about the nature of writing processes in classrooms. As students go from one classroom to another, they are presented with new speech situations, and they must determine what constitute appropriate ways of speaking and writing in each new territory. How do students, in the course of the semester, figure out what the writing requirements are in that discipline and for that teacher, and how do they go about producing it? In order to answer these questions the researcher followed one college student's writing experiences in one class per semester during his freshman and sophomore years. Follow-up data were collected during his junior year. Four research methods were used: observation, interviews, composing-aloud protocols, and text analysis. Conclusions are drawn from the data about how this student figured out what constituted acceptable writing in each classroom, and how he worked to produce it. Also presented are conclusions about what enhanced or denied his success in communicating competently in unfamiliar academic territories. Affecting his success were unarticulated social aspects of classroom contexts for writing as well as explicitly stated requirements and instructions.

Dave Garrison, a college junior and the focus of the present study, was asked how he would advise incoming freshmen about writing for their college courses. His answer was both homely and familiar.

"I'd tell them," he said, "first you've got to figure out what your teachers want. And then you've got to give it to them if you're gonna' get the grade." He paused a moment and added, "And that's not always so easy."

No matter how we teachers may feel about Dave's response, it does reflect his sensitivity to school writing as a social affair. Successful students are those who can, in their interactions with teachers during the semester,

Reprinted from *Research in the Teaching of English* (October 1987). Copyright 1987 by the National Council of Teachers of English. Reprinted with permission.

I am grateful to the participants who made this study possible and to Professors Linda Brodkey, Barbara McDaniel, Susan Lytle, and David Smith whose insights and support were invaluable.

determine what constitute appropriate texts in each classroom: the content, structures, language, ways of thinking, and types of evidence required in that discipline and by that teacher. They can then produce such a text. Students who cannot do this, for whatever reason—cultural, intellectual, motivational—are those who fail, deemed incompetent communicators in that particular setting. They are unable to follow what Britton calls the "rules of the game" in each class (1975, p. 76). As students go from one classroom to another they must play a wide range of games, the rules for which, Britton points out, include many conventions and presuppositions that are not explicitly articulated.

In this article, writing in college is viewed as a process of assessing and adapting to the requirements in unfamiliar academic settings. Specifically, the study examined how students figured out what constituted appropriate texts in their various courses and how they went about producing them. And, further, it examined what characterized the classroom contexts which enhanced or denied students' success in this process. This study was a 21-month project which focused on the writing experiences of one college student, Dave, in three of his courses, Freshman Composition in the spring of his freshman year, and, in his sophomore year, Introduction to Poetry in the fall and Cell Biology in the spring. Dave, a biology/pre-med major, was typical of students at his college in terms of his SAT scores (502 verbal; 515 math), his high school grades, and his white, middle-class family background.

As I followed Dave from one classroom writing situation to another, I came to see him, as he made his journey from one discipline to another, as a stranger in strange lands. In each new class Dave believed that the writing he was doing was totally unlike anything he had ever done before. This metaphor of a newcomer in a foreign country proved to be a powerful way of looking at Dave's behaviors as he worked to use the new languages in unfamiliar academic territories. Robert Heinlein's (1961) science fiction novel suggested this metaphor originally. But Heinlein's title is slightly different; his stranger is in a *single* strange land. Dave perceived himself to be in one strange land after another.

Background to the Study

The theoretical underpinnings of this study are to be found in the work of sociolinguists (Hymes, 1972a, 1972b; Gumperz, 1971) and ethnographers of communication (Basso, 1974; Heath, 1982; Szwed, 1981) who assume that language processes must be understood in terms of the contexts in which they occur. All language use in this view takes place within speech communities and accomplishes meaningful social functions for people. Community members share characteristic "ways of speaking," that is, accepted linguistic, intellectual, and social conventions which have developed over time and govern spoken interaction. And "communicatively competent" speakers in every community recognize and successfully employ these "rules of use," largely without conscious attention (Hymes, 1972a, pp. xxiv-xxxvi).

A key assumption underlying this study is that writing, like speaking, is a social activity. Writers, like speakers, must use the communication means considered appropriate by members of particular speech or discourse communities. And the writer's work, at the same time, may affect the norms of the community. As students go from one class to another, they must define and master the rules of use for written discourse in one classroom speech community after another. And their writing can only be evaluated in terms of that particular community's standards.

Some recent practical and theoretical work in writing studies has emphasized that writers' processes and products must be understood in terms of their contexts, contexts which are created as participants and settings interact (Bazerman, 1981; Bizzell, 1982; Cooper, 1986; Faigley, 1985; Whiteman, 1981). Studies of writing in non-academic settings have shown just how complex these writing environments are and how sophisticated the knowledge—both explicit and tacit—is that writers need in order to operate successfully in them (Odell & Goswami, 1985). And classrooms offer no less complex environments for writing. As Erickson (1982) points out, the classroom learning environment includes not only the teacher and the student, but also the subject matter structure, the social task structure, the actual enacted task, and the sequence of actions involved in the task. In addition, in many classrooms students may be provided with too few instructional supports to help them as they write (Applebee, 1984). Specifically, college classroom contexts for writing, Herrington (1985) argues, must be thought of in terms of several speech communities, viewed "in relation not only to a school community, but also to the intellectual and social conventions of professional forums within a given discipline" (p. 333). These overlapping communities influence the ways students think and write and interact in college classrooms, and will shape their notions of what it means to be, for example, an engineer or a biologist or a literary critic.

Research which has directly examined particular classroom contexts for writing has provided insight into their diversity (Applebee, 1984; Calkins, 1980; Florio & Clark, 1982; Freedman, 1985; Herrington, 1985; Kantor, 1984). Though these studies suggest that an individual student is likely to encounter a number of quite different classroom writing situations, there is also evidence that individual student writers may employ consistent patterns across tasks as they interpret assignments, reason, and organize their knowledge (Dyson, 1984; Langer, 1985, 1986).

What has not yet been done, however, is to follow individual college students as they progress across academic disciplines. In this study I offer information about how one college student fares in such a journey across the curriculum. That is, I detail how this student's behavior changed or remained constant across tasks in three classroom contexts and how those contexts influenced his success. Though this study is limited in scope to the experiences of a single student as he wrote for three college courses, it addresses questions central to much writing across the curriculum scholarship:

1. What are the tasks students encounter as they move from one course to another?
2. How do successful students interpret these tasks? Further, how do students determine what constitutes appropriate texts in that discipline and for that teacher, and how do they produce them?
3. What are the social factors in classrooms that foster particular writing behaviors and students' achievement of competence in that setting?

The ultimate aim of this study is to contribute to our understanding of how students learn to write in school. Findings from this study corroborate the notion that learning to write should be seen not only as a developmental process occurring within an individual student, but also as a social process occurring in response to particular situations.

Methods

The research approach was naturalistic. I entered the study with no hypotheses to test and no specially devised writing tasks. Rather, I studied the writing that was actually being assigned in these classrooms, working to understand and describe that writing, how it functioned in each classroom, and what it meant to people there. My purpose was to get as rich a portrait as possible of Dave's writing and his classroom writing contexts. To this end I combined four research tools: observation, interviews, composing-aloud protocols, and text analysis. The data provided by the protocols and text analysis served to add to, crosscheck, and refine the data generated by observation and interviews. Using this triangulated approach (Denzin, 1978), I could view Dave's writing experiences through several windows, with the strengths of one method compensating for the limitations of another.

The Courses

The college is a private, co-educational, liberal arts institution located in a large, northeastern city. Of its 2600 students nearly half are business, accounting, and computer science majors. Yet over half of students' courses are required liberal arts courses, part of the core curriculum. Two of Dave's courses in this study are core courses: Freshman Composition and Introduction to Poetry. The third, Cell Biology, is a course taken by biology majors; it was Dave's third semester of college biology. All three were one-semester courses. In the descriptions of these courses that follow, I use pseudonyms for the teachers.

In Freshman Composition, which met twice a week for 90 minutes, students were required to write a series of five, similarly structured essays on topics of their choice. These two or four page essays were due at regular intervals and were graded by the professor, Dr. Jean Carter. Classes were generally teacher-led discussions and exercises, with some days allotted for students to work together in small groups, planning their essays or sharing drafts. Dr. Carter held one individual writing conference with each student at mid semester.

Introduction to Poetry is generally taken by students during their sophomore year, and it, like Freshman Composition, met for 90 minutes twice a week. In this class students were also required to write a series of similar papers. These were three to six page critical essays on poems that students chose from a list given them by their professor, Dr. Charles Forson. These essays, like those in Freshman Composition, were due at regular intervals and were graded by the professor. The Poetry classes were all lectures in which Dr. Forson explicated poems. However, one lecture early in the semester was devoted entirely to writing instruction.

Cell Biology, which Dave took in the spring of his sophomore year, met three times a week, twice for 90-minute lectures and once for a three-hour lab. In this course, like the other two, students were required to write a series of similar short papers, three in this course. These were three to five page reviews of journal articles which reported current research in cell biology. Students were to summarize these articles, following the five-part scientific format in which the experiment was reported. They were then to relate the experiment to what they were doing in class. These reviews were graded by the professor, Dr. Tom Kelly.

The Participants

The participants in this study included these three professors, Drs. Carter, Forson, and Kelly. All were experienced college teachers who had taught these courses before. All talked willingly and with interest about the writing their students were doing, and both Dr. Carter and Dr. Forson invited me to observe their classes. Dr. Kelly said that it would not be productive for me to observe in his Cell Biology course because he spent almost no time talking directly about writing, so pressed was he to cover the necessary course material.

The student participants in this study were Dave and two of his friends. I first met these three young men in Dr. Carter's Freshman Composition class where I was observing regularly in order to learn how she taught the course, the same one I teach at the college. As I attended that course week after week, I got to know the students who sat by me, Dave and his friends, and I realized I was no longer as interested in understanding what my colleague was teaching as I was in understanding what these students were learning. As the study progressed, my focus narrowed to Dave's experiences, although none of the three students knew this. The contribution of Dave's friends to this study was to facilitate my understanding of Dave. At first, in their Freshman Composition class, these students saw my role as a curious combination of teacher and fellow student. As the study progressed, my role became, in their eyes, that of teacher/inquirer, a person genuinely interested in understanding their writing. In fact, my increasing interest and ability to remember details of his writing experiences seemed at times to mystify and amuse Dave.

At the beginning of this study Dave Garrison was an 18 year old freshman, a biology pre-med major who had graduated the year before from a parochial boys' high school near the college. He described himself as a "hands-on" person who preferred practical application in the lab to reading theory in books. Beginning in his sophomore year, Dave worked 13 hours a week as a technician in a local hospital, drawing blood from patients, in addition to taking a full course load. He "loved" his hospital work, he said, because of the people and the work, and also because difficulties with chemistry have made him worry about being accepted in medical school. In the hospital he was getting an idea of a range of possible careers in health care. The oldest of four children, Dave lived at home and commuted 30 minutes to campus. He is the first person in his family to go to college, though both of his parents enjoy reading, he said, and his father writes in his work as an insurance salesman. When Dave and I first met, he told me that he did not really like to write and that he was not very good, but he knew that writing was a tool he needed, one that he hoped to learn to see better.

Instrumentation and Analytic Procedures

I collected data from February, 1983, through November, 1985. A detailed, semester by semester summary is presented in Table 1.

Observation

I observed in all three classes in order to help me understand the contexts for writing in which Dave was working. During the observation I recorded field notes about the classroom activities and interactions I was seeing, and as soon as possible after the observation I read my notes and fleshed them out where possible. Returning to fill out the notes was particularly important when I had participated in the classroom activities as I did in Freshman Composition. In that class I participated in Dave's small group discussions of drafts and did the in-class writing exercises along with the students. I wrote my field notes on the right-side pages of a spiral notebook, leaving the pages opposite free for later notes.

Interviews

I interviewed Dave, his two friends, and the three professors in order to elicit their interpretations of the writing in each class. Questions were often suggested by the participants' earlier comments or by emerging patterns in the data that I wanted to pursue. Interviews with professors generally took place in their offices and centered on their assignments, their purposes for having students write, and the instructional techniques they used to accomplish their purposes.

The interviews with the students took place in my office on campus and lasted one hour. I chose to interview Dave and his friends together in a series of monthly interviews because I believed I could learn more from Dave in this way. The students often talked to and questioned each other, producing more from Dave than I believe I ever could have gotten from one-on-one sessions with him. I did on two occasions, however, interview Dave alone for

Table 1
Data Collection Record

Observation
> Freshman Composition (Freshman year. Spring, 1983)
> - Participant observation in 1 class per week for 9 weeks.
> - All class documents were collected and analyzed.
>
> Introduction to Poetry (Sophomore year. Fall, 1983)
> - Observation of the 90-minute lecture devoted to writing instruction.
> - All class documents were collected and analyzed.
>
> Cell Biology (Sophomore year. Spring, 1984)
> - Observation of a lab session for 15 minutes

Interviews
> Freshman Composition
> - Frequent conversations and 2 hour-long interviews with the professor, Dr. Carter.
> - Frequent conversations with the students before and after class.
>
> Poetry
> - 1 hour-long interview with the professor, Dr. Forson.
> - 4 hour-long interviews with the students at one-month intervals.
>
> Cell Biology
> - 2 hour-long interviews with the professor, Dr. Kelly.
> - 4 hour-long interviews with the students at one-month intervals.
>
> Junior Year Follow-up (Fall, 1984)
> - 2 hour-long interviews with the students.

Protocols with Retrospective Interviews
> Freshman Composition
> - 1 protocol and interview audiotaped as Dave composed the first draft of his fourth (next to last) essay.
>
> Poetry
> - 1 protocol and interview audiotaped as Dave composed the first draft of his third (last) paper.
>
> Cell Biology
> - 1 protocol and interview audiotaped as Dave composed the first draft of his third (last) review.

Text Analysis
> Freshman Composition
> - Dave's fourth essay with the teacher's responses was analyzed. All drafts of all essays were collected.
>
> Poetry
> - Dave's third paper with the teacher's responses was analyzed. All drafts of all essays were collected.
>
> Cell Biology
> - Dave's third review with the teacher's responses was analyzed. All drafts of all essays were collected.

one hour when I wanted to question him in a particularly intensive way.

During all interviews I either took notes or made audiotapes which I later transcribed and analyzed. All hour-long interviews with the students were taped.

Analysis of the Observations and Interviews

I read and reread my field notes and the interview transcripts looking for patterns and themes. These organized the data and suggested the salient features of writing in each context, its nature and meaning, and of Dave's experiences there. These patterns and themes then focused subsequent inquiry. I was guided in this process by the work of Gilmore and Glatthorn (1982) and Spradley (1979, 1980).

Composing-Aloud Protocols and Retrospective Interviews

Late in each of the three semesters, I audiotaped Dave as he composed aloud the first draft of a paper for the course we had focused on that semester. Dave wrote at the desk in my office, his pre-writing notes and his books spread out around him, and I sat nearby in a position where I could observe and make notes on his behaviors. The protocols lasted 30 minutes and were followed by a 30-minute retrospective interview in which I asked Dave to tell me more about the process he had just been through. I reasoned that in the retrospective interviews Dave's major concerns would be reemphasized, whereas the smaller issues that may have occupied him during composing would be forgotten. Because I followed Dave across time and collected all his written work for each assignment, I could examine what preceded and what followed the composed-aloud draft. I could thus see how the protocol draft related to Dave's entire composing process for a task.

The information provided by the protocols generally corroborated what he had said in the interviews. Of particular interest, however, were the points at which the protocol data contradicted the interview data. These points spurred further inquiry. Though composing-aloud was never easy for Dave, who characterized himself as a shy person, he became more and more comfortable with it as the semesters progressed. He did produce, in each of the protocol sessions, a useful first draft for his final paper in each course.

Analysis and Scoring of the Protocols and Retrospective Interviews

I analyzed the transcripts of the protocols and interviews, classifying and counting what I called the *writer's conscious concerns*. These concerns were identified as anything the writer paid attention to during composing as expressed by (1) remarks about a thought or behavior or (2) observed behaviors. I chose to focus on Dave's conscious concerns because I expected that they would include a broad range of writing issues and that they would reflect the nature and emphases of the classrooms for which he was writing. The protocols would thus provide the supporting information I needed for this study. In identifying and classifying the writer's conscious concerns, I was guided by the work of Berkenkotter (1983), Bridwell (1980), Flower and

Hayes (1981), Perl (1979), and Pianko (1979).

The analysis of the transcripts was carried out in a two-part process. First I read them several times and drew from them four general categories of writer's concerns, along with a number of subcategories. Then, using this scheme, I classified and counted the writer's remarks and behaviors. The first protocol was, of course, made during Dave's writing for Freshman Composition. The categories from that composing session were used again in analyzing the protocols from Poetry and Cell Biology. To these original categories were added new ones to describe the concerns Dave expressed as he composed for the later courses. In this way I could identify both concerns that were constant across courses as well as those that were specific to particular classroom writing situations.

I carried out the analyses of the protocols alone because of the understanding of the writing context that I brought to the task. I viewed this knowledge as an asset in identifying and classifying Dave's writing concerns. Thus, instead of agreement between raters, I worked for "confirmability" in the sense of agreement among a variety of information sources (Guba, 1978, p. 17).

Text Analysis

The final window through which I looked at Dave's writing experiences was text analysis. I analyzed the completed papers, with the professors' comments on them, of the assignments Dave had begun during the protocol sessions. If Dave is understood to be a stranger trying to learn the language in these classroom communities, then his teachers are the native-speaker guides who are training him. In this view, students and teachers in their written interactions share a common aim and are engaged in a cooperative endeavor. Their relationship is like that of people conversing together, the newcomer making trial efforts to communicate appropriately and the native speaker responding to them.

Thus, in order to examine the conventions of discourse in each classroom and get further insight into the interaction between Dave and his professors, I drew upon the model of conversation proposed by Grice (1975). Grice says that conversants assume, unless there are indications to the contrary, that they have a shared purpose and thus make conversational contributions "such as are required . . . by the accepted purpose or direction of the talk exchange in which they are engaged" (p. 45). He terms this the "Cooperative Principle." From the Cooperative Principle Grice derives four categories or conditions which must be fulfilled if people are to converse successfully: Quality, Quantity, Relation, and Manner. When conversation breaks down, it is because one or more of these conditions for successful conversation have been violated, either accidentally or intentionally. On the other hand, people conversing successfully fulfill these conditions, for the most part without conscious attention. Grice's four conditions for conversational cooperation provided my text analysis scheme. They are:

1. *Quality.* Conversants must speak what they believe to be the truth and that for which they have adequate evidence.
2. *Quantity.* Conversants must give the appropriate amount of information, neither too much nor too little.
3. *Relation.* The information that conversants give must be relevant to the aims of the conversation.
4. *Manner.* The conversants must make themselves clear, using appropriate forms of expression.

In my examination of Dave's last paper for each course, I considered both his work and his professor's response as conversational turns in which the speakers were doing what they believed would keep the Cooperative Principle in force. Dave's written turns were taken to display the discourse he believed was required in each setting so he would be deemed cooperative. I identified which of Grice's four conditions for successful conversation Dave paid special attention to fulfilling in each context. In this process I drew from the interview and protocol data as well as from the texts. I then counted and categorized Dave's teachers' written responses to his papers according to these same four conditions. A response was identified as an idea the teacher wanted to convey to Dave and could be as short as a single mark or as long as several sentences. Of particular interest were, first, the extent to which Dave and each teacher agreed upon what constituted cooperation, and, second, what the teacher pointed out as violations of the conditions of cooperation, errors that jeopardized the Cooperative Principle in that setting. Further, the form and language of each teacher's response provided insight into the ways of speaking in that particular discipline and classroom.

The text analysis data added to and refined my understanding of Dave's classroom writing situations. And, conversely, my analyses of Dave's texts were informed by what I knew of the classroom writing situations. For this reason, I again elected to work alone with the texts.

Validity of the findings and interpretations in this study was ensured by employing the following techniques. (1) Different types of data were compared. (2) The perspectives of various informants were compared. (3) Engagement with the subject was carried on over a long period of time during which salient factors were identified for more detailed inquiry. (4) External checks on the inquiry process were made by three established researchers who knew neither Dave nor the professors. These researchers read the emerging study at numerous points and questioned researcher biases and the bases for interpretations. (5) Interpretations were checked throughout with the informants themselves. (See Lincoln & Guba, 1985, for a discussion of validity and reliability in naturalistic inquiry.)

Results and Discussion

Information from all data sources supports three general conclusions, two concerning Dave's interpretation and production of the required writing tasks and one concerning social factors in the classrooms that influenced him as he wrote. First, although the writing tasks in the three classes were in many ways similar, Dave interpreted them as being totally different from each other and totally different from anything he had ever done before. This was evidenced in the interview, protocol, and text analysis data.

Second, certain social factors in Freshman Composition and Cell Biology appeared to foster Dave's writing success in them. Observation and interview data indicated that two unarticulated aspects of the classroom writing contexts influenced his achievement. These social factors were (1) the functions that writing served for Dave in each setting, and (2) the roles that participants and students' texts played there. These social factors were bound up with what Dave ultimately learned from and about writing in each class.

Third, Dave exhibited consistent ways of figuring out what constituted appropriate texts in each setting, in his terms, of "figuring out what the teacher wanted." Evidence from the interviews and protocols shows that he typically drew upon six information sources, in a process that was in large part tacit. These information sources included teacher-provided instructional supports, sources Dave found on his own, and his prior knowledge.

The Writing Assignments: Similar Tasks, Audiences, and Purposes

My analysis of the assignments, combined with the observation and interview data, showed that the writing in the three classes was similar in many ways. It was, in all cases, informational writing for the teacher-as-examiner, the type of writing that Applebee found comprised most secondary school writing (1984). More specifically, the task in Cell Biology was a summary, and in Freshman Composition and Poetry it was analysis, closely related informational uses of writing. Dave's audiences were identified as teacher-as-examiner by the fact that all assignments were graded and that Dave, as he wrote, repeatedly wondered how his teacher would "like" his work.

Further similarities among the writing in the three courses included the purpose that the professors stated for having their students write. All three said that the purpose was not so much for students to display specific information, but rather for students to become competent in using the thinking and language of their disciplines. Dr. Kelly, the biologist, stated this most directly when he explained to me why he had his students write reviews of journal articles: "I want students to be at ease with the vocabulary of Cell Biology and how experiments are being done. . . . Students need to get a feeling for the journals, the questions people are asking, the answers they're getting, and the procedures they're using. It will give them a feeling for the excitement, the dynamic part of this field. And they need to see that what they're doing in class and lab is actually *used* out there." Students' summaries of journal articles in Cell Biology were, in other words, to get them started speaking the language of that discourse community.

Learning the conventions of academic discourse was also the purpose of students' writing in Freshman Composition. Dr. Carter was less concerned with the content of the students' five essays than she was with their cohesiveness. She repeatedly stated that what would serve these students in their subsequent academic writing was the ability to write coherent prose with a thesis and subpoints, unified paragraphs, and explicitly connected sentences. In an interview she said, "Ideas aren't going to do people much good if they can't find the means with which to communicate them. . . . When these students are more advanced, and the ability to produce coherent prose is internalized, then they can concentrate on ideas. That's why I'm teaching the analytic paper with a certain way of developing the thesis that's generalizable to their future writing." Dr. Carter's goal was, thus, to help students master conventions of prose which she believed were central to all academic discourse.

And likewise in Poetry the purpose of students' writing was to teach them how people in literary studies think and write. In his lecture on writing, early in the semester, Dr. Forson stated this purpose and alluded to some of the conventions for thinking and writing in that setting. He told students, "The three critical essays you will write will make you say something quite specific about the meaning of a poem (your thesis) and demonstrate how far you've progressed in recognizing and dealing with the devices a poet uses to express his insights. You'll find the poem's meaning in the poem itself, and you'll use quotes to prove your thesis. Our concern here is for the *poem*, not the poet's life or era. Nor are your own opinions of the poet's ideas germane."

Dr. Forson then spent 20 minutes explaining the mechanical forms for quoting poetry, using a model essay that he had written on a poem by Robert Herrick. He ended by telling students that they should think of their peers as the audience for their essays and asking them not to use secondary critical sources from the library. "You'll just deal with what you now know and with the poetic devices that we discuss in class. Each group of poems will feature one such device: imagery, symbolism, and so forth. These will be the tools in your tool box."

Thus in all three courses Dave's tasks were informational writing for the teacher-as-examiner. All were for the purpose of displaying competence in using the ways of thinking and writing appropriate to that setting. And in all three courses Dave wrote a series of similar short papers, due at about three-week intervals, the assumption being that students' early attempts would inform their subsequent ones, in the sort of trial-and-error process that characterizes much language learning. Further, the reading required in Poetry and Cell Biology, the poems and the journal articles, were equally unfamiliar to Dave. We might expect, then, that Dave would view the writing for these three courses as quite similar, and, given an equal amount of work, he would achieve similar levels of success. This, however, is not what happened.

Dave's Interpretation of the Writing Tasks
The Writer's Concerns While Composing. In spite of the similarities among the writing tasks for the three courses, evidence from several sources shows that Dave interpreted them as being totally different from each other and

totally different from anything he had ever done before. Dave's characteristic approach across courses was to focus so fully on the particular new ways of thinking and writing in each setting that commonalities with previous writing were obscured for him. And interwoven with Dave's conviction that the writing for these courses was totally dissimilar was his differing success in them. Though he worked hard in all three courses, he made B's in Freshman Composition, D's and C's in Poetry, and A's in Cell Biology.

The protocol data explain in part why the writing for these classes seemed so different to Dave. Dave's chief concerns while composing for each course were very different. His focus in Freshman Composition was on textual coherence. Fifty-four percent of his expressed concerns were for coherence of thesis and subpoints, coherence within paragraphs, and sentence cohesion. By contrast, in Poetry, though Dave did mention thesis and subpoints, his chief concerns were not with coherence, but with the new ways of thinking and writing in that setting. Forty-four percent of his concerns focused on accurately interpreting the poem and properly using quotes. In Cell Biology, yet a new focus of concerns is evident. Seventy-two percent of Dave's concerns deal with the new rules of use in that academic discipline. His chief concerns in Biology were to accurately understand the scientific terms and concepts in the journal article and then to accurately rephrase and connect these in his own text, following the same five-part structure in which the published experiment was reported. It is no wonder that the writing for these classes seemed very different to Dave. As a newcomer in each academic territory, Dave's attention was occupied by the new conventions of interpretation and language use in each community. (See Table 2.)

The same preoccupations controlled his subsequent work on the papers. In each course Dave wrote a second draft, which he then typed. In none of these second drafts did Dave see the task differently or make major changes. He is, in this regard, like the secondary students Applebee (1984) studied who were unable, without teacher assistance, to revise their writing in more than minor ways. And Dave revised none of these papers after the teachers had responded.

We can further fill out the pictures of Dave's composing for the three classes by combining the protocol findings with the observation and interview data. In his first protocol session, in April of his freshman year, Dave composed the first draft of his fourth paper for Freshman Composition, an essay in which he chose to analyze the wrongs of abortion. To this session Dave brought an outline of this thesis and subpoints. He told me that he had spent only 30 minutes writing it the night before, but that the topic was one he had thought a lot about. As he composed, Dave was most concerned with, and apparently very dependent upon, his outline, commenting on it, glancing at it, or pausing to study it 14 times during the 30 minutes of composing. Dave's next most frequently expressed concerns were for coherence at paragraph and sentence levels, what Dr. Carter referred to as coherence of mid-sized and small parts. These were the new "rules of use" in this setting. Dave told me that in high school he had done some "bits and pieces" of

Table 2
Concerns Expressed During Composing-Aloud Protocols and
Retrospective Interviews

	Percent of Comments		
	Freshman Composition	Poetry	Cell Biology
Concerns Expressed in All Three Courses			
Features of Written Text Coherent thesis/ subpoint structure	22	18	0
Coherent paragraph structure	15	13	3
Cohesive sentences	17	8	3
Editing for mechanical correctness	9	3	3
Communication Situation (assignment, reader-writer roles, purpose)	8	6	5
On-Going Process	18	6	12
Emerging Text	11	2	2
Concerns Specific to Poetry			
Appropriately using quotes from poem	0	32	0
Making a correct interpretation of the poem	0	12	0
Concerns Specific to Cell Biology			
Following the 5-part scientific guidelines	0	0	20
Correctly understanding the content of the article being summarized	0	0	37
Rephrasing & connecting appropriate parts of the article	0	0	15
Total	100	100	100
Number of comments	64	62	60

writing and some outlines for history, but that he had never before written essays like this. The total time Dave spent on his abortion essay was five hours.

In Dave's Poetry protocol session seven months later, in November of his sophomore year, he composed part of the first draft of his third and last paper for that class, a six-page analysis of a poem called "Marriage" by contemporary poet Gregory Corso. To this session he brought two pages of notes and his *Norton Anthology of Poetry* in which he had underlined and written notes in the margins beside the poem. He told me that he had spent four hours (of an eventual total of 11) preparing to write: reading the poem many times and finding a critical essay on it in the library. During his pre-writing and composing, Dave's primary concern was to get the right interpretation of the poem, "the true meaning" as he phrased it. And as Dave wrote, he assumed that his professor knew the true meaning, a meaning, Dave said, that "was there, but not there, not just what it says on the surface." Further, Dave knew that he must argue his interpretation, using not his own but the poet's words; this was his second most frequently expressed concern.

As Dave composed, he appeared to be as tied to the poem as he had been to his outline in Freshman Composition the semester before. He seemed to be almost *physically* attached to the *Norton Anthology* by his left forefinger as he progressed down the numbers he had marked in the margins. He was, we might say, tied to the concrete material, the "facts" of the poem before him. Dave never got his own essay structure; rather, he worked down the poem, explicating from beginning to end. In the retrospective interview he said, "I didn't really have to think much about my thesis and subs because they just come naturally now. . . . But anyway it's not like in Comp last year. Here my first paragraph is the introduction with the thesis, and the stanzas are the subpoints." Dave's preoccupation with the poem and the new conventions of interpreting and quoting poetry resulted in a paper that was not an analysis but a summary with some interpretation along the way. His focus on these new rules of use appeared to limit his ability to apply previously learned skills, the thesis-subpoint analytical structure, and kept him working at the more concrete summary level.

This domination by the concrete may often characterize newcomers' first steps as they attempt to use language in unfamiliar disciplines (Williams, 1985). Dave's professor, Dr. Forson, seemed to be familiar with this phenomenon when he warned students in his lecture on writing: "You must remember that the poet ordered the poem. You order your essay with your own thesis and subtheses. Get away from 'Next. . . . Next'." But if Dave heard this in September, he had forgotten it by November. Dave's experience is consonant with Langer's (1984) finding that students who know more about a subject as they begin to write are likely to choose analysis rather than summary. And these students receive higher scores for writing quality as well.

In his writing for Cell Biology the following semester, Dave's concerns were again focused on the new and unfamiliar conventions in this setting. Before writing his last paper, a four-page review of an experiment on glycoprotein reported in *The Journal of Cell Biology*, Dave spent three hours preparing. (He eventually spent a total of eight hours on the review.) He had chosen the article in the library from a list the professor had given to students and had then read the article twice, underlining it, making notes, and looking up the definitions of unfamiliar terms. To the protocol session Dave brought these notes, the article, and a sheet on which he had written what he called "Dr. Kelly's guidelines," the five-part scientific experiment format that Dr. Kelly wanted students to follow: Background, Objectives, Procedures, Results, and Discussion.

In his composing aloud, Dave's chief concerns in Biology were, as in Poetry the semester before, with the reading, in this case the journal article. But here, unlike Poetry, Dave said the meaning was "all out on the table." In Poetry he had had to interpret meaning from the poem's connotative language; in Biology, by contrast, he could look up meanings, a situation with which Dave was far more comfortable. But as he composed for Biology, he was just as tied to the journal article as he had been to the poem or to his outline in previous semesters. Dave paused frequently to consult the article, partially covering it at times so that his own paper was physically closer to what he was summarizing at that moment.

Dave's first and second most commonly expressed concerns during the Biology protocol session were for rephrasing and connecting parts of the article and for following Dr. Kelly's guidelines. These were, in essence, concerns for coherence and organization, what Dave was most concerned with in Freshman Composition. But the writing for Biology bore little relation in Dave's mind to what he had done in Freshman Composition. In Biology he was indeed concerned about his organization, but here it was the five-part scientific format he had been given, very different, it seemed to him, than the thesis/subpoint organization he had had to create for his freshman essays. In fact, until I questioned him about it at the end of the semester, Dave never mentioned the freshman thesis/subpoint structure. And the concerns for coherence at paragraph and sentence levels that had been so prominent as he wrote for Freshman Composition were replaced in Biology by his concern for rephrasing the article's already coherent text. In Freshman Composition Dave had talked about trying to get his sentences and paragraphs to "fit" or "flow" together. In Biology, however, he talked about trying to get the article into his own words, about "cutting," "simplifying," and "combining two sentences." Again, it is no wonder that Dave believed that this writing was totally new. It took one of Dave's friend's and my prodding during an interview to make Dave see that he had indeed written summaries before. Lots of them.

The Nature of Cooperation in the Three Courses. The text analysis data provide further insight into why Dave perceived the writing in these courses as so dissimilar. The data provide information about what was, in Grice's terms, essential to maintaining the Cooperative Principle in these written exchanges. Analyses of the teachers' responses to Dave's papers show that his concerns in each class generally did match theirs. Put differently, Dave had figured out, though not equally well in all classes, what counted as "co-operation" in each context, and what he had to do to be deemed a competent communicator here. (See Table 3.)

Analysis of Dave's finished essay for Freshman Composition suggests that his concerns for textual coherence were appropriate. Dave knew that to keep the Cooperative Principle in force in Dr. Carter's class, he had to pay special attention to fulfilling the condition of *Manner,* to making himself clear, using appropriate forms of expression. He succeeded and was deemed cooperative by Dr. Carter when she responded to his contribution with a telegraphic reply on the first page: "18/20." Apart from editing two words in Dave's text, she made no further comments, assuming that Dave and she shared an understanding of what constituted cooperation in her class and of what her numbers meant. (She had explained to students that she was marking with numbers that semester in an attempt to be more "scientific," and she had defined for them the "objective linguistic features of text" to which her numbers referred.) Dave did understand the grade and was, of course, very pleased with it.

In an interview, Dr. Carter explained her grade to me. "Though his content isn't great," she said, "his paper is coherent, not badly off at any place. . . . He gave a fair number of reasons to develop his paragraphs, he restated his point at the end, and there is no wasted language. It's not perfectly woven together, but it's good." Though Dr. Carter mentioned the "reasons" Dave gave as evidence for his contentions, she was concerned not so much with their meaning as with their cohesiveness. Cooperation in this setting thus depended upon fulfilling the condition of *Manner*. Dave knew this and expected only a response to how well he had achieved the required form, not to the content of his essay.

In his writing for Poetry the following semester, Dave was attempting to keep the Cooperative Principle in force by paying special attention to two conditions, *Quality* and *Manner*. That is, first he was attempting to say what

Table 3
Teachers' Responses to Dave's Papers

	Number of Responses Indicating Violations of Conditions for Cooperation				*Grade*
	Quality	Quantity	Relevance	Manner	
Composition	0	0	0	2	18/20
Poetry	8	0	0	11	C+
Cell Biology	0	0	0	14	96

was true and give adequate evidence, and, second, he was attempting to use proper forms of expression. This is evidenced in the interview and protocol as well as the text data. Analysis of Dr. Forson's 19 responses to Dave's paper shows that Dave's concerns matched those of his teacher, that Dave had figured out, though only in part, what counted as cooperation in that setting. Dr. Forson's responses all referred to violations of the same conditions Dave had been concerned with fulfilling, *Quality* and *Manner*. In seven of his eight marginal notes and in an endnote, Dr. Forson disagreed with Dave's interpretation and questioned his evidence, violations of the *Quality* condition. Mina Shaughnessy (1977) says that such failure to properly coordinate claims and evidence is perhaps the most common source of misunderstanding in academic prose. The ten mechanical errors that Dr. Forson pointed out were violations of the condition of *Manner*, violations which may jeopardize the Cooperative Principle in many academic settings. Dave's unintentional violations in Poetry of the *Quality* and *Manner* conditions jeopardized the Cooperative Principle in that exchange, resulting in the C+ grade.

Dr. Kelly's responses to Dave's writing in Biology were, like those in Freshman Composition, much briefer than Dr. Forson's. Dr. Kelly's 14 marks or phrases all pointed out errors in form, unintentional violations of the Gricean condition of *Manner*. But these were apparently not serious enough to jeopardize the aims of the written conversation in Biology; Dave's grade on the review was 96.

This application of Grice's rubric for spoken conversation to student-teacher written interaction gives further insight into the differences in these classroom contexts for writing. It is evident that successfully maintaining the Cooperative Principle was a more complicated business in Poetry than in Freshman Composition or Biology. In Biology, Dave was unlikely to violate the condition of *Quality*, as he did in Poetry, because he was only summarizing the published experiment and thus only had to pay attention to the condition of *Manner*. In Poetry, by contrast, he was called upon to take an interpretive position. This assumed that he had already summarized the poem. He had not. Thus his analytical essay took the form of a summary, as we have seen. In Biology, on the other hand, the writing was supposed to be a summary that then moved to a comparison of the summarized experiment to what was going on in class.

For Dave, the latter assignment was more appropriate. Novices in a field may need the simpler summary assignment that helps them understand the new reading, the new language that they are being asked to learn. They may then be ready to move to analysis or critique. One wonders if Dave's success in Poetry would have been enhanced if he had been asked to write out a summary of the poem first. He could then have worked from that summary as he structured his own critical essay.

Similarly, in Freshman Composition, Dave was unlikely to violate the condition of *Quality*, to say something untrue or provide inadequate evidence for his claim. Though Dave did have to provide evidence for his subpoints, he was not evaluated for his content, and thus he concentrated on the condition of *Manner*. Further, the writing in Freshman Composition did not require Dave to master unfamiliar texts as it did in both Poetry and Biology. And for Dave the task of integrating new knowledge from his reading into his writing in those courses was his salient concern, as we have seen.

The apparent absence of attention paid in any of these classes to fulfilling the conditions of *Quantity* or *Relation* is puzzling. Perhaps Dave's prior school writing experience had trained him to include the right amount of information *(Quantity)* and stay on topic *(Relation)*.

The text analysis data, then, show that what counted as cooperation in these three classes was indeed quite different. Dr. Forson, in his extensive responses, apparently felt it necessary to reteach Dave how people think and write in his community. This is understandable in light of Dave's numerous unintentional violations of the Cooperative Principle. Further, though Dr. Forson told students that he was being objective, finding the meaning of the poem in the text, he told me that his responses to students' papers were to argue his interpretation of the poem and, thus, to justify his grade.

The differing language and forms of these professors' responses probably also added to Dave's sense that in each classroom he was in a new foreign land. Response style may well be discipline-specific as well as teacher-specific, with responses in literary studies generally more discursive than in the sciences. Further, Dr. Forson's responses were in the informal register typically used by an authority speaking to a subordinate (Freedman, 1984). His responses to Dave's paper included the following: "You misfire here." "I get this one. Hurrah for me!" "Pardon my writing. I corrected this in an automobile." The informality, and the word "corrected" in particular, leave little doubt about the authority differential between Dr. Forson and Dave. By contrast, Dave seemed to interpret the numerical grade in Biology as more characteristic of a conversation between equals. In a comment that may say more about their classroom interaction than their written interaction, Dave spoke of Dr. Kelly's brief responses to his review: "Yeah. He's like that. He treats us like adults. When we ask him questions, he answers us." Dave's apparent mixing of his spoken and written interaction with Dr. Kelly emphasizes the point that students' and teachers' writing for each other in classrooms is as fully contextualized as any other activity that goes on there.

Before Dave turned in his last papers in Poetry and Biology, I asked him to speculate about the grade he would get. When he handed in his six-page paper on the Corso poem, "Marriage," on which he had spent eleven hours, he told me that he hoped for an A or B: "I'll be really frustrated on this one if the grade's not good after I've put in the time on it." A week later, however, he told me in a resigned tone and with a short laugh that he'd gotten a C+ . By contrast, when he turned in his last review in Biology, he told me he knew he would get an A. When I questioned him, he replied, "I don't know how I know. I just do." And he was right: his grade was 96. Dave obviously understood far better what constituted cooperation in Biology than he did in Poetry.

Social Aspects of the Classrooms that Influenced Dave's Writing

Why was Dave's success in writing in these classrooms so different? The answers to this question will illuminate some of the dimensions along which school writing situations differ and thus influence student achievement. It would be a mistake to think that the differing task structure was the only reason that Dave was more successful in Biology and Freshman Composition than he was in Poetry. Assignments are, as I have suggested, only a small part of the classroom interaction, limited written exchanges that reflect the nature of the communication situation created by participants in that setting. Two unarticulated qualities in the contexts for writing in Freshman Composition and Biology appeared to foster Dave's success in those classes. These were (1) the social functions Dave's writing served for him in those classes, and (2) the roles played by participants and by students' texts there.

The Functions Dave Saw His Writing as Accomplishing. It has been argued that the social functions served by writing must be seen as an intrinsic part of the writing experience (Clark & Florio, 1983; Hymes, 1972a, 1972b; Scribner & Cole, 1981). Evidence from interviews and observations indicates that the writing in Freshman Composition and Biology was for Dave a meaningful social activity, meaningful beyond just getting him through the course. Further, Dave and his teachers in Freshman Composition and Biology mutually understood and valued those functions. This was not the case in Poetry. The data show a correlation not only between meaningful social functions served by the writing and Dave's success with it, but also between the writing's social meaning and Dave's ability to remember and draw upon it in subsequent semesters.

In Freshman Composition Dave's writing served four valuable functions for him. He articulated all of these:

1. Writing to prepare him for future writing in school and career
2. Writing to explore topics of his choice
3. Writing to participate with other students in the classroom
4. Writing to demonstrate academic competence

In Biology Dave also saw his writing as serving four valuable functions:

1. Writing to learn the language of Cell Biology, which he saw as necessary to his career
2. Writing to prepare him for his next semester's writing in Immunology
3. Writing to make connections between his classwork and actual work being done by professionals in the field
4. Writing to demonstrate academic competence

Evidence from interviews and observation shows that Dr. Carter and Dr. Kelly saw writing in their classes as serving the same four functions that Dave did.

On the other hand, in Poetry, though Dave's professor stated four functions of student writing, Dave saw his writing as serving only one function for him: writing to demonstrate academic competence. Dave, always the compliant student, did say after he had received his disappointing grade in Poetry that the writing in Poetry was probably good for him: "Probably any kind of writing helps you." Though he may well be right, Dave actually saw his writing for Poetry as serving such a limited function—evaluation of his skills in writing poetry criticism for Dr. Forson—that he was not really convinced (and little motivated by the notion) that this writing would serve him in any general way.

Dave contended that any writing task was easy or difficult for him according to his interest in it. When I asked him what he meant by interesting, he said, "If it has something to do with my life. Like it could explain something to me or give me an answer that I could use now." Writing must have, in other words, meaningful personal and social functions for Dave if it is to be manageable, "easy," for him. These functions existed for Dave in Freshman Composition and Biology, providing the applications and personal transaction with the material that may be generally required for learning and forging personal knowledge (Dewey, 1949; Polanyi, 1958).

Dave's Poetry class, however, served no such personally meaningful functions. Six weeks after the Poetry course was finished, I asked Dave some further questions about his last paper for that course, the discussion of the Corso poem on which he had worked 11 hours. He could remember almost nothing about it. When I asked him to speculate why this was, he said, "I guess it's because I have no need to remember it." By contrast, when I asked Dave in the fall of his junior year if his Cell Biology writing was serving him in his Immunology course as he had expected, he said, "Yes. The teacher went over how to write up our labs, but most of us had the idea anyway from last semester because we'd read those journal articles. We were already exposed to it."

Of course the functions of his writing in Biology served Dave better than those in Poetry in part because he was a biology major. The writing for Cell Biology fit into a larger whole: his growing body of knowledge about this field and his professional future. The material in Cell Biology was for Dave a comprehensible part of the discipline of Biology which was in turn a comprehensible part of the sciences. Dave was, with experience, gradually acquiring a coherent sense of the language of the discipline, how biologists think and speak and what it is they talk about. And his understanding of the language of biology was accompanied by an increasing confidence in his own ability to use it. Both of these are probably necessary foundations for later, more abstract and complex uses of the language (Piaget, 1952; Perry, 1970; Williams, 1985).

In the required one-semester Poetry class, however, the poems seemed to Dave to be unrelated to each other except for commonly used poetic devices, and his writing about them was unrelated to his own life by anything at all beyond his need to find the "true meaning" and get an acceptable grade.

Dave's different relationship to the languages of these disciplines was shown when he said, "In Biology I'm using what I've *learned*. It's just putting what I've learned on paper. But in Poetry, more or less each poem is different, so it's not *taught* to you. You just have to figure it out from that poem itself and hope Dr. Forson likes it." Nor, in Poetry, was Dave ever invited to make personally meaningful connections with the poems. And he never did it on his own, no doubt in part because he was so preoccupied with the new ways of thinking and speaking that he was trying to use.

In Freshman Composition the social function of writing that was perhaps most powerful for Dave was writing to participate with other students in the classroom. In his peer writing group Dave, for the first time ever, discussed his writing with others. Here he communicated personal positions and insights to his friends, an influential audience for him. That an important social function was served by these students' work with each other is suggested by their clear memory, a year and a half later, both of their essays and of each other's reactions to them.

The four social functions that Dave's writing in Freshman Composition accomplished for him enhanced his engagement with and attitude toward the writing he did in that class. This engagement is reflected in Dave's memory not only of his essays and his friends' reactions to them, but also in his memory and use of the ideas and terms from that course. When Dave talked about his writing during his sophomore and junior years, he used the process terms he had learned in Freshman Composition: prewriting, revision, and drafts. He also used other language he had learned as a freshman, speaking at times about his audience's needs, about narrowing his topic, about connecting his sentences, providing more details, and choosing his organizational structure. This is not to say that Dave had mastered these skills in every writing situation nor that he always accurately diagnosed problems in his own work. In fact, we know that he did not. It is to say, however, that Dave did recognize and could talk about some of the things that writing does involve in many situations. Thus, the value of this course for Dave lay not so much in the thesis/subpoint essay structure. Rather, Dave had, as a result of his experiences in Freshman Composition, learned that writing is a process that can be talked about, managed, and controlled.

Thus the social functions that writing served for Dave in each class were viewed as an intrinsic part of his writing experiences there. Where these functions were numerous and mutually understood and valued by Dave and his teacher, Dave was more successful in figuring out and producing the required discourse. And then he remembered it longer. In Poetry, where his writing served few personally valued ends, Dave did less well, making a C on the first paper, a D on the second, and a C+ on the third. It should be noted, in addition, that grades themselves serve a social function in classrooms: defining attitudes and roles. Dave's low grades in Poetry probably further alienated him from the social communication processes in that classroom community and helped define his role there.

The Roles Played by the Participants and by Students' Texts. Other social aspects of these classroom contexts for writing which affected Dave's experiences were the roles played by the people and texts in them. Such roles are tacitly assigned in classroom interaction and create the context in which the student stranger attempts to determine the rules of language use in that territory. Here we will examine (1) Dave's role in relation to the teacher, (2) Dave's role in relation to other students in the class, and (3) the role played by students' texts there.

Dave's Role in Relation to the Teacher. This is a particularly important role relationship in any classroom because it tacitly shapes the writer-audience relation that students use as they attempt to communicate appropriately. In all three classes Dave was writing for his teachers as pupil to examiner. However, data from several sources show that there were important variations in the actual "enactments" (Goffman, 1961) of this role-relationship.

In Composition, both Dave and his professor played the role of writer. Throughout the semester Dr. Carter talked about what and how she wrote, the long time she spent in prewriting activities, the eight times she typically revised her work, and the strategies she used to understand her audience in various situations. She spoke to students as if she and they were all writers working together, saying such things as "I see some of you write like I do," or "Let's work together to shape this language." And, as we have seen, she structured the course to provide opportunities for students to play the role of writer in their peer groups. She also asked them to describe their writing processes for several of their essays. Dave told me in an interview during his junior year, "In high school I couldn't stand writing, but in Comp I started to change because I knew more what I was doing. I learned that there are steps you can go through, and I learned how to organize a paper." As a freshman, Dave understood for the first time something of what it feels like to be a writer.

In Biology both Dave and his teacher, Dr. Kelly, saw Dave as playing the role of newcomer, learning the language needed for initiation into the profession. Dr. Kelly played the complementary role of experienced professional who was training Dave in the ways of speaking in that discipline, ways they both assumed Dave would learn in time.

In Poetry, on the other hand, Dave played the role of outsider in relationship to his teacher, the insider who knew the true meanings of poetry. And Dave stayed the outsider, unable ever to fully get the teacher's "true meaning." This outsider/insider relationship between Dave and Dr. Forson was created by a number of factors: (1) Their spoken and written interaction, (2) the few meaningful social functions served for Dave by the writing in that class, (3) the demanding nature of the analytic task, combined with (4) the limited knowledge Dave commanded in that setting, (5) the limited number of effective instructional supports, and (6) the low grades Dave got, which further alienated him from the communication processes in that class. (To the instructional supports provided in Poetry we will return below.) Because

Dave's outsider role was not a pleasant one for him, he seemed increasingly to separate his thinking from his writing in Poetry, saying several times that he had the right ideas, the teacher just did not like the way he wrote them.

Dave's Role in Relationship to Other Students. Students' relationships with each other, like those between students and teachers, are created as students interact within the classroom structures the teacher has set up. These classroom structures grow out of teachers' explicit and tacit notions about writing and learning. What specifically were the relationships among students in Freshman Composition, Biology, and Poetry?

In Composition, as we have seen, students shared their writing and responded to each other's work. The classroom structure reflected Dr. Carter's perhaps tacit notion that writing is a social as well as intellectual affair. However, in neither Poetry nor Biology was time built into the class for students to talk with each other about their writing. Dave lamented this as he wrote for Poetry early in his sophomore year, because, he said, he now realized how valuable the small group sessions had been in Freshman Composition the semester before.

In Biology, Dave told me students did talk informally about the journal articles they had selected and how they were progressing on their summaries. Dr. Kelly, who circulated during lab, was at times included in these informal talks about writing. And it is no surprise that students discussed their writing in this way in Biology in light of Dr. Kelly's notions about writing. It is, he believes, an essential part of what scientists do. He told me that it often comes as a rude shock to students that the way biologists survive in the field is by writing. He said, "These students are bright, and they can memorize piles of facts, but they're not yet good at writing. They know what science *is*," he told me, "but they don't know what scientists *do*." Thus, writing up research results is seen by Dr. Kelly as an integral part of a biologist's lab work. No wonder his students talked about it.

In Poetry, however, there was little talk of any kind among students. Classes were primarily lectures where Dr. Forson explicated poems and explained poetic devices. Only occasionally did he call on one of the 22 students for an opinion. This lack of student interaction in Poetry was in line with the image of the writer that Dr. Forson described for students, an image that may be widely shared in literary studies: A person alone with his or her books and thoughts. Dr. Forson did, however, tell students that he himself often got his ideas for writing from listening to himself talk about poems in class. Yet, in conversation with me, he said that he did not want students discussing the poems and their writing with each other because he feared they would not think for themselves. Dave picked up on this idea very clearly. It was not until the fall of his junior year that he admitted to me that he and his girlfriend had worked together on their papers. They had discussed the interpretations of the poems and how they might best write them, but, he told me, they had been careful to choose different poems to write about so that Dr. Forson wouldn't know they had worked together. This absence of student interaction in Poetry may have contributed to the outsider role that Dave played in that class.

Throughout this study I was amazed at the amount of talk that goes on all the time outside class among students as they work to figure out the writing requirements in various courses. What Dave's experience in Poetry may suggest is that where student collaboration in writing is not openly accepted, it goes on clandestinely.

The Roles Played by Students' Texts. What were students' texts called and how were they handled? Interview and observation data show that students' texts were treated quite differently in these three courses, and this affected how Dave saw the assignments, and, perhaps more important, how he saw himself as writer.

In Freshman Composition Dave wrote what he referred to as "essays"; in Biology, "reviews"; in Poetry, "papers." This latter term is commonly used, of course, but it is one that Emig (1983, p. 173) says suggests a low status text: "Paper"—as if there were no words on the sheet at all. In Poetry the high status texts, the ones that were discussed and interpreted, were the poems. Students' works were just more or less successful explications of those. Furthermore, in Poetry the one model essay the students read was written by the teacher. Though students were told they should think of their peers as their audience, in fact they never read each other's essays at all. Students' texts were, rather, passed only between student and teacher as in a private conversation.

In Biology, student texts enjoyed a higher status. Excellent student reviews were posted and students were encouraged to read them; they were to serve as models. Some student writers were thus defined as competent speakers in this territory, and the message was clear to Dave: This was a language that he too could learn given time and proper training.

And in Freshman Composition, of course, student texts were the *objects* of study. The class read good and flawed student texts from former semesters and from their own. This not only helped Dave with his writing, it also dignified student writing and elevated his estimation of his own work. Student texts were not, in short, private affairs between teacher and student; they were the subject matter of this college course.

Thus the roles that were enacted by teachers, students, and students' texts were quite different in each classroom and were an integral part of Dave's writing experiences there. The participants' interaction and the social functions that writing serves are important factors working to create the communication situation. And this communication situation, it has been suggested, is the fundamental factor shaping the success of writing instruction (Langer & Applebee, 1984, p. 171).

The Information Sources Dave Drew Upon

In a process that was in large part tacit, Dave drew upon six sources for information about what constituted successful writing in Freshman Composition, Poetry, and Biology. These included teacher-provided instructional supports, sources Dave found on his own, and his prior experience. Many of these have been mentioned above. They are summarized in Table 4.

Of particular interest are the information sources Dave drew upon (or failed to draw upon) in Poetry, the course in which the writing assignment was the most demanding and in which Dave did least well in assessing and producing the required discourse. The information source that Dr. Forson

Table 4
Information Sources Dave Drew Upon
in Assessing Required Discourse

Information Sources	Freshman Composition	Poetry	Cell Biology
What teachers said in class about writing	Constant lectures & exercises about process & products	-One lecture -General statements to the class about their papers when returning them	-Ten minutes giving "guidelines" when returning 1st set of reviews -Informal comments in lab
Model texts	Many, including flawed models	-One, written by teacher -One, written by professional (from library)	-The articles being summarized served as models. -Posted student reviews
Talk with other students	Frequent groups in class	With friend outside class	Informal, in class
Teachers' written responses to writing	Read responses & revised early essays accordingly	Read. No revision required	Read. No revision required
Dave's prior experience	The extent to which Dave drew upon prior experience is difficult to say. In each class he believed he had no prior experience to draw from. However we know he had had related prior experience.		
Personal talk with teacher	One conference with teacher	None	None

intended to be most helpful to students, the instructional support on which he spent a great deal of time, was his response to their papers. However his extensive comments did not help Dave a great deal in learning how to communicate in that setting. Dave said that the comments on his first paper did help him some with his second, but he really did not refer to Dr. Forson's responses on the second paper as he wrote the third. Nor did Dave use the comments on the third paper when preparing for the essay question on the final exam. Dr. Forson required no revision in direct response to his comments, and the expected carry-over of his responses from one paper to the next did not occur. Rather, Dave repeated similar mistakes again and again. The assumption that trial and error will improve students' writing across a series of similar tasks did not hold true for Dave's work in Poetry.

Neither was the model text in Poetry, Dr. Forson's analysis of the Herrick poem that he went over in lecture, as useful an information source for Dave as Dr. Forson had hoped it would be. Dave told me that though he had looked at Dr. Forson's model critical essay as he wrote his first paper, it had not helped him a great deal. "Seeing how someone else did it," he said, "is a lot different than doing it yourself." In Freshman Composition and Biology, however, the model texts, both excellent and flawed ones, were more numerous. And in Biology, the model provided by the article Dave was summarizing was virtually inescapable. Model texts are, it seems reasonable, particularly important to newcomers learning the conventions of discourse in a new academic territory.

An information source which Dave was not adept at using in any course was direct questioning of the professor, the native-speaker expert in each setting. Dave never voluntarily questioned a teacher, though in October of his sophomore year, when he was doing poorly in Poetry, he did make an attempt to speak with Dr. Forson at his office. But when Dr. Forson was not there, Dave waited only a short time and then left—relieved, he said. He did not return. In Freshman Composition, however, Dave was required to interact with Dr. Carter individually in his mid-semester conference. That interview provided an additional information source upon which Dave could draw as he assessed and adapted to the writing requirements in that class.

Discussion

What, then, can be learned from Dave's experiences? First, this study adds to existing research which suggests that school writing is not a monolithic activity or global skill. Rather, the contexts for writing may be so different from one classroom to another, the ways of speaking in them so diverse, the social meanings of writing and the interaction patterns so different, that the courses may be for the student writer like so many foreign countries. These differences were apparent in this study not only in Dave's perceptions of courses but in his concerns while writing and in his written products.

Second, the findings of this study have several implications for our understanding of writing development. This study suggests that writing development is, in part, context-dependent. In each new classroom community, Dave in many ways resembled a beginning language user. He focused on a limited number of new concerns, and he was unable to move beyond concrete ways of thinking and writing, the facts of the matter at hand. Moreover, skills mastered in one situation, such as the thesis-subpoint organization in Freshman Composition, did not, as Dave insisted, automatically transfer to new contexts with differing problems and language and differing amounts of knowledge that he controlled. To better understand the stages that students progress through in achieving competence in academic speech communities, we need further research.

Dave's development across his freshman and sophomore years, where he was repeatedly a newcomer, may also be viewed in terms of his attitude toward writing. Evidence over 21 months shows that his notion of the purpose of school writing changed very little. Though there were, as we have seen, other functions accomplished for Dave by his writing in Freshman Composition and Biology, he always understood the purpose of his school writing as being primarily to satisfy a teacher-examiner's requirements. A change that did occur, however, was Dave's increased understanding of some of the activities that writers actually engage in and an increased confidence in his writing ability. As a freshman, he had told me that he did not like to write and was not very good, but by the fall of his junior year he sounded quite different. Because of a number of successful classroom experiences with writing, and an ability to forget the less successful ones, Dave told me, "Writing is no problem for me. At work, in school, I just do it."

Whether Dave will eventually be a mature writer, one who, according to Britton's (1975) definition, is able to satisfy his own purposes with a wide range of audiences, lies beyond the scope of this study to determine. We do know, however, that Dave did not, during the period of this study, write for a wide range of audiences. Nor did he, in these classes, define his own audiences, purposes, or formats, though he did in Freshman Composition choose his topics and in Poetry and Biology the particular poems and articles he wrote about. What this study suggests is that college undergraduates in beginning-level courses may have even less opportunity to orchestrate their own writing occasions than do younger students. Balancing teachers' and students' purposes is indeed difficult in these classrooms where students must, in 14 weeks, learn unfamiliar discourse conventions as well as a large body of new knowledge.

The findings of this study have several implications for the teaching of writing. They suggest that when we ask what students learn from and about writing in classrooms, we must look not only at particular assignments or at students' written products. We must also look at what they learn from the social contexts those classrooms provide for writing. In Freshman Composition, Dave learned that writer was a role he could play. In Biology, writing was for Dave an important part of a socialization process; he was the newcomer being initiated into a profession in which, he learned, writing counts for a great deal. From his writing in Poetry, Dave learned that reading poetry was not for him and that he could get through any writing task, no matter how difficult or foreign. This latter is a lesson not without its value, of course, but it is not one that teachers hope to teach with their writing assignments.

This study also raises questions about how teachers can best help student "strangers" to become competent users of the new language in their academic territory. Because all writing is context-dependent, and because successful writing requires the accurate assessment of and adaptation to the demands of particular writing situations, perhaps writing teachers should be explicitly training students in this assessment process. As Dave researched the writing requirements in his classroom, he drew upon six information sources in a process that was for him largely tacit and unarticulated. But Dave was actually in a privileged position in terms of his potential for success in this "figuring out" process. He had, after all, had years of practice writing in classrooms. Furthermore, he shared not only ethnic and class backgrounds with his teachers, but also many assumptions about education. Students from diverse communities may need, even more than Dave, explicit training in the ways in which one figures out and then adapts to the writing demands in academic contexts.

For teachers in the disciplines, "native-speakers" who may have used the language in their discipline for so long that is it partially invisible to them, the first challenge will be to appreciate just how foreign and difficult their language is for student newcomers. They must make explicit the interpretive and linguistic conventions in their community, stressing that theirs is one way of looking at reality and not reality itself. As Fish (1980) points out, "The choice is never between objectivity and interpretation, but between an interpretation that is unacknowledged as such and an interpretation that is at least aware of itself" (p. 179). Teachers in the disciplines must then provide student newcomers with assignments and instructional supports which are appropriate for first steps in using the language of their community. Designing appropriate assignments and supports may well be more difficult when the student stranger is only on a brief visit in an academic territory, as Dave was in Poetry, or when the student comes from a community at a distance farther from academe than Dave did.

Naturalistic studies like the present one, Geertz says, are only "another country heard from . . . nothing more or less." Yet, "small facts speak to large issues" (1973, p. 23). From Dave's story, and others like it which describe actual writers at work in local settings, we will learn more about writers' processes and texts and how these are constrained by specific social dynamics. Our generalizations and theories about writing and about how people learn to write must, in the final analysis, be closely tied to such concrete social situations.

References

Applebee, A. (1984). *Contexts for learning to write: Studies of secondary school instruction.* Norwood, NJ: Ablex.

Basso, K. (1974). The ethnography of writing. In R. Bauman and J. Sherzer (Eds.), *Explorations in the ethnography of speaking* (pp. 425-432). New York: Cambridge University Press.

Bazerman, C. (1981). What written knowledge does: Three examples of academic discourse. *Philosophy of the Social Sciences, 11,* 361-87.

Berkenkotter, C. (1983). Decisions and revisions: The planning strategies of a publishing writer. *College Composition and Communication, 34,* 156-169.

Bizzell, P. (1982). Cognition, convention, and certainty: What we need to know about writing. *PRE/TEXT, 3,* 213-243.

Bridweil, L. (1980). Revising strategies in twelfth grade students' transactional writing. *Research in the Teaching of English, 14,* 197-222.

Britton, J., Burgess, T., Martin, N., McLeod, A., & Rosen, H. (1975). *The development of writing abilities 11-18.* London: Macmillan.

Calkins, L. (1980). Research update: When children want to punctuate: Basic skills belong in context. *Language Arts, 57,* 567-573.

Clark, C., & Florio, S., with Elmore, J., Martin, J., & Maxwell, R. (1983). Understanding writing instruction: Issues of theory and method. In P. Mosenthal, L. Tamor, & S. Walmsley (Eds.), *Research on writing: Principles and methods* (pp. 236-264). New York: Longman.

Cooper, M. (1986). The ecology of writing. *College English, 48,* 364-375.

Denzin, N. (1978). *Sociological methods.* New York: McGraw-Hill.

Dewey, J. (1949). *The child and the curriculum and the school and society.* Chicago: University of Chicago Press.

Dyson A. (1984). Learning to write/learning to do school: Emergent writers' interpretations of school literacy tasks. *Research in the Teaching of English, 18,* 233-264.

Emig, J. (1983). *The web of meaning: Essays on writing, teaching, learning, and thinking.* Upper Montclair, NJ: Boynton/Cook.

Erickson, F. (1982). Taught cognitive learning in its immediate environments: A neglected topic in the anthropology of education. *Anthropology & Education Quarterly, 13* (2), 148-180.

Faigley, L. (1985). Nonacademic writing: The social perspective. In L. Odell & D. Goswami (Eds.), *Writing in nonacademic settings* (pp. 231-248). New York: Guilford Press.

Fish, S. (1980). Interpreting the Variorium. In J. Tompkins (Ed.), *Reader response criticism: From formalism to post-structuralism.* Baltimore: Johns Hopkins University Press.

Florio, S., & Clark, C. (1982). The functions of writing in an elementary classroom. *Research in the Teaching of English, 16,* 115-130.

Flower, L., & Hayes, J. (1981). The pregnant pause: An inquiry into the nature of planning. *Research in the Teaching of English, 15,* 229-244.

Freedman, S. (1984). The registers of student and professional expository writing: Influences on teachers' responses. In R. Beach & L. Bridwell (Eds.), *New directions in composition research* (pp. 334-347). New York: Guilford Press.

Freedman, S. (1985). *The acquisition of written language: Response and revision.* New York: Ablex.

Geertz, C. (1973). *The interpretation of cultures.* New York: Basic Books.

Gilmore, P., & Glatthorn, A. (1982). *Children in and out of school: Ethnography and education.* Washington, DC: Center for Applied Linguistics.

Goffman, E. (1961). *Encounters: Two studies in the sociology of interaction.* New York: Bobbs-Merrill.

Grice, H. (1975). *Logic and conversation.* 1967. William James Lectures, Harvard University. Unpublished manuscript, 1967. Excerpt in Cole and Morgan (Eds.), *Syntax and semantics, Vol. III: Speech acts* (pp. 41-58). New York: Academic Press.

Guba, E. (1978). *Toward a method of naturalistic inquiry in educational evaluation.* Los Angeles: Center for the Study of Evaluation, University of California at Los Angeles.

Gumperz, J. (1971). *Language in social groups.* Stanford, CA: Stanford University Press.

Heath, S. B. (1982). Ethnography in education: Defining the essentials. In P. Gilmore & A. Glatthorn (Eds.), *Children in and out of school: Ethnography and education* (pp. 33-55). Washington, DC: Center for Applied Linguistics.

Heinlein, R. (1961). *Stranger in a strange land.* New York: Putnam.

Herrington, A. (1985). Writing in academic settings: A study of the contexts for writing in two college chemical engineering courses. *Research in the Teaching of English, 19,* 331-359.

Hymes, D. (1972a). Introduction. In C. Cazden, V. P. John, & D. Hymes (Eds.), *Functions of language in the classroom* (pp. xi-lxii). New York: Teachers College Press.

Hymes, D. (1972b). Models of the interaction of language and social life. In J. Gumperz & D. Hymes (Eds.), *Directions in sociolinguistics* (pp. 35-71). New York: Holt, Rinehart, & Winston.

Kantor, K. (1984). Classroom contexts and the development of writing intuitions: An ethnographic case study. In R. Beach & L. Bridwell (Eds.), *New directions in composition research* (pp. 72-94). New York: Guilford.

Langer, J. (1984). The effects of available information on responses to school writing tasks. *Research in the Teaching of English, 18*, 27-44.

Langer, J. (1985). Children's sense of genre: A study of performance on parallel reading and writing tasks. *Written Communication, 2,* 157-188.

Langer, J. (1986). Reading, writing, and understanding: An analysis of the construction of meaning. *Written Communication, 3*, 219-267.

Langer, J., & Applebee, A. (1984). Language, learning, and interaction: A framework for improving the teaching of writing. In A. Applebee (Ed.), *Contexts for learning to write: Studies of secondary school instruction* (pp. 169-182). Norwood, NJ: Ablex.

Lincoln, Y., & Guba, E. (1985). *Naturalistic inquiry.* Beverly Hills, CA: Sage Publications.

Odell, L., & Goswami, D. (1985). *Writing in nonacademic settings.* New York: Guilford Press.

Perl, S. (1979). The composing process of unskilled college writers. *Research in Teaching of English, 13*, 317-336.

Perry, W. G. (1970). *Forms of intellectual and ethical development in the college years.* New York: Holt, Rinehart, and Winston.

Piaget, J. (1952). *The origins of intelligence in children.* New York: International Universities Press.

Pianko, S. (1979). A description of the composing processes of college freshman writers. *Research in the Teaching of English, 13*, 5-22.

Polanyi, M. (1958*). Personal knowledge: Towards a post-critical philosophy.* Chicago: University of Chicago Press.

Scribner, S. & Cole, M. (1981). Unpackaging literacy. In M. F. Whiteman (Ed.), *Variation in writing: Functional and linguistic-cultural differences* (pp. 71-88). Hillsdale, NJ: Lawrence Erlbaum.

Shaughnessy, M. (1977). *Errors and expectations.* New York: Oxford University Press.

Spradley, J. (1979). *The ethnographic interview.* New York: Holt, Rinehart and Winston.

Spradley, J. (1980). *Participant observation.* New York: Holt, Rinehart and Winston.

Szwed, J. (1981). The ethnography of literacy. In M. F. Whiteman (Ed.), *Variation in writing: Functional and linguistic-cultural differences* (pp. 13-23). Hillsdale, NJ: Lawrence Erlbaum.

Whiteman, M. F. (1981). *Variation in writing: Functional and linguistic-cultural differences.* Hillsdale, NJ: Lawrence Erlbaum.

Williams, J. (1985, March). *Encouraging higher order reasoning through writing in all disciplines.* Paper presented at the Delaware Valley Writing Council-PATHS Conference, Philadelphia.

Section 4:
Writing in the Disciplines

What Written Knowledge Does:
Three Examples of Academic Discourse[*]

by Charles Bazerman

Knowledge produced by the academy is cast primarily in written language—now usually a national language augmented by mathematical and other specialized international notations.[1] Language, however, is not an inert vessel. The ancient philosophic and aesthetic debate over the relationship of form and content should caution us to consider the influences the languages of knowledge might have on the shaping of knowledge.[2] Recently linguistic interest in scientific language has produced several descriptions of the syntax of scientific prose in English (Huddleston; Gopnik; Lee).[3] Syntactical studies, however, are concerned only with the patterns of symbols stripped of context and meaning. To understand what language conveys we must look to the contexts in which language operates and to which language refers. Statements do things and talk about things. To put it more formally, we may say that documents serve specific functions within historical and social situations to continue, add to, and transform a group interaction.[4] In carrying on the

---

Reprinted from *Philosophy of the Social Sciences* 11 (1981): 361-387. Used by permission of Sage Publications, Inc.

[*]Fred Baumann, Robert Merton, Norman Storer, Harriet Zuckerman, and members of the Seminar in the Sociology of Science at Columbia University deserve credit for their extensive comments and suggestions on an earlier version of this paper. Responsibility for errors and opinions remains, of course, mine.

[1] The limitation of this paper to consideration of the formal printed documents that comprise the permanent record of knowledge excludes consideration of the significant role of informal communication—both spoken and written—in the creation and dissemination of knowledge. Within limited communities informal communication may even serve as the primary channel of publication: informal communication also seems to influence citation patterns (and perhaps patterns of cognitive influence) in formal printed publications. See Diana Crane, *Invisible Colleges*, Chicago 1972; and Donald Edge and Michael Mulkay, *Astronomy Transformed: The Emergence of Radio Astronomy in England*, New York 1976. On the other hand, it may be argued that because talk and other informal communication rely on the prior literature of the field and are aimed at the eventual production of a new document, informal communication must be understood in relation to formal publication. The work of sorting out the full set of relations between formal and informal communication remains to be done.

[2] The cognitive consequences of the advent of written forms of language are explored in Jack Goody, *The Domestication of the Savage Mind*, Cambridge 1977; and Eric Havelock, *The Greek Concept of Justice*, Cambridge, Mass. 1978, and *Origins of Western Literacy*, Toronto 1976. The cognitive consequences of the advent of printing are explored in Elizabeth Eisenstein, *The Printing Press as an Agent of Change*, 2 vols., Cambridge 1979.

[3] R. D. Huddleston, *The Sentence in Written English*, Cambridge 1971; Myrna Gopnik, *Linguistic Structures in Scientific Texts*, The Hague 1972; and Lee Kok Cheong, *Syntax of Scientific English*, Singapore 1978.

[4] See Ludwig Wittgenstein, *Philosophical Investigations*, New York 1953; J. L. Austin, *How to do Things with Words*, Cambridge, Mass. 1962; and John R. Searle, *Speech Acts*, Cambridge 1969.

interaction, nevertheless, documents—particularly knowledge-bearing documents—make representations of objects, actions, and knowledge that exist beyond confines of the interaction. Fleck, Kuhn, Popper, Toulmin, and Ziman have each developed a theoretical model defining the respective roles of social situation and reference to the objects of nature within scientific communications.[5] More recently, Latour and Woolgar, and Knorr have examined actual texts to establish models of scientific activity.[6]

This essay continues the investigation of knowledge-bearing texts, but from a different vantage point. Rather than working from a theory of scientific activity, this essay starts with a minimal theory of language—actually little more than an orientation towards texts—in order to discover what the texts reveal about themselves. In particular, the texts are examined in relationship to four contexts: the object under study, the literature of the field, the anticipated audience, and the author's own self.[7] By examining how these four contexts are brought together in each text, we can see what is embodied in the language of the statement of knowledge. This method, although it gives no firm evidence about the actual intentions of the authors and the actual understanding of the readers, does nonetheless reveal the intentions and meanings available in the text.

This essay also ranges beyond the scientific paper to examine knowledge-bearing texts in other disciplines in order to explore the possibilities of variation in what constitutes a statement of knowledge and to accentuate textual features through contrast. The differences in the examples reveal the resources of language to mediate the four contexts examined. The examples are not claimed to be typical of their disciplines, nor are the analyses to be taken as a simple model of the spectrum of knowledge.

How a text refers to, invokes, or responds to each context is explored here through specific features of language. First, the lexicon of an article is examined to find the types of information conveyed about the objects under discussion. The nature of the symbolization, the frameworks in which the objects are identified, the precision of identification, and the tightness of fit between name and object indicate the quality of tie between text and the world.

Second, explicit citation and implicit knowledge indicate an article's

---

[5] Ludwik Fleck, *Genesis and Development of a Scientific Fact*, Chicago 1979; Thomas S. Kuhn, *The Structure of Scientific Revolutions*, Chicago 1962; Karl R. Popper, *Objective Knowledge*, Oxford 1979; Stephen Toulmin, *Human Understanding*, Princeton 1972; John Ziman, *Public Knowledge*, Cambridge 1968.

[6] Bruno Latour and Steve Woolgar, *Laboratory Life: The Social Construction of Scientific Facts*, Beverly Hills, 1979; Karin D. Knorr, 'Producing and Reproducing Knowledge: Descriptive or Constructive?', *Social Science Information*, 16, 1977, 669-96; and Karin D. Knorr and Dietrich W. Knorr, 'From Scenes to Scripts: On the Relationship Between Laboratory Research and Published Paper in Science', forthcoming.

[7] This four part analysis is based on a modification of the model of communication process presented in James Kinneavy, *A Theory of Discourse*, Englewood Cliffs, N.J. 1971. Kinneavy sees language (or a text) mediating among an encoder (or writer), a decoder (or audience), and reality; I have added a fourth item to be mediated by language, the literature.

relationship to the previous literature on the subject.[8] About explicit references questions arise concerning the precision of meaning conveyed by the reference, the relationship of the reference to the claim of the article, the use made of the reference, and the manner of discussion of the reference.[9] About implicitly used knowledge, questions arise concerning the extent of codification and the role the knowledge takes in the argument.[10]

Third, each article's attention to the anticipated audience can be seen in the knowledge and attitudes the text assumes that the readers will have, in the types of persuasion attempted, in the structuring of the argument, and in the charge given by the author to the readers (i.e., what the author would like the readers to do after being convinced by the article).[11]

Finally, the author is represented in several ways within the text. The human mind stands between the reality it perceives and the language it speaks in; statements reflect the thoughts, purposes, observations, and quirks of the individual. The individual can be seen in the breadth and originality of the article's claims, in the idiosyncracies of cognitive framework, in reports of introspection, experience, and observation, and in value assumptions. These features add up to a persona, a public face, which makes the reader aware of the author as an individual statement-maker coming to terms with reality from a distinctive perspective.

Although the four contexts (and the features that indicate them) are separated here for analysis, they are mutually dependent in each text. An observation concerning one has implications for the others. The depth of the interdependence is evident if one considers that the perception and thought of both author and audience are shaped for the most part by the same literature, and that literature provides the accepted definition of the objects discussed. On the other hand, shared interest in and observation of objects of study draw the literature, author, and audience together.

An author, in deciding which words to commit to paper, must weigh these

---

[8] Karl Popper in 'Epistemology Without a Knowing Subject' in *Objective Knowledge* (see note 5) argues similarly that knowledge once created becomes largely autonomous, something separate from either reality or our subjective sense of it. Once created, knowledge can be treated as an object, upon which further intellectual operations may be made, much as a spider web once woven becomes an object in the world. In like manner, I consider the literature of the field as a fact in itself, a fact with which all new publications must contend, just as they must contend with the objects they presume to study. With respect to new publication the literature of a field has a status beyond simply the record of past subjective perception. The new publication, in criticizing, correcting, extending, and simply using the prior literature treats that literature as the 'third world' Popper describes.

[9] See also G. Nigel Gilbert, 'Referencing as Persuasion', *Social Studies of Science*, **7**, 1977, 113-22; and Henry G. Small, 'Cited Documents as Concept Symbols', *Social Studies of Science*, **8**, 1978, 327-40.

[10] Harriet Zuckerman and Robert Merton discuss codification on pages 510-19 of 'Age, Aging, and Age Structure in Science', in Norman Storer (ed.), *The Sociology of Science*, Chicago 1973. Merton also discusses the implicit use of knowledge, or what he calls 'obliteration by incorporation', in *Social Theory and Social Structure*, New York 1968, chapter one; and in *Sociological Ambivalence and Other Essays*, New York 1976, p. 130.

[11] Latour and Woolgar, and Knorr (see note 6) seem most interested in the persuasive and other effects texts have on their audiences; the process of text creation is seen to have the primary goal of persuasion. In this they follow Joseph Gusfield, 'The Literary Rhetoric of Science', *American Sociological Review*, **41**, 1976, 16-34.

four contexts and establish a workable balance among them. A text is, in a sense, a solution to the problem of how to make a statement that attends through the symbols of language to all essential contexts appropriately. More explicitly, an article is an answer to the question, 'Against the background of accumulated knowledge of the discipline, how can I present an original claim about a phenomenon to the appropriate audience convincingly so that thinking and behaviour will be modified accordingly?' A successful answer is rewarded by its becoming an accepted formulation.

Each of the contexts, when abstracted from the writer's task of embodying complex meaning in a specific text and when viewed singly as a theoretical problem in communication, can appear to raise overwhelming epistemological difficulties. The kinds of difficulties that arise from such monochrome analysis are suggested by a slight renaming of the four factors we have been considering: language and reality; language and tradition; language and society; and language and mind. Exclusive concern with the language-creating mind leads to a subjective view of knowledge which makes uncertain the reality perceived and which rejects the cognitive growth of cultures. Viewing in isolation the effect of tradition on statement-making may lead one to misjudge accumulated statements—whether called paradigms or authority—as juggernauts, flattening out observed anomalies and individual thought. Perceiving statements only within the process of social negotiation of a socially constructed reality ignores the individual's powers of observation and language's ability to adjust to observed reality. But the most common errors arise from language considered only in relation to reality: on one side the naive error of assuming that language is an unproblematic reflection of reality, and on the other side the sophistry that language is arbitrary, radically split from nature, with no perceiving cognitive selves and no trace of rational community to heal the split.

The three texts examined below represent three different solutions to the problem of writing knowledge: James Watson and Francis Crick, 'A Structure for Deoxyribose Nucleic Acid'; Robert K. Merton, 'The Ambivalence of Scientists'; and Geoffrey H. Hartman, 'Blessing the Torrent: On Wordsworth's Later Style'. The different balance of contexts established in each article derives in part from the differences in contexts—different types of objects studied, differently structured literatures, audiences of differing homogeneity, and different role expectations for the authors. The origin of the papers in separate fields (molecular biology, sociology, and literary criticism) representing the three traditional divisions of the academy (sciences, social sciences, and humanities) of course accentuates the differences on all fronts; however, these examples should not be over-read as typical of large divisions of knowledge. They represent only three spots on the map of knowledge, and it is as yet unclear where on the map they lie, or even what the map looks like.

I

The article 'A Structure for Deoxyribose Nucleic Acid' (see appendix) primarily describes a geometric model, elaborated in quantitative and qualitative terms, that is claimed to correspond to the structure of a substance found in nature. This act of geometric naming depends on the substance being discrete and robust and its structure being consistent through repeated observations, for otherwise the names will not convey a distinct and stable meaning to all observers.[12] Thus the primary context explicitly attended to by the language of the paper is the context of the objects of nature.

All other contexts are subordinated to this primary one so that the article may appear to speak univocally about nature. The previous literature on the subject is sorted out according to the criterion of closeness of fit between the observed phenomena and the claims made, and the accepted claims in the literature become assimilated into the language used to describe the phenomena. The audience is assumed to share the same criteria of closeness of fit, discreteness, robustness, and reproducibility for acceptance of claims (or symbolic formulations) about phenomena; therefore, the audience can be relied on to have much the same assessment of the literature as the author does, and persuasion may proceed by maintaining apparent focus on the object of study.[13] Further, because the audience has a well established frame of reference in which to fit the new claim, they do not need to be given much guidance about the claim's implications. Finally, the authors' apparent presence is minimized by the common pursuit of authors, literature, and audience to establish a common, codified, symbolic analogue for nature. The authors seem only to be contributing a filler for a defined slot, and they are only in competition with a few other authors who are trying to fill the same slot. The persona, although proud among colleagues, is humbled before nature.

The above generalizations, to be specified through analysis of the text shortly, represent only the appearance of the document itself, and not the full range of actual activity of the scientists. The complex processes of discovery, isolation of phenomena, and interaction with colleagues are well known to involve many psychological, sociological and even random elements which do not appear in the final article.[14] Nonetheless, the role of the conventions of formal presentations should not be discounted as an important factor in sorting out these so-called 'non-scientific' elements of scientific work. The mechanisms of formal scientific communication may encourage the produc-

---

[12]Here I am not concerned with the reproducibility of individual experiments, but rather with the appearance of the phenomenon under a variety of circumstances. The more situations in which the phenomenon unmistakeably appears, the more certain is the identification of its discrete existence.

[13]Latour and Woolgar (see note 6), pp. 75-76, suggest that scientific persuasion is successful when attention is drawn away from the circumstances of statement creation toward a 'fact', which appears to be above the particularities of a specific circumstance. In the authors' terms, 'the processes of literary inscription are forgotten'.

[14]The complex sociological, psychological, and historical specifics of the process of discovery in the case of D.N.A. are extensively recounted in James Watson, *The Double Helix*, New York 1968; Anne Sayre, *Rosalind Franklin and DNA*, New York 1975; and Horace Freeland Judson, *The Eighth Day of Creation*, New York 1979.

tion of knowledge that extends beyond the human and social circumstances of its creation.

The opening sentence of Watson and Crick's article sets the task: 'We wish to suggest a structure for the salt of deoxyribose nucleic acid'. The task of identifying a structure assumes, first, that there is a distinct substance which can be isolated and inspected and which has qualities distinguishing it from other substances. By 1944 Avery, MacLeod, and McCarty had extracted a substance which they called 'the transforming principle' and the method of extraction was standard by the time Watson and Crick began work.[15] Further, this substance is assumed to preexist the historical, human act of isolating and identifying the substance.

The ability to isolate the substance under repeatable conditions gives an ostensiveness to the name. Since the name only serves to point out or tag something distinctly and unmistakeably observable, the name need not convey any particular information. It can be arbitrary, whimsical, eponymic, or otherwise accidental; it need only be distinctive. The name, however, can do double service, conveying information as well as identifying. The name deoxyribose nucleic acid identifies elements of structure—e.g., the ribose configuration without an oxygen—as well as letting us know that the substance is to be found within cell nuclei. Thus the name is in this case overdetermined with respect to reality; we know more about the substance than we need to for purely identification purposes.

At this point we can see how the accumulated knowledge of the field (represented by the literature) is incorporated into the language. The isolation of elements and the theory of chemical combination, as well as the idea that substances can be analyzed chemically, are all implicit in the name of the object. More than that, the name reveals the gradually emerging orientation of chemistry to describe most features and processes through structure. Even the linguistically oldest component of the name, *acid* has been transformed through redefinition as chemical knowledge and orientation have changed. In Bacon's day the word *acid* meant only sour-tasting; then it came to mean a sour tasting substance; then, a substance which reddens litmus; then, a compound that dissociates in aqueous solution to produce hydrogen ions; then, a compound or ion that can give protons to other substances; and most recently, a molecule or ion that can combine with another by forming a covalent bond with two electrons of the other.[16] The tasting and taster vanish as the structure emerges.

The task of assigning a structure relies on a further assumption, that nature arranges itself in geometrical ways; theories of forces account for this remarkable correspondence between the symbolic representation of geometric

---

[15]Ibid., p. 36. D.N.A. was, in fact, first extracted by Johann Friedrich Miescher in 1869 (ibid., p. 28).
[16]*Oxford English Dictionary*, compact edition, New York 1971, p. 20; *Webster's New Collegiate Dictionary*, Springfield, Mass. 1953, p. 8; *American Heritage Dictionary*, Boston 1976, p. 10.

shapes and the repeating arrangement of matter in nature. Geometry as a study is the product of human consciousness, but geometric forms are claimed to preexist human invention. Thus the task of the molecular biologist is not to create a structure that approximates nature, but to discover and express in human terms the actual structure resulting from all the forces and accounting for the behaviour and appearance of the molecule. The claim of representing an actual structure rather than creating an approximate model results in a strong requirement for correspondence between data and claim. This correspondence, as we shall see below, is the main criterion of persuasion offered to the audience.

The few words of text discussed so far convey much about the object and the knowledge developed through the history of chemistry and biology, yet such compact transmission of information reveals no literary genius on the part of the authors. The dense communication is inherent in the names of objects and tasks. That a mere naming of parts conveys such precise and full meaning indicates how much the historical genius of the discipline is embodied in the development of its language.

The analysis of the first sentence is not yet finished. The first five words, 'we wish to suggest a . . . ,' reveal much about the joint persona and contribution of the two authors. Despite the usual convention of avoiding the first person in scientific papers, the authors do assert their presence through the word *we*. That direct presence, however, is immediately subordinated to the object under consideration, the structure of D.N.A. Moreover, the authors are only *suggesting*, and the suggestion has only an indefinite article; whether *a* suggestion turns out to be *the* structure depends on nature. *Wish to suggest* is a form which implies humility before the facticity of the object, yet the phrase also has the boldness of the authors' presumption that their claim indeed will be confirmed by nature. Mild speech is possible because the suggestion will gain all the force it needs from the observation of reality; nature will stand up for scientists. The locution *wish to suggest*, appropriate here, might sound pompous in a branch of knowledge which does not find such immediate confirmation in nature.

Science will as well stand up for scientists, for the authors also subordinate themselves to scientific knowledge as currently constituted. By identifying their subject within the language of scientific disciplines, they are implicitly putting their original contribution within the framework of existing scientific knowledge. The placement and titling of the paper itself suggest how much the originality of the paper is subsumed within a highly structured framework of knowledge. The article is within a section entitled 'Molecular Structure of Nucleic Acids' and is followed by another article of the same class, 'Molecular Structure of Deoxypentose Nucleic Acid'.[17] The Watson-

---

[17]*Nature*, **171** (April 25, 1953), pp. 737, 738.

Crick article discusses only one particular substance in a larger class of substances, all being studied by colleagues to determine the same type of information.

The second sentence—'This structure has novel features which are of considerable biological interest'—places the chemical claim in the context of biological knowledge; this added context identifies the great importance of the paper. The knowledge of one field is not treated as the hermetic creation of that field, liable only to internal consistency within that field. Rather, other disciplines are subject to the discoveries about nature. Yet the specific implications of the discovery need not be discussed, for once the novel features of the structure are made known and referred to the codified knowledge of biology, any competent biologist would see a wide range of implications. Later in the article the authors comment, 'It has not escaped our notice that the specific pairing we have postulated immediately suggests a copying mechanism for the genetic material'. This brief comment invokes the knowledge of genetics and cellular mechanics and tells the biologist where to fit this structure into the open claims of the field. The single added piece of information will allow biology to move forward in directions determined by its own logic. It would be presumptuous, tedious, and unnecesary for Watson and Crick to lecture on the subject.

It is worth noting that although the subject of the paper is structural, the consequences and import are functional. From the shape of things, one can better understand how things happen.

It is also worth noting that all the uses of the first person are to indicate intellectual activities: statement making (opening words of paragraphs one and four), making assumptions (later in paragraph four), criticizing statements (paragraph two), and placing knowledge claims within other intellectual frameworks (paragraphs eleven and twelve). None of the first person uses imply inconstancy in the object studied, but only changes or development of the authors' beliefs of what the appropriate claims about the object should be. The object is taken as given, independent of perception and knowing; all the human action is only in the process of coming to know the object—that is, in constructing, criticizing, and manipulating claims.

Once the claim about the object has been placed into its chemical slot, to define the inquiry, and its biological slot, to define the significant consequences, the competing claims that would fill the same slots must be eliminated. If the codified literatures of the relevant disciplines aim to represent the way nature is, a multiplicity of claims about the same phenomenon indicates an unresolved issue. Until a univocal formulation that describes the phenomenon in all its features is found, the phenomenon is not fully understood.

The grounds on which the two competing structures for D.N.A. are rapidly dismissed in the second and third paragraphs reveal the central role of specific knowledge about the object of study. How any claim fits with what is or can be known about the object forms the chief constraint for originality, codification of the literature, and persuasion of the readers. The Pauling and

Corey model, defined by a quick geometric description, is dismissed as impossible on two counts, both based on knowledge of features of such molecules well established in the literature: binding forces and van der Waals distances. Because Watson and Crick do not present their exact calculations, their criticisms must rely on the presumption that the features they invoke are commonly accepted and similarly understood well enough to allow reproducible calculations that will satisfy other researchers in the field. The codified knowledge about all aspects of the object presents clear constraints that must be met by any potential model. If a model does not match existing theory which is believed to accurately describe nature, then the model must be dismissed. If later the dismissed model is strongly supported by other evidence, the dismissing theory must be called into question.

The dismissal of the Fraser model on the grounds that it is 'rather ill-defined' is even more interesting, for the ill-definition does not allow calculations of the kind invoked for the Pauling-Corey model. The Fraser model is not consequential enough. Since the model cannot then be discussed against the framework of codified knowledge or against measurable aspects of the object, there is no profit looking into it.

With the competition disposed of, Watson and Crick can proceed to the core of the paper, their suggested structure. The diagram to the left of the fourth paragraph gives the geometrical essence of the solution; the fourth through eighth paragraphs cast the geometry into words, add details, and clarify elements of the structure through reference to accepted causal statements, prior work, and other models. The five paragraphs are descriptive, recreating physical presence through the symbolic systems of words and numbers, but the symbols are more than approximate metaphors. The names point to discrete objects, and the geometry is of nature itself. Scientific language, as a symbolic system with a commitment to reform itself in accordance with replicable observation of nature, becomes more than an arbitrary symbolic system.[18]

After this long description of the model, only brief mention is made in paragraphs nine and eleven of the evidence in hand that confirms the model and the evidence still needed to provide a rigorous test. Acceptance of the model depends on the confirming evidence; therefore, the sketchiness of the discussion of evidence might seem surprising. But once the model is described, the existing evidence needs only be referred to because it is

[18]Harriet Zuckerman, 'Cognitive and Social Processes in Scientific Discovery: Recombination in Bacteria as a Prototypical Case' (unpublished manuscript, 1974; revised 1975), discusses the resistances to discovery created by misleading names and the processes by which definition is corrected through discovery. The inaccurate naming impedes, but does not prevent, discovery; ultimately observation of the object leads to corrected knowledge. In the case Zuckerman studies, 'bacteriologists believed that bacteria were asexual *by definition*' (emphasis hers) because bacteria were classified as schizomycetes, from the Greek meaning 'fission fungi' (p. 8). In 1946 Joshua Lederberg's discovery of sexual recombination in the bacteria *E. coli.*, however, led to a revised definition of the classification schizomycetes, despite the literal meaning of the etymology.

generally available and can be interpreted by any competent molecular biologist. Similarly, the construction of new tests is within current technology. The other researchers must satisfy themselves that the model fits past evidence and new tests. It is up to nature to persuade the readers, not the authors.

Just as the ninth and eleventh paragraphs present only limited persuasion, the tenth paragraph presents only limited guidance to the readers about how the model might be applied. The comment that the model is probably not applicable to R.N.A. may be primarily to eliminate R.N.A. as a competitor for the biological slot of genetic carrier (as was then thought more likely than D.N.A.).

After mentioning the genetic implications of the structure, the paper has finished its primary scientific business. The thirteenth paragraph promises greater detail in later publication. This later publication primarily was devoted to spelling out the genetic copying mechanisms.[19] Nonetheless, it is this first short article that counts as the primary statement of knowledge and is the one usually cited.

The last paragraph pays its respects to some aspects of the social system of science: prepublication criticism, access to unpublished evidence and ideas, and funding. To those who know the history of this discovery, these few thanks and the earlier criticisms of competitive work recall a web of social intricacies and inchoate psychological reaching toward discovery.[20] These prepublication facts of life are recognized by working scientists as necessary preconditions of publishable work; nonetheless, these preconditions of discovery do not enter the actual argument of the publication. In the article, competition is dealt with only in cognitive terms, discovery is presented as a fait accompli, and the social system is appended only as a courtesy, a polite nod at the end.

Dependence on the community of the discipline is even more fundamental in the language used, the prior knowledge, and the accepted perception of the object of study, yet even this cognitive dependence on the scientific community is not given explicit recognition. The article cites only work immediately relevant to the assessment of claims made in the article. The six footnotes document only articles presenting competing claims that were criticized or offering supporting data.

In order to maximize the tightness of fit between nature and its symbolic representation, all the relations between language and other contexts—the literature, the audience, and the authors—are both harnessed to and driven by

---

[19]J. D. Watson and F. H. C. Crick, 'Genetical Implications of the Structure of Deoxyribonucleic Acid', *Nature*, **171**, May 30, 1953, 942-67; J. D. Watson and F. H. C. Crick, 'The Structure of DNA', *Cold Spring Harbor Symposia on Quantitative Biology*, **18**, 1953, 123-31; and F. H. C. Crick and J. D. Watson, 'The Complementary Structure of Deoxyribonucleic Acid', *Proceedings of the Royal Society*, **A223**, 1954, 80-96.
[20]See note 14.

the relationship between language and nature. Society, self, and received knowledge are present in the research report, but they are subordinated to the representation of nature. The criterion of correspondence between statement and object governs all of the contexts.

II

Robert K. Merton's essay in the sociology of science, 'The Ambivalence of Scientists' (see appendix), presents a different kind of linguistic solution to a different kind of linguistic problem. In the D.N.A. paper, except for the specific structure proposed, all aspects of the symbolic formulation are shared by author, audience, and literature. At the beginning of the ambivalence paper much less is shared; Merton must establish the ground on which his claim is to rest. The phenomenon which is the object of study is not universally recognized as a discrete phenomenon, and much of the language needed in the discussion does not have unmistakable ostensive reference. The literature of the field does not provide a generally recognized framework in which to place the current claim. The criteria the audience will apply are not clear-cut and universal, nor is it certain what intellectual framework they will bring to the reading. The author's perspective is, then, in many respects individual; nonetheless, through the medium of the paper he hopes to establish his claims as shared knowledge.

The particular subject of the article—the ambivalence of scientists (including social scientists) in observing and reporting certain aspects of behaviour—adds an additional level of problem to be solved in the paper. The subject concerns the process of statement making and applies in a self-exemplifying fashion to the author's work in this essay, the statements in the literature, and the statements made by the readers. Thus, if the claims of the paper are correct, then the literature must be reinterpreted, the author must take into account his own ambivalence, and the readers must question their own statement-making. Not only must Merton establish the grounds of the claim, he must carry the claim across shifting grounds.

In this article a wide range of linguistic choice is open to the author; little is predetermined by a knowledge of reality codified in language, literature, and criteria of judgement. Merton must develop at length original formulations to represent the phenomenon, to assemble and interpret the relevant literature, to establish his perspective, and to attend to the audience's perception.

The first specific difficulty faced by the essay is the identification of the topic and its placement in the discipline. Unlike the Watson-Crick topic, which is located at the intersection of two terms already within the lexicon of the discipline (i.e., 'structure' and 'D.N.A.'), Merton's topic is doubly alien to his discipline. First, the topic depends on the recognition of a prior topic—multiples and priorities—not previously in the discipline; then the topic inquires into why the prior topic has not obtained due recognition. Merton's solution to the importation of a topic which he claims to be indigenous, necessary just to set the stage for the true topic of the paper, is to rely on his own prior work on multiples and priorities and then to suggest that enough evidence already existed within documents familiar to the field such that the topic should have been raised earlier, except for the impeding mechanism of ambivalence.

The fact that the prior topic of multiples and priorities has a clear and substantial place in the author's own framework of knowledge, but does not yet have a fixed place in the codified literature of the discipline, leads to three consequences common in the social sciences. First, for clarification, readers are referred to the author's own works rather than the shared knowledge of the discipline. Second, the readers must be persuaded not only of the specific claims of the essay, but of the author's larger framework of thought in which the claims are placed. Finally, the author's new construction of the knowledge of the field requires a reconsideration of the validity of wide parts of the literature and not just of the specifically competing claims. Without a fixed, codified literature to place and constrain topics and claims, authors are both free and encouraged to frame their contributions in broad revolutionary terms, reordering large segments of knowledge. Paradoxically, the great power and broad implications of Watson and Crick's structure of D.N.A. result from the claim's tight constraint within a highly elaborated framework of thought; the narrow claim reverberates through the whole system. A broader claim in a less tightly strung system may have a more damped effect.

In order to establish the phenomenon to be discussed, the opening paragraph of the ambivalence paper asks the scholarly reader to recall a wide range of evidentiary documents: 'the diaries and letters, the notebooks, the scientific papers, and biographies of scientists' as well as the scholarly discussion of these documents. The reader of the Watson-Crick article must only make a highly directed scan of codified knowledge to locate and accept the topic. Here, however, the reader must review the literature from a critical perspective incorporating a new topic of priorities before he can place and accept the topic of ambivalence as worthy of study. Indeed, the large quantity of examples of the phenomenon cited throughout the essay are, in part, necessary to confirm to the reader that this topic does exist.

Since the topic of ambivalence involves a critique of the field, the writer has a special problem with respect to the scholarly audience, all of whom presumably are subject to the cognitive lapse which is under discussion. Merton must challenge the readers while still maintaining their good will and attentiveness. To overcome audience resistance and ease the shock of self-recognition, Merton creates a strong presence of his own viewpoint and an atmosphere of camaraderie that assumes temporarily that the audience is already with him. He begins with statements of great certitude and only later fills in the background of concepts that make the opening statement possible. This technique bears similarity to the way Hemingway opens *To Have and Have Not*: 'You know how it is there early in the morning in Havana with the bums still asleep against the walls of the buildings; before even the ice wagons come by with ice for the bars'.[21] The reader is drafted into a club, and only gradually is he filled in on the experience he presumably shared from the beginning. The reader is companionably drawn into the world populated by sleeping bums and bars and early morning adventures in Havana. In Merton's essay, the atmosphere of agreement takes the edge off the challenge and creates enough good will for the argument to unfold. Further, Merton withholds explicit discussion of sociologists' group involvement in the problem until the entire mechanism has been laid out, the giants of science implicated, a few confessions cited, and dispassion praised. Moreover, eminent psychologists and sociologists are identified as having the courage of self-examination on this matter before the readers are asked to consider their own cases.

After introducing the problem, in the second paragraph Merton identifies the mechanism of the ambivalence, thereby localizing the phenomenon in a theory of the operations of science. The metaphor of conflict of forces is drawn from physics, and Merton is careful to label it as metaphor by the phrase 'can be conceived of'. There is no claim here of measurable forces as there would be in physics. Metaphors are underconstrained in meaning; by their nature they are only suggestive and approximate. One resorts to metaphor only when the thing to be described is partially or imprecisely known, and one must look to correspondences with better known objects. Even in the best of metaphors the correspondence between the thing being described and the metaphorical representation is only partial. In any specific case, however, the metaphor may be the best available description and, when combined with other underconstrained terms and contextual clues, may create a web of approximate meanings surrounding the actual thing, such that a meaning develops adequate to the situation. The second sentence provides a second underconstrained meaning to support the metaphor of resistance: 'Such resistance is a sign of malintegration of the social institution of science which incorporates potentially incompatible values. . . .' Of all the sentences in the article, this sounds the most typically sociological, precisely because it attaches the topic to familiar sociological concepts. The terms of this sentence, however, are abstract, some of variable or disputed meaning, some metaphoric, and all in a complex syntactical relationship that makes the imprecision additive, if not geometrical. Further, resistance is only 'a sign', not a particular sign or the only sign. Here the indefinite article is a true indefinite, unlike Watson and Crick's 'a structure', where near at hand observations of nature can fix the structure as unique.

Such underdetermination of language provides further reason for requiring the good will of the audience. A sympathetic audience is more likely to expend the effort to reconstruct from partial indicators the meaning most congruent to the argument—a process that may be called reading in the intended spirit. The unsympathetic reader, however, can find in underconstrained

---

[21]Ernest Hemingway, *To Have and Have Not*, New York 1937, p. 1.

meanings enough inconsistency, contradiction, and unacceptable thought to mount a serious attack. Even such ordinary appearing terms as 'scientific accomplishment' or turns of phrases as 'as happy as a scientist can be' rely on many loosely defined conceptual assumptions; they can easily disintegrate under a hostile reading.

In the third paragraph the author turns from an invisible social structure which is claimed to generate the ambivalence to the more visible 'overt behavior that can be interpreted as expressions of such resistance'. Even these overt manifestations of trivialization and distortion, nonetheless, are not directly measurable and discrete. Distortion, for example, is a conceptual term, requiring comparative judgements against a normative model, application of judgement criteria, imputation of thought, and similar interpretive procedures. The interpretation of the concrete evidence of contradictory statements by or about scientists on the matter of priorities requires the kind of analysis employed by psychologists and literary critics. Simple claims become indications of internal processes within the makers of the claims. Even the simple claims, that Halsted was overmodest about his work or Freud found questions of priority boring, are based on human judgement and the imputation of attitude.

The only direct evidentiary statements of the primary phenomenon of ambivalence are the confessions of the professionals of introspection, Freud and Moreno. On the less deeply embarrassing emotional conflicts discussed in the latter part of the paper—fear of the joy of discovery being dashed and fear of unconscious plagiary—Merton is able to cite direct confessions of ambivalence by less trained observers of themselves. But even the evidence of introspection involves judgement, conceptual categories, and the naming of transitory and evanescent phenomena by the introspector. Claims of reproducibility of phenomena within the self require a kind of phenomenological sense memory, and claims of similarity between observers raises even greater difficulties of matching affect to language. On many levels we have only the introspectors' words to go by.

As the essay reaches its mid-point, the samples of irrational statement-making (analyzed as evidence of ambivalence) start coming from sociological sources: the literature of the discipline has become the evidentiary document. The practice of imputing psychological phenomena into the very record of the discipline is justifiable on the basis of social science's own discoveries, but it makes for great difficulties in establishing a codified body of knowledge from the literature. To draw the paradox more strongly, the desire to establish a professional literature that rises above the cognitive and perceptual limitations of individuals leads to self examination, but that reflexivity only reveals the difficulty of codifying statements made by humans about human behaviour.

Once Merton has indicated a similarity of structure in many examples and has moved the examples to the readers' discipline, he is ready to call on the readers for further analysis of this issue. Before the final peroration on the therapeutic value of the study of multiples, he has already steeled the courage and minds of those he wants to carry forth the investigation. He has also suggested the method: dispassionate observation of the self and others, aided upon occasion by collaboration. The final charge to the audience is quite directive: have courage to overcome your own ambivalence to begin a systematic study of priorities, for not only will this study add to knowledge, it will be therapeutic for all of science, including sociology. This kind of 'follow my lead' is very different than the implicit charge to the reader offered by Watson and Crick: gather more evidence to see if we are right, then use the knowledge to advance science according to its own dictates.

The strength of Merton's directiveness at the end is typical of the entire essay, for he must establish a perception of reality and terms of discourse not universally shared in the discipline. He must persuade the readers not just of a specific claim, but an entire framework of knowledge. Language, rather than being highly determined by the discipline's shared perception of reality as it is in the Watson-Crick article, must be carefully shaped by the author to turn his own vision into the shared one of the discipline. Because of the originality of formulations, the author's presence is inevitably strong. If this were typical of the social sciences, one might see the consequences in authors being noted for a point of view or method of perception rather than a specific claim and in a greater tendency for schools to be formed around the most original authors. The differences in formulations among original authors may make reconciliation of viewpoints difficult, and many researchers may find the clearest direction by following in the footsteps of only a limited number of originators. There are, of course, many other economic, social, and cognitive reasons for the formation of schools in all disciplines.

III

Unlike the previous two articles, Geoffrey Hartman's 'Blessing the Torrent: On Wordsworth's Later Style' (see appendix) unfixes our knowledge of its subject (a poem), to suggest an experience that goes beyond any claim we can make. Rather than taming its subject by creating a representation that will count as knowledge, the essay seeks to reinvigorate the poem by aiding the reader to experience the imaginative life embodied in it. Insofar as the poem can be reduced to easily understood, verifiable claims—'normalized', in Hartman's term—the poem is of little interest.

This concern with the aesthetic moment of the poem requires that an existential bond be created among poet, critic, and reader. In the process of conveying the poetic moment, the critic's sensibility plays the central role. The poem, the literature, and the audience's perception are all mediated through the critic's vision. The critic perceives new dimensions of the poem, uses the literature to allude to his own aesthetic experience, and asks the audience to accept a new way of reading the poem. The poetic text and its context, the accumulated experience of literary criticism and literary texts, and the audience's critical judgment and expectation of poetry do constrain what the critic can persuasively state, yet the critic has considerable power to transform all of them.

In one sense the object of investigation, a sonnet entitled 'To the Torrent at the Devil's Bridge, North Wales, 1824', is a known and discrete phenomenon. It is printed in the collected works of William Wordsworth; apparently no scholar has questioned the attribution to Wordsworth, the dating, or the purity of the text. The poem is easily reproduced, as is done at the beginning of the essay. Moreover, some elementary literary techniques and a few well-known biographical facts seem to explain the apparent features of the poem, as Hartman demonstrates in the third through the sixth paragraphs. The topic of the essay, consequently, appears to be fixed in a framework even more complete than that which surrounds D.N.A., to the point where the topic appears trivial. Here, though, the essay sets the framework aside as not revealing the important knowledge of the poem.

That important knowledge is a complex state of mind beyond naming. Hartman can only try to reevoke it through description, contrast, analogy, and reconstruction of context. As Hartman states at the end of the second paragraph in what is the closest approximation of a thesis in the essay, 'Uncertainty of reference gives way to a well-defined personal situation, that is easily described, though less easily understood'. The outside of the situation, captured in the description, is distinguished from the inside of the moment, which counts as understanding. The poem, as verbal artifice, conveys something beyond the words.

The title of the essay indicates the true subject: 'Blessing the Torrent' is an act accomplished through the poem. Six of the essay's seven sections are devoted to recreating the existential moment of blessing. The subtitle 'On Wordsworth's Later Style' indicates that the act of this poem is similar to the acts of others of Wordsworth's later poems, but this similarity is only discussed in the last section of the paper, and no other poem is examined in sufficient detail to establish that it is the vessel of a similar moment. This reading of one sonnet can only provide an analogy for the reading of others, making the other poems more accessible; any more specific claim of equivalence among poems would suggest a reductive normalization. Each poetic moment is itself and no other.

The essay is structured to make the poet's state of mind accessible in all its fullness to the reader, to widen gradually the reader's consciousness of the central issue of the poem. The essay opens with a consideration of the literal meaning of the opening question of the poem: 'How art thou named?' Each of the following sections grows out of an issue raised in the previous one in order to open up the central, opening question. In a sense, each section progressively uncontains the flood.

The epigraphs of Hölderlin, Stevens, and Joyce prepare a first reading of the poem by setting the river in motion as one of a poetic family of floods, puzzling and uncontainable. The first section by raising issues of form—the untitled, unplaceable fragment versus the named, closed sonnet—localizes this particular flood, but raises the problem of understanding the localization. The second section takes up the theme of localization to examine biographical information that raises problems about what the poet could be meaning. At this point the critic brings in other samples of Wordsworth's writing to show the poet's way of thinking about these issues. The writings of other poets are examined to show what Wordsworth did not mean. By the end of the second section the formal solution to naming collapses as the critic points to the inadequacy of the poet's diction to fulfill the domesticating function of the sonnet.

The third section examines this dilemma through the text of the first half of the poem, where the poet explains the problem and proposes a first, inadequate solution. The fourth section discusses the acceptance of the inability of language to localize, as developed in the second half of the poem. Against this reading of the whole poem, Hartman reexamines a few phrases that appear to be clichés, but which now are seen to have unexpected depth, particularly in the context of Wordsworth's other writing. These phrases lead to a return to the problem of naming in the sixth section. Only after the full dynamics of the poem are revealed is the poem seen to represent a key part of Wordsworth's consciousness in his later career, deriving from the realizations of *The Prelude*.

The structure of Hartman's essay differs substantially from the structures of the two essays discussed earlier. In both of the earlier cases the arguments are built on claims to be placed, established, and applied—thereby achieving closure within a framework of knowledge. The two earlier essays differ primarily in the amount and directiveness of text required to define the framework and phenomenon, to establish the claim, and to indicate the applications of the claim. Hartman's essay, however, denies the reader the closure of a specific claim fixed within a coherent framework of knowledge. The essay only prepares the reader's sensibility to relive imaginatively the Wordsworthian sensibility. The essay ends with a method of reading and a promise of pleasure: 'The later poems often require from us something close to a suppression of the image of creativity as "burning bright" or full of glitter and communicated strife. Wordsworth's lucy-feric style, in its discretion and reserve, appears to be the opposite of luciferic. Can we say there is blessing in its gentle breeze?'

The essay also denies closure in another way. The final test of Hartman's argument is whether it illuminates the poems. No hard evidence will determine whether he is right or wrong. Certain kinds of evidence are available to convince the reader of the plausibility of the argument, which evidence the critic violates only at his own risk. Hartman must show his reading is consistent with the wording and structure of the poems and harmonious with what we know of the poet and his period. Further, each interpretation has an implicit psychology and aesthetic which cannot, without extensive rationale, violate readers' ideas of how people read and write poems; in his extensive writings on Wordsworth, Hartman has presented an intriguing and plausible phenomenological aesthetic, based on the Wordsworthian endeavour to feel a connectedness with nature through the poetic imagination.[22] But all the argument is based on plausibility with no hard, provable answers. And even notions of plausibility can be changed if the essay succeeds in expanding the reader's poetic imagination.

As the object of investigation, the poem only gains importance in its subjective experience, so also with the literature, of which there are four relevant types. First is the critical literature, toward which Hartman's essay contributes. Yet the critical literature is used neither as a groundwork out of which the ideas of the essay grow nor as an orderly body of information into which the essay fits. The accumulated knowledge of the critical literature is implicitly dismissed in several ways, and the whole of Wordsworth criticism is treated as so inconsequential as not to require explicit discussion. First, in finding this one poem (and most of the other later poems as well) worth serious study, Hartman challenges the conventional wisdom which sees a collapse in Wordsworth's poetic powers after *The Prelude*. Second, Hartman criticizes a normalized reading—i.e. conventional criticism—as inadequate to the poem. Finally, by locating the genesis of the later style in the perceptions of *The Prelude*, Hartman reverses the common view that the epic was the culmination of the early period and that Wordsworth almost immediately turned away from the great poem's realizations. In the text of the essay no explicit mention of Wordsworth criticism is made, and in the notes the only reference to any critics are to Longinus and Kenneth Burke, both of whom discussed concepts analogous to Hartman's. The references are brief, and serve only to illuminate Hartman's ideas. D. V. Erdman is also thanked for calling Hartman's 'attention to a topographical tract published in London, 1796'.

The second type of literature, used more extensively, provides contextual information, such as Wordsworth's activities at the time of the poem's composition and the typography of the poem's setting. These documents date primarily from Wordsworth's time. The argument does rely on this historical, non-literary information, but only in service of Hartman's literary perception.

Third is the corpus of world poetry, quoted substantially throughout. The works of other poets are used to illuminate Wordsworth's work by analogy and contrast. Wordsworth's poetic moment is identified by setting it against other poetic moments. Even though a Hölderlin poem may shed light on a Wordsworth poem, however, they remain separate, with separate lives to be evoked and with no fixed relationship to each other. Hartman does not even attend to the historical task of tracing influence and literary tradition, which would establish at least some formal connections between poems.

The last type of literature is the testimony of Wordsworth and his intimates concerning his state of mind and poetic intentions. This category includes letters, journals, and Wordsworth's other poems when they are used in an evidentiary way. As with the previous types of literature, these

---

[22]See, for example, Geoffrey H. Hartman, *Wordsworth's Poetry 1787-1814*, New Haven, Conn. 1964.

documents are used only to illuminate Hartman's perception of the dynamics of the poem under study, and they are interpreted through that perception. Thus Hartman uses a letter in which Wordsworth copied the poem not as an honest reflection of the poet's state of mind, but to recall another time when Wordsworth criticized just such attitudes as expressed in the letter. This juxtaposition, not at all evident in Wordsworth's letter by itself, prepares Hartman's criticism of the absurdity of the conventional reading and introduces the existential paradox which becomes Hartman's theme. Thus all the references, from the most scholarly historical geography to the most poetic evocations, serve only to recreate the consciousness Hartman perceives embodied in the poem.

The critical and poetic literatures have an additional important, but implicit, role: the language of the essay invokes and evokes concepts and aesthetic experiences from the entire history of poetry and poetic criticism. The literary vocabulary on one level appears to be purely technical, not unlike the technical vocabularies of molecular biology or sociology. Terms such as *topos, apostrophe, sonnet, turn, enjambment* and *sublime* are the critic's basic conceptual equipment, learned as part of professional training. On another level, however, the literary terms are more than technical, for each reverberates with former uses and examples. One can know and understand *deoxyribose* on the basis of modern chemistry alone, but to understand the *sublime* one must not only have read Longinus and be familiar with the ensuing critical debate to modern times, one must have experienced a wide range of poems that embody the development and variation of that concept. Even terms that do not refer directly to experience—*sonnet*, for example—rely on wide literary experience. That a poem has fourteen lines, particular rhymes and meters, and a turn is of some outward interest, but of greater importance is that the poem stands in a tradition that began as a representation of love, became increasingly introspective and confessional, then took on religious and philosophic concerns, fell into disuse as uncongenial to the concerns of the eighteenth century, and was finally revived by the romantics. To understand the term sonnet is to be sensitive to the wide range of consciousness and experience it has served to realize. Moreover, to understand the term's use in a phrase such as 'Though the sonnet as a form is a domesticating device . . .' one must remember the courtly lover torn by love yet graceful in his meters, Donne in religious turmoil tearing at the form, Herbert turning the sonnet in on itself, and Milton in grief, blindness, and civil war finding repose for the space of fourteen lines. In comparison, the sociological and psychological terms used by Merton—e.g., *ambivalence*, *denial*, and *integration*—do have histories in the literature, and familiarity with the original texts helps reveal how the terms are used, yet the history of the field and the experience of reading the entire corpus is not evoked in the use of the terms.

Because the experience embodied in the poetic literature and interpreted through the critical literature is implicit in the literary vocabulary, the terms take on an added subjective element. Not only does Hartman use the critical vocabulary to elucidate the subjective experience of the poem as he perceives it, his use embodies his own entire experience of literature—his experience of Longinus, Milton, and even Joyce. Moreover, in trying to communicate his perceptions he is relying on the subjective experiences each of his readers have of literature. Each reader has intimate familiarity with a different range of literature, and each reader gives each text a different reading. One's personal anthology personally interpreted comprises the individual's share of the corporate knowledge and is the basis of that individual's sensibility.

In the chain of consciousness from poet to critic to reader, the enterprise rests on the quality of the mediating critic's sensibility. Of course one can read a poem without benefit of a mediating critic, and some schools of thought suggest the best reading is the least tutored. If one turns to a critic, however, the reader must believe that the critic perceives things that would not be apparent to the reader. A critic's persuasiveness, therefore, depends in part on establishing a persona of perceptivity, if not brilliance. Reputation, which is prior to any given article, no doubt plays a significant role in fostering the persona. The content of the essay itself also provides a substantive basis for judging insight. But a persona of sensitivity and brilliance can also be fostered by stylistic habits. Hartman uses several techniques to increase the appearance of density of thought. First, like many critics, he prefers the elliptical argument to the fully delineated. Consider, for example, this sentence: 'The word "Viamala" has punctuated a pathfinding movement of thought and suggests a final station or resting point as it turns the sonnet toward the description of a single scene—though a scene that turns out to be a prospect rather than a terminus, with features that reach beyond time'. The single sentence moves through many concepts cast in metaphorical terms, modifying and by the end even reversing the original imagery. A number of the key phrases, such as *pathfinding movement* and *features that reach beyond time*, are neither prepared for earlier in the paper nor spelled out later. No specifics are attached to any of the generalizations of the sentence; the reader is left to figure out how the complex point of the sentence applies to both the rest of the article and to the poem. The interpretation required of the reader is increased because the metaphor of the critical sentence turns the imagery of the poem around, suggesting that the poet, and not the river, is on a pathfinding journey. The sentence can suggest many thoughts to the reader, not all of which may be intended or supported by the argument. In contrast, although the Watson and Crick article does employ ellipsis, the items not spelled out, such as *van der Waals distances*, do have specific, univocal meanings with clear-cut application to the argument of the paper. The ellipsis runs through a single meaning rapidly rather than reverberating with many possible suggested meanings.

In the literary essay reverberative density is also achieved through allusive language, invoking concepts and experiences of other poets and implying connections between words. The *capable negativity* Hartman mentions at the beginning of section III is a Spoonerism for Keats' term 'negative capability'. The verbal play suggests a deep transformation of Keats' poetics, but the phrase seems actually to have only the simple meaning in the essay that the poem recognizes the impossibility of its task. The last sentence of the essay—'Can we say there is a blessing in its gentle breeze?'—refers to the opening line of *The Prelude* and the title of the essay as well as a contrast to the torrent. Puns run throughout the essay from the first epigraph (where the double meaning of the German *entsprungen* ties the river to a puzzle), through 'the chasm that is like a chiasmus' in the fourth section, to the contrast of *luciferic* and *lucy-feric* (referring to Wordsworth's Lucy poems) in the next to the last sentence of the essay. A plethora of connections attests to the fertile sensibility of the critic, and sensibility is essentially what the critic has to offer in the essay.

To recapitulate the major points of comparison among the three texts analyzed is to notice that the three statements of knowledge are three different things. In mediating reality, literature, audience, and self, each text seems to be making a different kind of move in a different kind of game. All three texts appear to show interest in phenomena which form the topics for the essays (as well as provide the titles). But the phenomena are not equally fixed prior to the essays. The substance D.N.A. and the concept genetic carrier were well known (although not agreed to be synonymous) prior to Watson and Crick's essay. The Wordsworth poem was also well known, but Hartman claims what was known should not count as true knowledge, which can only come in the subjective recreation of the poetic moment. In the ambivalence essay Merton must first establish that the phenomenon exists and is consequential.

The chemical and biological literatures are codified and embedded in the language, problematics, and accepted modes of argumentation; consequently, the D.N.A. essay does not need to discuss explicitly most of the relevant literature except for claims and evidence immediately bearing on the essay's claim. The sociological literature on scientific behaviour is more diverse, unsettled, and open to interpretation; therefore, the essay must reconstruct the literature to establish a framework for discussion. The author attempts codification because codification is not a fact going into the essay. The literatures of poetry and its criticism tend to be particularistic and used in particularistic ways; the Wordsworth essay invokes both literatures idiosyncratically and only in support of the critic's vision of the particular poetic moment of consciousness being investigated. Codification, if it can be called that, is entirely personal.

The biological and biochemical audiences share an acceptance of much knowledge, evidence gathering techniques, and criteria of judgement against which to measure Watson and Crick's claims and to suggest how the claims might be applied; therefore, the authors do not urge, but rather leave the audience to judge and act according to the dictates of science. The sociological audience, sharing no uniform framework of thought or criteria of proof, must be urged, persuaded, and directed along the lines of the author's thoughts. The literary audience, concerned with private aesthetic experience, must find the critic's comments plausible, but more important must find the comments enriching the experience of reading; evocation of the richest experience is persuasion.

In their essay Watson and Crick take on a humble yet proud authorial presence: the humble servants of nature and their discipline, filling in only a small piece of a vast puzzle and subject to the hard evidence of nature and the cold judgement of their peers—yet the proud originators of claims that have the potential ring of natural truth and nearly universal professional acceptance. Merton stands more uncertainly before his discipline and nature, neither of which holds the promise of clear-cut judgement and unequivocal support, yet through the force of argument he hopes to establish some certainty. Curiously, the literary critic Hartman, who has the least responsibility to establish certainty, must take on the most demanding role: appearing to have insight greater than that of his readers. Since his contribution cannot be measured in terms of a claim to be judged right or wrong, the quality of his whole sensibility is up for judgement.

As stated at the beginning of the essay, the texts examined are not necessarily typical of their fields and the contrasts revealed by analysis cannot be taken as defining the features of a spectrum of knowledge. We cannot even begin to speculate on what uniformities with what variations exist within disciplines or whether patterns of differences emerge among disciplines until many more examples have been examined and statistical indicators found to test the generality of conclusions. This analysis, nonetheless, does suggest terms on which typicality can be explored and through which the symbolic knowledge of different disciplines can be compared. The terms of the analysis here provide concrete means for investigating the character of the endeavours of different disciplines, at least as those endeavours appear through the public record of publication.

Moreover, the terms of this analysis suggest how texts serve as dynamic mediating mechanisms, creating those elusive linguistic products we call knowledge. In focusing attention on texts, this analysis looks through the texts to the realms represented in the texts. Texts bring together worlds of reality, mind, tradition, and society in complex and varying configurations, and knowledge is in those words that sit in the middle.

Appendix

I   J. D. Watson and F. H. C. Crick, 'A Structure for Deoxyribose Nucleic Acid', *Nature*, **171**, April 25, 1953, pp. 737-38, complete.

II   Robert K. Merton, 'The Ambivalence of Scientists' in Norman Storer (ed.), *The Sociology of Science*, Chicago 1973, pp. 383-412. Excerpted, pp. 383-85.

III Geoffrey H. Hartman, 'Blessing the Torrent: On Wordsworth's Later Style', *Publications of the Modern Language Association*, **93**, March 1978, pp. 196-204. Excerpted, pp. 196-97.

Molecular Structure of Nucleic Acids
A Structure for Deoxyribose Nucleic Acid

We wish to suggest a structure for the salt of deoxyribose nucleic acid (D.N.A.). This structure has novel features which are of considerable biological interest.

A structure for nucleic acid has already been proposed by Pauling and Corey[1]. They kindly made their manuscript available to us in advance of publication. Their model consists of three intertwined chains, with the phosphates near the fibre axis, and the bases on the outside. In our opinion, this structure is unsatisfactory for two reasons: (1) We believe that the material which gives the X-ray diagrams is the salt, not the free acid. Without the acidic hydrogen atoms it is not clear what forces would hold the structure together, especially as the negatively charged phosphates near the axis will repel each other. (2) Some of the van der Waals distances appear to be too small.

Another three-chain structure has also been suggested by Fraser (in the press). In his model the phosphates are on the outside and the bases on the inside, linked together by hydrogen bonds. This structure as described is rather ill-defined, and for this reason we shall not comment on it.

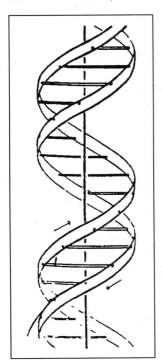

This figure is purely diagrammatic. The two ribbons symbolize the two phosphate—sugar chains, and the horizontal rods the pairs of bases holding the chains together. The vertical line marks the fibre axis.

We wish to put forward a radically different structure for the salt of deoxyribose nucleic acid. This structure has two helical chains each coiled round the same axis (see diagram). We have made the usual chemical assumptions, namely, that each chain consists of phosphate diester groups joining β-D-deoxyribofuranose residues with 3',5' linkages. The two chains (but not their bases) are related by a dyad perpendicular to the fibre axis. Both chains follow right-handed helices, but owing to the dyad the sequences of the atoms in the two chains run in opposite directions. Each chain loosely resembles Furberg's[2] model No. 1; that is, the bases are on the inside of the helix and the phosphates on the outside. The configuration of the sugar and the atoms near it is close to Furberg's 'standard configuration,' the sugar being roughly perpendicular to the attached base. There is a residue on each chain every 3·4 A. in the z-direction. We have assumed an angle of 36° between adjacent residues in the same chain, so

[1] Pauling, L., and Corey, R. B., *Nature.* **171**, 346 (1953); *Proc. U.S. Nat. Acad. Sci.*, **39**, 84 (1953).
[2] Furberg, S., *Acta Chem. Scand.*, **6**, 634 (1952).

that the structure repeats after 10 residues on each chain, that is, after 34 A. The distance of a phosphorus atom from the fibre axis is 10 A. As the phosphates are on the outside, cations have easy access to them.

The structure is an open one, and its water content is rather high. At lower water contents we would expect the bases to tilt so that the structure could become more compact.

The novel feature of the structure is the manner in which the two chains are held together by the purine and pyrimidine bases. The planes of the bases are perpendicular to the fibre axis. They are joined together in pairs, a single base from one chain being hydrogen-bonded to a single base from the other chain, so that the two lie side by side with identical z-co-ordinates. One of the pair must be a purine and the other a pyrimidine for bonding to occur. The hydrogen bonds are made as follows: purine position 1 to pyrimidine position 1; purine position 6 to pyrimidine position 6.

If it is assumed that the bases only occur in the structure in the most plausible tautomeric forms (that is, with the keto rather than the enol configurations) it is found that only specific pairs of bases can bond together. These pairs are: adenine (purine) with thymine (pyrimidine), and guanine (purine) with cytosine (pyrimidine).

In other words, if an adenine forms one member of a pair, on either chain, then on these assumptions the other member must be thymine; similarly for guanine and cytosine. The sequence of bases on a single chain does not appear to be restricted in any way. However, if only specific pairs of bases can be formed, it follows that if the sequence of bases on one chain is given, then the sequence on the other chain is automatically determined.

It has been found experimentally[3, 4] that the ratio of the amounts of adenine to thymine, and the ratio of guanine to cytosine, are always very close to unity for deoxyribose nucleic acid.

It is probably impossible to build this structure with a ribose sugar in place of the deoxyribose, as the extra oxygen atom would make too close a van der Waals contact.

The previously published X-ray data[5, 6] on deoxyribose nucleic acid are insufficient for a rigorous test of our structure. So far as we can tell, it is roughly compatible with the experimental data, but it must be regarded as unproved until it has been checked against more exact results. Some of these are given in the following communications. We were not aware of the details of the results presented there when we devised our structure, which rests mainly though not entirely on published experimental data and stereochemical arguments.

---

[3] Chargaff, E., for references see Zamenhof, S., Brawerman, G., and Chargaff, E., *Biochim. et Biophys. Acta*, **9**, 402 (1952).

[4] Wyatt G. R., *J. Gen. Physiol.*, **36**, 201 (1952).

[5] Astbury, W. T., Symp. Soc. Exp. Biol. 1, Nucleic Acid, 66 (Camb. Univ. Press, 1947).

[6] Wilkins, M. H. F., and Randall, J. T., *Biochim. et Biophys. Acta*, **10**, 192 (1953).

It has not escaped our notice that the specific pairing we have postulated immediately suggests a possible copying mechanism for the genetic material.

Full details of the structure, including the conditions assumed in building it, together with a set of co-ordinates for the atoms, will be published elsewhere.

We are much indebted to Dr. Jerry Donohue for constant advice and criticism, especially on interatomic distances. We have also been stimulated by a knowledge of the general nature of the unpublished experimental results and ideas of Dr. M. H. F. Wilkins. Dr. R. E. Franklin and their co-workers at King's College, London. One of us (J. D. W.) has been aided by a fellowship from the National Foundation for Infantile Paralysis.

J. D. Watson
F. H. C. Crick
Medical Research Council Unit for the
Study of the Molecular Structure of
Biological Systems,
Cavendish Laboratory, Cambridge. April 2.

The Ambivalence of Scientists
1963

Many of the endlessly recurrent facts about multiples and priorities are readily accessible—in the diaries and letters, the note-books, scientific papers, and biographies of scientists. This only compounds the mystery of why so little systematic attention has been accorded the subject. The facts have been noted, for they are too conspicuous to remain unobserved, but then they have been quickly put aside, swept under the rug, and forgotten. We seem to have here something like motivated neglect of this aspect of the behavior of scientists and that is precisely the hypothesis I want to examine now.

This resistance to the study of multiples and priorities can be conceived as a resultant of intense forces pressing for public recognition of scientific accomplishments that are held in check by countervailing forces, inherent in the social role of scientists, which press for the modest acknowledgment of limitations, if not for downright humility. Such resistance is a sign of malintegration of the social institution of science which incorporates potentially incompatible values: among them, the value set upon originality, which leads scientists to want their priority to be recognized, and the value set upon due humility, which leads them to insist on how little they have in fact been able to accomplish. To blend these potential incompatibles into a single

First published as a part of "Resistance to the Systematic Study of Multiple Discoveries in Science," *European Journal of Sociology* 4 (1963): 250-82; reprinted with permission. A condensed version of part of this paper appears under this title in the *Bulletin* of the Johns Hopkins Hospital, 112 (February 1963): 77-97.

orientation and to reconcile them in practice is no easy matter. Rather, as we shall now see, the tension between these kindred values creates an inner conflict among men of science who have internalized both of them. Among other things, the tension generates a distinct resistance to the systematic study of multiples and often associated conflicts over priority.[1]

Various kinds of overt behavior can be interpreted as expressions of such resistance. For one thing, it is expressed in the recurrent pattern of trying to trivialize or to incidentalize the facts of multiples and priority in science. When these matters are discussed in print, they are typically treated as though they were either rare and aberrant (although they are extraordinarily frequent and typical) or as though they were inconsequential both for the lives of scientists and for the advancement of science (although they are demonstrably significant for both).

Understandably enough, many scientists themselves regard these matters as unfortunate interruptions to their getting on with the main job. Kelvin, for example, remarks that "questions of priority, however interesting they may be to the persons concerned, sink into insignificance" as one turns to the proper concern of advancing knowledge.[2] As indeed they do: but sentiments such as these also pervade the historical and sociological study of the behavior of scientists so that systematic inquiry into these matters also goes by default. Or again, it is felt that "the question of priority plays only an insignificant role in the scientific literature of our time"[3] so that, once again, this becomes regarded as a subject which can no longer provide a basis for clarifying the complex motivations and behavior of scientists (if indeed it ever was so regarded).

Now the practice of seeking to trivialize what can be shown to be significant is a well-known manifestation of resistance. Statements of this sort read almost as though they were a paraphrase of the old maxim that the law does not concern itself with exceedingly small matters; *de minimis non curat scientia* [*lex*]. Not that there has been a conspiracy of silence about these intensely human conflicts in the world of the intellect and especially in science. These have been far too conspicuous to be denied altogether. Rather, the repeated conflict behavior of great and small men of science has been incidentalized as not reflecting any conceivably significant aspects of their role as scientists.

Resistance is expressed also in various kinds of distortions: in motivated misperceptions or in an hiatus in recall and reporting. It often leads to those wish-fulfilling beliefs and false memories that we describe as illusions. And

---

[1] This paragraph draws upon a fuller account of the workings of these values in the social institution of science in "Priorities in Scientific Discovery," chapter 14 of this volume.

[2] Silvanus P. Thompson, *The Life of William Thomson, Baron Kelvin of Largs* (London: Macmillan, 1910), 2:602.

[3] Otto Blüh, "The Value of Inspiration: A Study of Julius Robert Mayer and Josef Poppel-Lynkeus," *Isis* 43 (1952): 211-20, at 211.

of such behavior the annals that treat of multiples and priorities are uncommonly full. So much so that I have arrived at a rule of thumb that seems to work out fairly well. The rule is this: whenever the biography or autobiography of a scientist announces that he had little or no concern with priority of discovery, there is a reasonably good chance that, not many pages later in the book, we shall find him deeply embroiled in one or another battle over priority. A few cases must stand here for many:

Of the great surgeon, W. S. Halsted (who together with Osler, Kelly, and Welch founded the Johns Hopkins Medical School), Harvey Cushing writes: he was "overmodest about his work, indifferent to matters of priority."[4] Our rule of thumb leads us to expect what we find: some twenty pages later in the book in which this is cited, we find a letter by Halsted about his work on cocaine as an anesthesia: "I anticipated all of Schleich's work by about six years (or five). . . . [In Vienna,] I showed Wölfler how to use cocaine. He had declared that it was useless in surgery. But before I left Vienna he published an enthusiastic article in one of the daily papers on the subject. It did not, however, occur to him to mention my name."[5]

Or again, the authoritative biography of that great psychiatrist of the Salpêtrière, Charcot, approvingly quotes the eulogy which says, among other things, that despite his many discoveries, Charcot "never thought for a moment to claim priority or reward." Alerted by our rule of thumb, we find some thirty pages later an account of Charcot insisting on his having been the first to recognize exophthalmic goiter and, a little later, emphatically affirming that he "would like to claim priority" for the idea of isolating patients who are suffering from hysteria.[6]

But perhaps the most apt case of such denial of an accessible reality is that of Ernest Jones, writing in his comprehensive biography that "although Freud was never interested in questions of priority, which he found merely boring"—surely this is a classic case of trivialization at work—"he was fond of exploring the source of what appeared to be original ideas, particularly his own."[7] This is an extraordinarily illuminating statement. For, of course, no one could have "known" better than Jones—"known" in the narrowly cognitive sense—how very often Freud turned to matters of priority: in his own work, in the work of his colleagues (both friends and enemies), and in the history of psychology altogether.

---

[4] In his magisterial biography, *Harvey Cushing* (Springfield: Charles C. Thomas, 1946), pp. 119-20, John F. Fulton describes Cushing's biographical sketch of Halsted, from which this excerpt is quoted, as "an excellent description."

[5] Ibid., p. 142.

[6] Georges Gullain, *J.-M. Charcot: His Life, His Work*, ed. and trans. Pearce Bailey (New York: Paul B. Hoeber, 1959), pp. 61, 95-96, 142-43.

[7] Ernest Jones, *Sigmund Freud: Life and Work*, 3 vols. (London: Hogarth Press, 1957), 3:105. Contrast David Riesman, who takes ample note of Freud's interest in priority, in *Individualism Reconsidered* (Glencoe: The Free Press, 1954), pp. 314-15, 378.

Blessing the Torrent:
On Wordsworth's Later Style
by Geoffrey H. Hartman

Ein Räthsel ist Reinentsprungenes
                                        Hölderlin
            The river is fateful,
    Like the last one. But there is no ferryman.
    He could not bend against its propelling force.
                                        Wallace Stevens
riverrun, past Eve and Adam's

                                        James Joyce

I

How art thou named? In search of what strange land,
From what huge height, descending? Can such force
Of waters issue from a British source,
Or hath not Pindus fed thee, where the band
Of Patriots scoop their freedom out, with hand
Desperate as thine? Or come the incessant shocks
From that young Stream, that smites the throbbing rocks,
Of Viamala? There I seem to stand,
As in life's morn; permitted to behold,
From the dread chasm, woods climbing above woods,
In pomp that fades not; everlasting snows;
And skies that ne'er relinquish their repose;
Such power possess the family of floods
Over the minds of Poets, young or old!

If the two opening lines of this sonnet had been an untitled fragment,
their referent would be uncertain. Whom is the poet talking to, what "thou" is
addressed? Is the force natural or divine? And why should the act of naming
be important?

But the lines are part of a sonnet titled specifically "To the Torrent at the
Devil's Bridge, North Wales, 1824."[1] Moreover, as line 2 runs into line 3, the
"force" is identified as a "force of waters," that is, a river or, more precisely,
a waterfall. ("Force" was dialect in the North of England for "waterfall.")
Describing the impact of a different sight, though it also involves naming or
labeling, Wordsworth writes: "My mind turned round / As with the might of

---

[1] *The Poetical Works of William Wordsworth*, ed. E. de Selincourt and Helen Darbishire (Oxford:
Clarendon, 1946), III, 43. The "1824" in the title is not found till 1836.
[2] See 1850 *Prelude* VII.643-44, the encounter with the blind beggar in London.

waters."[2] In the present poem the verse line itself turns round and naturalizes the poet's wonderment. Uncertainty of reference gives way to a well-defined personal situation that is easily described, though less easily understood.

II

In September 1824 Wordsworth traveled through North Wales on one of the many sentimental journeys he was fond of taking. They were sentimental in the sense of covering old ground in order to reflect on the changes time had wrought in him or the scene; and "Tintern Abbey" was the earliest and most remarkable issue of such memorial visits. On this particular trip Wordsworth saw a friend of his youth, Robert Jones, who had shared with him two determining moments in his life: the ascent of Snowdon in 1791 and the tour of 1790 through revolutionary France and the Alps, with its complex seeding in his mind of experiences in the Simplon/Viamala region. Both journeys were now over thirty years old, and had already been described: the Snowdon climb in Book XIII of the unpublished *Prelude*, and the Continental tour in Book VI, as well as in *Descriptive Sketches* (1793). In 1820, moreover, Wordsworth retraced his journey through the Alps with his sister, Dorothy, and his wife, Mary, both of whom kept journals of the visit.

On a portion of this new trip to Wales the poet was accompanied by Robert Jones; and it was with him (as well as with Mary and Dora Wordsworth) that he viewed the waterfall described in the sonnet. No wonder, then, that as he stands at the torrent's edge, he feels he is back "in life's morn," and what he sees with the eyes of an aging man (he is fifty-four years old) is not a local river but "the young stream that smites the throbbing rocks, / Of Viamala," which had giddied him when his own mind was young and in turmoil.

We can normalize this sonnet then; and the fact that it is a sonnet, one of so many written during the poet's later career, tempts us to give it a nod of esteem and pass on. There is little on first reading to hold the attention. Formal features of a conventional sort abound: opening and closing apostrophes; a first half comprising a cascade of questions that receive their resolution or coda in the second half, which is introduced by an efficient turn in the eighth line; enjambments that reflect the passion or perplexity of the utterance; and the abbreviated effect of sublimity created by a broken series of descriptive phrases characterizing his memory of the Viamala region (LL. 10-12).

In line with this we can also normalize the initial "How art thou named?" as a rhetorical or animating movement that is a residue of sublime style and so risks bathos. The poet must have known the name; he is obtruding the question to express a momentary ecstacy or disorientation. Still, this trace of sublime diction makes us uneasy; and the discomfort spreads if we read the letter Wordsworth wrote to his noble painter friend, Sir George Beaumont. We learn that "It rained heavily in the night, and we saw the waterfalls in perfection. While Dora was attempting to make a sketch from the chasm in

the rain, I composed by her side the following address to the torrent."[3] There
is a calming or distancing effect in the phrase "waterfalls in perfection" that
reminds us of Wordsworth's own earlier critique of the picturesque artist's
superficial mastery of landscape; there is also the subdued paradox of making
"a sketch from the chasm" and "composing" an "address to the torrent."

Even if "compose" is used here without the overtone of "repose," two
further sonnets written during the visit to Wales stress that "expression of
repose" with which nature or time endows wild places.[4] And there is, I would
suggest, something faintly absurd about an "address to the torrent." How does
one address a *torrent*? To do so, one hears Alice or some Wonderland
Creature saying—to do so one must have its name and know where it lives.
And, indeed, Wordsworth is not asking for an actual name. His opening
question is in search of something existential rather than informational. If
Lucy lives among untrodden ways near the Springs of Dove, where do I live?
Where now, in 1824? Near what springs or feeding-sources? Like the torrent
itself, he seems uncertain of origin or direction, and the questioning mood of
the next lines confirms that.

Yet his opening cry is not "What art thou?" nor as in a moving poem of
Hölderlin's "Where art thou?" ("Wo bist Du? Trunken dämmert die Seele mir
...."). It is "How art thou named?" What force, then, lies in the naming of a
force? One of the other sonnets written in Wales describes a stream that
mingles with the Dee and flows along the "Vale of Meditation," or "Glyn
Myrvr"—a "sanctifying name," comments Wordsworth. As in his early
"Poems on the Naming of Places" (1800), he then invents a name in Welsh
for the place he wishes to single out. Yet the sonnet before us bestows no
name, even though "Devil's Bridge" and "Viamala" might have encouraged a
man called Wordsworth.

To "address the torrent" means, clearly enough, to domesticate the
sublime: to contain it in the form of picturesque sketch or reflective sonnet;
and the opening exclamation, at once perplexed and marveling, is expressive
of Wordsworth's problem. The sublime, moreover, is not a quality of place
alone but also of time: a bewildering memory seems to decompose the name
of the torrent or any that might be given. Though the sonnet as a form is a
domesticating device and though Wordsworth emulates Milton's "soul-
animating strains" when he first chooses the sonnet as a verse instrument, his
diction falters or condenses under the strain. But the significance of this
cannot be discussed without attending carefully to the strangeness of
Wordsworth's later verse, indeed to the verbal style of the sonnet in its
entirety, from title to final exclamation. The title already suggests the
problems of (1) naming and (2) localization. It anticipates the question of how
a "force" can be localized in place, time, or language.

---

[3] *The Letters of William and Dorothy Wordsworth: The Later Years*, ed. E. de Selincourt (Oxford:
Clarendon, 1939) I, 155.
[4] "Composed among the Ruins of a Castle in North Wales" and "To the Lady E. B. and the Hon. Miss P."
The Poetical Works of William Wordsworth, III, 42-43.

The Social Construction of Two Biologists' Proposals

by Greg Myers

Two anthropologists who studied the researchers at the Salk Institute describe the scientists and technicians there as "a strange tribe who spend the greatest part of their day coding, marking, altering, correcting, reading, and writing" (Latour & Woolgar, 1979). Literary critics describe some of the texts of the scientific tribe, but only those that seem literary; they approach this tribe as collectors of primitive art. Most rhetorical and linguistic studies of scientific writing focus on the individual and treat the process as another variant of a general writing process; it is as if an anthropologist treated every tribe's religious rituals as a debased form of Episcopalianism. Sociologists of science, on the other hand, give us ways of talking about the structure of the discipline as a whole, but they seldom discuss texts; it is as if an anthropologist ignored the artifacts of the tribe as of little interest. I would like to read two scientific texts as products of a community of researchers, to see what they can tell us about composing as a process of social construction (Knorr-Cetina, 1981; Gilbert & Mulkay, 1984). My examples will be grant proposals, the most obviously rhetorical writing scientists do, and the writing that has the most immediate effects on the structure of the discipline.

Most academic scientific research in the United States is funded by the National Institutes of Health (NIH) and the National Science Foundation (NSF), through a procedure of peer review in which researchers' written proposals are evaluated by panels of researchers from the same general field. Nonscientists have often raised questions about the fairness of such a system. John B. Conlan, a former congressman from Arizona, has charged, "It is an incestuous buddy system that frequently stifles new ideas and scientific breakthroughs" (Cole, Rubin, & Cole, 1977), and Michael Kenward quotes an observer who says it is like a murder trial with "a jury of axe murderers from the same gang" (Kenward, 1984). There has been a great deal of study of the peer review procedures of these agencies, both by social scientists and by in-house committees (Cole et al., 1977; Cole and Cole, 1979; Cole, Cole, and Simon, 1981; Van den Beemt and Le Pair, 1983). Both the criticisms and the studies have focused on what happens in the funding after the proposals are

Reprinted from *Written Communication* 2 (1985): 219-45. Used by permission of Sage Publications, Inc.

submitted and have asked what role factors besides "quality of science" play
in the decision to fund or not to fund a project; they ask, for instance, if there
is an "old boy network," or if the panels tend to reject "high-risk" proposals
(NIH, 1983). But the funding process starts before the panel even sees the
proposal. I will argue that the writing of proposals, which takes up such a
large proportion of the active researcher's time, is part of the consensus-
building process essential to the development of scientific knowledge. To use
the metaphor that the critic Kenward quotes, it brings the axe-murderers into
the gang.

Most researchers would grant that proposal writing is a rhetorical activity
in which the writer seeks a strategy for persuading a reluctant audience. There
is a paradox here because the proposal format, with its standard questions
about background and goals and budget, and the scientific report style, with
its passives and impersonality, do not allow for most types of rhetorical
appeals; one must persuade without seeming to persuade. Yet almost every
sentence is charged with rhetorical significance. In classical rhetorical terms,
the forms of appeal in the proposal are ethical and pathetic as well as logical;
one shows that one is able to do the work, and that the work is potentially
interesting to one's audience of other researchers, as well as showing that one
is right. In textual terms, one describes the work so as to create a persona and
insert the work into the existing body of literature. One has a special problem
if one sees one's work as new or falling between two specialized fields; one
must either present a persona as an established member of one of the fields,
or redraw the fields around the work. In either case, one places the potentially
dissenting idea within a new context. The process of writing a proposal is
largely a process of presenting—or creating—in a text one's role in the
scientific community. Thus the texts of proposals may have something to tell
us about how science changes and defines itself, as well as about how it is
funded and how it is communicated.

Methods

I have collected all major drafts of proposals by two biologists working
on two controversial research programs. In one case, these were successive
proposals submitted to several agencies over the course of eighteen months;
in the other, they were drafts of one proposal written and rewritten over the
course of the ten months before its submission. In both cases, the authors had
comments of readers from which to revise, one using the peer-reviews of
previous attempts, the other getting comments from coworkers, so I collected
these comments and the writers' responses to the comments. The proposals
were part of a web of other writing, so I also collected drafts of articles on
the research proposed, and comments on them. Thus I worked with three
readings of the proposals: the writers', the readers', and my own.

For each proposal, I noted changes between drafts (first to second, second
to third, and so on), sometimes following handwritten changes on the drafts,
but usually comparing one printout to the next. I categorized changes by what

seemed to motivate them and noted especially those that seemed to indicate the writer's self presentation or relation to the research community. I also noted changes of the content of the proposals, but as we will see, there were few such changes. In addition to these revisions, they made many of the improvements in readability any good writer might make. The changes affecting persona or context in the community are largely specific to the field, and as a nonspecialist, I had to have some clue from the writers or commenters to interpret them. These categories are themselves matters of interpretation; my categorization of revisions represents one view of the text, which changed as I read on and as I tested my reading against other readings.[1] After assigning categories, I interviewed the writers about my interpretation of selected revisions, and also had them check, at various stages of my writing, the views in the essay as a whole.[2]

The Writers

The researchers I studied are, in some respects, representative of biologists at large research universities: They both supervise laboratories and have published many articles, and they both have received grants in the past and have reviewed grant applications themselves. But I chose to work with them partly because they were atypical: They were presenting work based on new models that put them between two well-established subspecialties of research. Judging by the response to articles presenting these models, their work is controversial. The fact that they assumed resistance to their proposals may have made them more self-conscious about their writing processes, and certainly made the rhetorical features of their proposals more apparent to a nonspecialist. In the proposals I am studying, they faced quite different rhetorical problems: One was taking his well-known and respected research in a new theoretical direction; the other was entering a new field in which he was unknown.

For David Crews, an Associate Professor of Zoology and Psychology at the University of Texas at Austin, the problem was getting continuing support for his large and productive laboratory during a period of very selective funding. Dr. Crews came to the University of Texas two years ago after receiving a Ph.D. at Rutgers, a post-doc at Berkeley, and teaching at Harvard.

---

[1] I noticed, for instance, that in my earlier notes, I tended to interpret almost all revisions as improving readability or accuracy, whereas later I tended to see more revisions as related to the author's self-presentation or relation to the community. This shift may reflect a real difference between earlier and later drafts, as I show in discussing the authors' changes in strategy. They may also reflect a change in my reading in the course of the study. I began as a technical writing teacher, especially aware of ease of reading and precision of statements. As I read more drafts, comments, and letters, and especially as I interviewed the writers, I became aware of the context in which these changes were made.

[2] Often the biologists gave a different interpretation of the change than mine. This shows not that they were right and I was wrong, but that the interpretation depends on the point of view, knowledge, and purpose of the reader, as well as the motivation of the writer. I should note that the biologists also pointed out a number of mechanical errors in the English teachers' writing.

He does lab and field studies of the reproductive physiology of reptiles, and is author or coauthor of about 15 papers a year. His lab, with two post-docs, several graduate students, and half a floor of a building, is now funded by grants from NSF (for one species), NIH/NICHHD (for two other species), and an NIMH Research Scientist Development Award (for him). I studied his proposal for a competitive renewal, after five years, of his current NIH grant.

Although Dr. Crews had a strong record as a researcher, he was concerned about the scarcity of research funds. His panel would not be the same one that awarded him the earlier grant, and his work would not be the same work. While he was writing his proposal (September 1982 to July 1983), he was also giving talks and he submitted an article on the theoretical model of the relation between hormones and behavior that guides his research (Myers, 1984). Thus he knew that the model was controversial, at least in some quarters. Reviewers of the article were either very enthusiastic or very critical, and he could not afford even one critical review of the proposal. He would either have to face or to sidestep this resistance. Also, the increased competition for federal funds (Mandel, 1983; NIH, 1983) meant he needed to prepare for close scrutiny according to the interests of NIH. He would have to show that his work on lizards had fairly direct application to problems of human reproduction. He would have to justify his field work on behavior, a type of work for which he thought NIH had little enthusiasm, and he would have to show that the large number of experiments he proposed all made a single coherent research project. Because heavily funded researchers are getting increased scrutiny, he would have to justify the funding of his lab by both NSF and NIH, clearly separating his work on one species from his work on the others.

Dr. Crews's proposal is necessarily a long one, with more than ninety pages of text and detailed lists of experiments and procedures. He took about four months, spending two nights a week, writing the first draft that he would circulate to his research group. He began with his earlier, successful proposal and reviewers' comments on it, the NIH guidelines, a list of topics he wanted to include, some boilerplate (the technical writer's term for material that can be reused on many proposals) on materials and methods, and several of his recent review articles. For the main part of his proposal, the prospectus of experiments, he drew on summaries each of his assistants had written, describing their current work and plans. A letter he had recently written in support of his career award contained arguments on the benefits of his work to humans; this proved helpful in drafting the section on "Significance." After about two dozen drafts (done using a text-processing program from his handwritten revisions), he gave a version to his research group. He included the guidelines and reviews of his earlier proposal, because he considered the proposal-writing process part of the education of the post-docs and graduate students working with him. He explained the competitive situation: "This has got to be an orgasmic experience for a reproductive biologist."

For David Bloch, a Professor of Botany, the main problem of the proposal was to demonstrate his competence in a specialty different from that for which he had been funded in the past. Dr. Bloch studied at Wisconsin and Columbia and taught at UCLA before coming to the University of Texas in 1961. Most of his published articles are on cell biology, most recently on flow cytometric studies. His lab is supported by an NIGMS grant and an NSF grant for these studies. But since 1981, he has also been working in a quite different field, identifying homologies in rRNA and tRNA for indications of the evolution of nucleic acids. As these studies developed, he applied to NSF (twice) and to NASA for support, not getting funded but apparently getting much closer. Now he is applying to the Public Health Service and reapplying to NSF.

To some reviewers, Dr. Bloch seemed to be a latecomer to the biology of nucleic acids, but his interest in them has a long history. As a graduate student, he, like so many other molecular biologists, was fascinated by Erwin Schrodinger's *What is Life?* A back injury thirty years later gave him time for reflection and reading in this area. He offered a graduate course in what he calls "The Evolution of Evolution," in which he and his students devised what seemed to them to be a plausible model for the origins of nucleic acids. He set out to test this model, using published data and a computer program written by one of his graduate students, and worked without outside funding except university grants for computer time and a semester off from teaching.

Dr. Bloch had in his favor a successful laboratory and an original idea on a topic of great theoretical interest. He also had a fresh familiarity with the literature, and a demonstrated expertise with, and access to, computers. All this impressed his more favorable reviewers. But he had not gone through a conventional apprenticeship in nucleic acid research; he was not known to the leaders in the field, and he was not oriented toward the structure and function studies that occupy most researchers in nucleic acid sequencing. The most critical of his early reviewers bluntly rejected his proposal as that of a newcomer to a field already full of people doing structure-function research. Until recently, his articles in this area could be listed only as "submitted" (Bloch, 1983). He had a clear enthusiasm for one model, which left him open to charges of a premature drawing of conclusions from insufficient data. Dr. Bloch was well aware of his rhetorical strengths and vulnerabilities from the responses he had gotten to his papers at conference, to the articles he had submitted for publication, and to his proposals to various agencies. Like Dr. Crews, he was acutely conscious of increased competition for research funds. Dr. Bloch's proposals have the same sections as Dr. Crews's, but because he does not have a long series of separate experiments to describe and justify, they are much shorter, following PHS page limits, with about ten pages of text. His collaborators in his group contribute comments and criticism, but he is entirely responsible for the writing. He has now been working on the project for more than two years, with countless drafts (on a text processor) of four articles, and five submitted proposals, in addition to applications to the university. Later versions of the proposal did not go through as many drafts, but sections within them changed as he accumulated more and more data in his sequence searches and as he responded to or adapted to criticism. The proposals did not grow larger. As we will see, the increasingly detailed discussions of data that he had gathered substitute for passages that described the model.

The Writer's Persona and
The Discipline's Literature

The instructions for writing the body of the proposal included with the NIH application emphasize the panel's concern with ethos and pathos—the character of the writer as researcher, and the interest of his or her work to other researchers:

> Organize sections A-D of the research plan to answer the following questions. (A) What do you intend to do? (B) Why is the work important? (C) What has already been done? (D) How are you going to do the work? (NIH, 1984)

Dr. Crews and Dr. Bloch are mainly concerned with questions (C) and (B), defining their persona and their relation to the literature. Both these criteria involve contradictions. The form of scientific reports, the syntax of scientific prose, and the persona of the scientific researcher all work against self-assertion. The definition of scientific importance requires both that the work be original and that it be closely related to the concerns and methods of current research. We will see these contradictions presented and resolved in the course of the authors' revisions.

The number of revisions each writer made is remarkable considering that the first draft I studied, in each case, was itself the result of many drafts. The number of drafts means little when the writers are using word processors, but in the five versions of Dr. Crews's proposal and the four of Dr. Bloch's that I studied, there averaged five to ten large or small changes on each page of each draft, and hardly a sentence remained unchanged over the course of revision. Many of the changes would have been suggested by any editor. Both writers had served on grant panels and had learned from the experience of reading piles of proposals that, in Dr. Bloch's words, they have to "get the idea across efficiently," and in Dr. Crews' words, "they have to be made exciting." For instance, Dr. Crews wants his sentences to "flow" (see Cooper and Odell, 1976), so he deletes such unnecessary words as "causal agents" in the phrase, "Disorders of human sexuality are causal agents responsible for . . ." Both authors cut jargon wherever they recognize it, so Dr. Crews changes "low temperature dormancy" to "hibernation." A reader criticizes his use of the term "therapy," which implies he is doing the lizard a favor with these injections of hormones; Dr. Crews substitutes the more neutral term "treatment." Both authors are cautious with neologisms, so Dr. Bloch, having apparently coined the term "forward complementarity," changes it to "reverse complementarity" when a reviewer is confused. Both authors correct, with the help of their readers, dangling participles, faulty parallelism, and the like, though they do not identify these errors by these names.

Another category of revision we might expect to see, besides revisions affecting persona, relation to the discipline, and readability, is that of substantive changes in the research proposed. But neither of these authors significantly alters his plan of work to counter possible criticism. Other NIH applicants do add to, delete from, or modify their methods sections, especially if they have gotten detailed criticisms on their pink sheets (the summaries of the study section's evaluation of the proposal, sent out after the decision). That Dr. Bloch and Dr. Crews do not may indicate their relations to the specialties of the study section members, relations in which they are quite different from each other. Dr. Bloch's research is so unusual and so isolated from the mainstream that he gets little detailed criticism. Reviewers suggest some statistical tests he uses, but their own work in microbial genetics seems to give them little to help Dr. Bloch with his broad evolutionary questions. Dr. Crews, on the other hand, has been working for five years on the project for which he is requesting continuing funding, and has fifty or so pages of detailed descriptions of experimental work in progress; his specific methods have already proven themselves to the study group members, and if questions are raised, they are likely to be questions of logistics and management rather than experimental design.

The important studies of funding decisions by Cole, Cole, and Rubin take as given the applicant's status in the research community, as determined by institution, publications, citations, and previous funding. Additionally, the writer cannot do much in writing a proposal to change these facts, the most powerful arguments for his or her competence. But the tone of almost every sentence of a proposal can be revised to show that one is cautiously but competently scientific. Often, because of the contradictions of self-assertion in scientific prose, the most effective means of self-presentation is understatement, toning down—not one's claims for one's research, but one's language. When Dr. Crews questions the received idea that "courtship behavior . . . is dependent on androgens," he rephrases it as "courtship behavior . . . might depend on androgens." He must be particularly careful about claims of priority. He changes "the implications of this observation have been unappreciated" to "have not been fully appreciated." Asked about this change, he says that the assertion of "total originality" is "sure death" with the review committee. One of the ways he defines his place in the community is by his choice of research animal, so he must be extremely cautious, even in apparently innocent comments on lizards (see Crews, 1975). He changes the phrase "More is known about the green anole lizard than about any other reptile," which could only tempt fans of other species to object, to "A great deal is known . . ." He must be especially cautious in using the findings of other fields outside his area of research, for instance, those of clinical research on humans. He adds the cautious note to the statement that "sexual experience appears to be the most important factor" in human sexual function, because he thinks a more definite statement, though supported by his reading, "could have gotten nailed."

Dr. Bloch also strengthens his argument by backing off from his claims in ways that are more interesting rhetorically than scientifically. One ratio is followed, in the first version, by "We proposed that." The ratio was questioned by some reviewers of the article; the explanation of it in a later version begins, "One interpretation would be that." One of his bolder objectives in the first proposal was to "determine, if feasible, the rates of evolutionary divergence and . . . approximate time of synthesis." But this was criticized by a panel member as a "notoriously difficult" project. The later version says, more cautiously, that he would "use the reconstruction as a guide in studying the early evolution of the coding mechanism," and he refers to "the distant goal of reconstruction." In general, later versions present the interpretation suggested by his model as one hypothesis among several others.

The revisions do not, however, show that the meek shall inherit the grants. As both authors temper their claims, they also assert their authority in their specific areas of research, and point to their previous accomplishments. Often this change means just a shift from passive to active voice. Dr. Crews changes "mechanisms are revealed" to "I have been able to reveal," and "New light will be shed" to "I will shed new light." Similarly, Dr. Bloch adds paragraphs on data gathered "using a program written in this laboratory." He changes "the finding of increased numbers of homologies" to "our finding, in nearly half the searches." This change emphasizes the success of the project so far and emphasizes what his own lab, which has not been funded to do its own sequencing (the experimental determination of the order of bases on the nucleic acid), has contributed. As part of this self-assertion, the writers sometimes go out on a limb. Dr. Crews adds the loaded phrase "I predict that" before a claim, showing that his hypothesis is, in Karl Popper's term, falsifiable. Apparently this risky language is expected at certain points; Dr. Bloch's proposals are full of such explicit predictions, and are praised for being "testable."

Perhaps the most powerful component of self-presentation is the tone of the proposal. Tone is not easily traced in textual terms, but clearly both authors are concerned with sounding scientific as well as being scientific. For example, Dr. Crews explains a change from "highlighted" to "shed new light on," which was mystifying to me, by saying that the first expression was "too catchy—sounds unscientific." Dr. Bloch makes a change in tone when he refers to the object of his search as "an early precursor to both molecules," tRNA and rRNA, rather than as a "primordial molecule," which suggests more strongly his concern with the origin of things. Interestingly, they both allow themselves to vary their subdued tone when revising sections on the implications of their research. Dr. Bloch ends his latest proposal with a paragraph on broadly suggested "spinoffs." Dr. Crews adds to his introduction a paragraph of data on the effects of the stress of concentration camp life on women's menstruation cycles, data he had used in an earlier letter showing the relevance of work on environment and sex hormones to humans. As he explains it, this addition, with its social and emotional weight, was made to support his technical argument. "I wasn't going to use it," he says, "because everybody uses it, but when I reread it, I saw that it was making a valid point about *extreme* stress."

The first major section of the application for an NIH grant must show the significance of the research proposed. But significance only has meaning in relation to the existing body of literature of the field. Thus there is a tension in defining one's claim as in defining one's persona; it must be original to be funded, but must follow earlier work to be science. These writers find their place in the community by making their texts fit in in two ways—with their citations and with their terminology.

In both writers we see a rhetoric of citations, though they use these citations in different ways. Dr. Bloch usually demonstrates his familiarity with the latest work in the field; Dr. Crews highlights his own contributions. Dr. Bloch does cite his own articles, at whatever stage of review they have reached as he writes, and he attaches a manuscript as an appendix. As he accumulates data, he is able to refer more often to his own studies. He does not usually cite authors to refute them, but rather to show that he is aware of parallels and contributors of data to his own work. Nor does he cite articles to establish a theoretical base, an authority for his own approach; the only major cited contribution to his method is a program and a data-base from Los Alamos. Many citations are tactical. The most hostile referee of an early version of the article compared Bloch's model to that of Eigen, and the editor of the journal that accepted it compared the model to that of Fitch. So Eigen and Fitch are both cited in a later version of the proposal in a way that shows the difference between their approaches and Dr. Bloch's. This strategy seems to have paid off; one panel's summary of an intermediate version of the proposal says, "The authors have considered alternative explanations and designed their analyses accordingly."

When Dr. Crews adds citations to those in his early draft, they are usually to his own work. For instance, he expands his assertion that estrogen "plays a critical role in yolk deposition" into a two-stage description of the depletion and production of vitellogenin, bringing in more references to his successful line of previous work. This sort of change is not done just to display his productivity; that is obvious enough from the section required by the proposal format using five pages to list four years of publications related to the grant by his group. He is known mainly for his laboratory and field work, and he cites this work to support certain theoretical views, he says, "to make a point, to associate myself with these perspectives." There are risks to this approach; a critical referee on one of his articles notes disapprovingly that most of the data supporting the theory are his own. But this may just show that the rhetoric of citations in a review article, which claims to speak for the entire research program or subspecialty, must be more circumspect than that of a proposal, which is expected to give some coherence to one's own previous work. Dr. Crews's problem as an established researcher is, then, the opposite of Dr. Bloch's as a new researcher; he must interpret his empirical work to associate himself with a new theoretical line, whereas Dr. Bloch must present his untried theoretical approach as potentially productive of new data. One cites himself, one cites others, but both are trying to insert new work into an existing literature.

The addition or deletion of terms with meanings or connotations specific to a discipline may be another, more subtle way of indicating one's place in the community. I have noted that they cut jargon wherever they recognize it, but they also add or change some loaded terms. A reviewer of Dr. Bloch's earliest proposal says, "Most laboratories that *do research* with either tRNA or rRNA are already analyzing not only homologies but *real* structure-function correlates" (emphasis in the original). The implication is that Dr. Bloch's researches are not research (perhaps because he is using published data), that his correlates for molecular structures are not real (because they are selected to study evolution, not to study the biological functions), and that, as the reviewer continues, "the homology results are an offshoot of the main business." After this, if not because of this, Dr. Bloch is careful to relate his homology work to the "main business" of sequencing research. He is also careful to account for the possibility of convergent evolution (which would fit better with this "main business"), and to use prominently the word "function" even though origin, not function, is his main concern.

In the latest version of the proposal, Dr. Bloch makes another significant change in terms; for almost every occurrence of the word, "homologies"—the central term of his project—he substitutes, "matching sequences" or some equivalent. He had stumbled onto the problem, common in interdisciplinary work, of a term that has a more restricted meaning in one field than in another. In molecular biology, as the reviewer's usage quoted in the previous paragraph shows, the word indicates any structural similarity. In evolutionary biology, the word can indicate only those structural similarities that result from common origins. If Dr. Bloch used the word in this sense while trying to prove common origins, he would be begging the question. The editor of the journal that published the article pointed out the ambiguity, and Dr. Bloch changed his terminology willingly, in the article and in later proposals, glad to restore some precision of meaning to the word. But precision is not all that is at issue here; the change is part of the consensus-making process of proposal writing. The editor says, in asking for the change in usage, "Molecular biologists must also be biologists, too." To use the word in this more restricted sense is to acknowledge, or to assert, that one belongs to both the specialty of molecular biology and the broader discipline.

Dr. Crews's many changes in diction suggest how meanings may vary between members and nonmembers of a discipline. Thus minor revisions improving precision can be seen as part of the adaptation of the writer's style to the literature of the discipline. One zoologist finds his use of "cycles" rather than "phases" jarring in a certain context, and she draws a distinction between them; Dr. Crews responds by changing his terminology throughout. She also points out the vagueness, to an ethologist who must observe these activities, of the phrases "behaviorally inactive" and "sexual behavior." Dr. Crews substitutes phrases that have more specific meanings to an ethologist: "non-courting" and "courtship and copulatory behavior." One of his changes shows, like Dr. Bloch's deletion of "homology," the lines between disciplines or approaches. I had interpreted his substitution of reproductive "processes" for reproductive "behavior" as an attempt to describe his comprehensive approach more accurately by using a more general term. In fact, he says, the change is tactical. He believes that studies of behavior, especially field studies, are not being funded by NIH, whereas studies of physiology (which are what the words "reproductive processes" imply in this instance) are more attractive to them. What seems a minor revision relates to the changing fortunes of that notoriously loaded word "behavior" through the 1970s, and indicates the researcher's keen sense of the connotation of the word in various disciplines.

Changing Strategies of Presentation

We have seen that many of these writers' revisions affect their personae as researchers and relate their work to the literature and the discipline. If we look at successive versions of one short but crucial part of the proposal—Dr. Bloch's "Abstract" and Dr. Crews's "Specific Aims"—we can see how in the processes of writing and rewriting the writers respond to and develop consensus in the field. These carefully composed sections are the writers' chance to present the main purposes of their research programs without burying them in detailed methods and data; some reviewers may not read the rest as carefully, especially if the proposal is as long as Dr. Crews's. We will see that, late in the revision process, Dr. Bloch and Dr. Crews come to opposite strategies of self-presentation. Dr. Bloch tries to play down the more "speculative" theoretical aspects of his program and emphasize the data he has collected so far, whereas Dr. Crews decides at last to emphasize the larger and more controversial implications of his study. Each shows, in his last version, a closer fit between his work as he presents it and his discipline as he presents it. Both strategies shown in these processes of revision are attempts to deal with increased competition for health-related research funds by relating the proposed work to the consensus in the field.

We have seen that Dr. Bloch is criticized by reviewers for being too committed to his model, for being too speculative, and for wandering from the "main business" of structure-function studies. In the three versions of his abstract (see Appendix), we note that the model is first played down and then finally removed, that the accumulation of data is emphasized more than the larger implications, and that alternative explanations for the matches, including function, are given more consideration. The revision of the opening sentence reflects this change in strategy. In the first version he says, "A search is being conducted for sequence homologies"; the subject of the sentence is the author's action, and the tone, as in the last sentence ("An attempt is being made"), sounds merely hopeful. The opening of the second version is at once more impersonal and more confident; there he presents data from the research so far as posing a striking problem requiring solution: "Ribosomal RNA is peppered with tracts that are homologous with regions found among different transfer RNAs." The lively verb "peppered" suggests that these data are too insistent to be overlooked, and the reference to "different transfer RNAs" suggests a broad scope of data. In the third version, this lively but still vague statement is replaced by a statement suggesting comprehensive and quantifiable findings from many species: "A large minority of tRNAs from all species of organisms studied have stretches whose base sequences are identical or nearly so to stretches found in rRNAs."

Dr. Bloch's accommodation of the discipline and his presentation of his work in terms of its consensus is apparent also in his revisions of organization and sentence structure. In the first abstract, the model occupies the central and longest paragraph. He immediately states that he is looking for evidence of common origins, not just explaining homologies; here he tips his hand and lets his critics see his larger program. The rest of the abstract is organized, logically enough, by the researcher's effort: theory, model, predictions. One methodological problem is evident in the gap between sentences 7 and 8; his data are, of course, on existing rRNA and tRNA, but he applies them to what he calls primordial RNA. That his data and hypothesis remain in separate sentences suggests that he has not yet found the syntax to make the connection. This gap will prove to be important to reviewers.

The second version gives a longer discussion of the homologies (sentences 4-7) before presenting the model he uses to explain them; the focus is on the matches rather than on the researcher and the theory until "our work" in sentence 6. Now he mentions function as a possible alternative explanation for the homologies, and offers a test for convergence to determine its role. Still, he can only say at this point that this complicating factor "cannot yet be ruled out." The description of the model and prediction is tightened (sentence 10), giving it fewer words and less emphasis. The gap in the first version between present-day data and primordial hypothesis is not bridged but eliminated; here it is clear that the model only predicts homologies in present-day tRNA and rRNA, and needs no inferential leap into the past.

In the third version, the model is not mentioned explicitly at all, though it is still implied in his analysis of the homologies. This version is organized by the sequence of ideas rather than by the narrative of the researcher's efforts; it offers a sort of theoretical flowchart. Dr. Bloch says, more cautiously than before, that the homologies might be due either to function or to common origins. If function is the explanation, it might be either on the DNA or on the RNA level, and if origin is the explanation, it might be the result of either primordial or relatively recent conditions. Now the assertion of the ancient origin of these homologies is in the passive, and is after the data so that the data, not Dr. Bloch, suggest it. The potentially troublesome statement that he is searching for ancestral RNA starts with a long noun phrase that may defuse some resistance and uses cautious verbs: The overlapping and overlays "suggest" that further identification "should permit" reconstruction. Finally, whereas the first two versions end with this prediction, the third version ends by emphasizing "the correct functions of the transcription-translation mechanism." That is, he emphasizes the possible health applications, which were not mentioned in the earlier NSF versions.

Dr. Crews has also been criticized for favoring a "speculative" model that is inconsistent with much of current research, but in the revisions of his "Specific Aims" section, we see a strategy different from that of Dr. Bloch, a movement toward emphasizing his controversial model. This change was made in a very late draft after many other changes, most of them to improve readability, had led to a draft he labeled "final final final draft." In this draft, he still cautiously plays down the model that proposes dissociated as well as associated reproductive tactics. A two-sentence introduction to his general field and specific interest is followed by a two-paragraph comparison of the green anole lizard to the red-sided garter snake. The model is subordinated to the unexceptionable comparison of two species that happen to exhibit these tactics. His own methods of investigation are not stressed. The third paragraph says that the difference in reproductive tactics has implications, but leaves those implications for the next section, where they are less prominent.

In the later version, Dr. Crews highlights his more controversial approaches. The safe statement, "I will continue my study of two reptile species," is replaced with a sentence beginning, "The general objectives of my research are," that introduces immediately the ecological views disputed by some reviewers. Further sentences in the first paragraph emphasize his distinctiveness as a researcher, as shown by his comparative approach and his combination of laboratory and field experiments. The second paragraph, which had been organized around the comparison of two species, is now organized around two reproductive tactics, further emphasizing his theoretical framework. He highlights the definitions of the terms he has coined by putting them in separate sentences (returning to the phrasing of a much earlier draft, written before he had started downplaying the newness of his work). No specific species are mentioned yet; the lizard and the snake are introduced only in the last paragraph, as "one representative species of each reproductive tactic." His "goal is to compare the two tactics," to look for broad knowledge of mechanisms rather than just specific knowledge on one or two species. He emphasizes the "broad approach" and the search for important generalizations. The concluding sentence of the earlier version had put direct, immediately applicable findings first, with fundamental concepts in the second part of the sentence; here it is the direct findings that come after the "also," in the position of secondary importance to the fundamental concepts.

Though the two researchers follow different tactics, they both try to relate the proposed work to the consensus in the field. Dr. Bloch saw that his proposals and articles were getting more favorable reviews as he gathered more data and discussed alternative explanations. Thus he presents himself as a new but well-informed and cautious member of the existing RNA sequencing program, and plays down wherever he can what he feels are the controversial aspects of his project. He need not insist on the newness of his thesis; its boldness will be apparent, to anyone likely to accept it, from the striking tendencies in the data collected so far. But he is not just persuading the panel and the discipline with these tactical changes; his reviewers are persuading him in some ways as well. Because he must discuss the alternatives to his model, he becomes more involved with structure-function relations if only to dismiss their influence here, so the context of his research is changed by the process of applying for funding.

Dr. Crews's last-minute revisions may seem to indicate a strategy of defiance of the consensus of his subspecialty, just as the previous version seems to indicate a tactical appeal through the less controversial elements of his research. But these changes may also be seen as part of a consensus-making process, one that goes beyond the boundaries of the subspecialties of herpetology and classical neuroendocrinology to include an audience of comparative biologists and evolutionary theorists. To put this strategy in more practical terms, he may have reasoned that if only about 5% of the proposals to this panel were to be funded, no amount of interesting new data on anole lizards and red-sided garter snakes would be considered worth funding if it just supported existing models based on other species. If he stuck to the consensus, he might not be criticized, and might even get favorable comments from the reviewers, but he would not generate enough enthusiasm to get him across what the reviewers call "the payline," the priority score cutoff for funding. He would have to present a bold idea and present himself as a researcher capable of a uniquely broad and ambitious project. He knew, after a few hostile reviews of his related article, that in taking this approach he risked a rejection if the panel was persuaded by one of his critics. But that risk was apparently preferable to cautious dullness.

My study ends with these submitted versions of the proposals, because I am interested in how the researchers write the proposal, not in how the decision to fund is actually made. But the decisions, in this case, support the researchers' senses of appropriate strategy. The "pink sheet" summarizing the decision on Dr. Bloch's application shows that the study section members were intrigued by the homologies he pointed out, but were suspicious of his advocacy of a model attributing these homologies to a common ancestor. The summary says he needs to consider critically the other possibilities, especially convergence due to function. Thus he has not convinced them that his work gives sufficient attention to the work being done on structure-function relations. The major criticism of the proposal, though, is that it lacks a sufficiently detailed theoretical framework, specifically a lack of explanation for how he will relate the present-day homologies to the ancestor molecule, how he will cross that gap noted in the structure of the first summary. This too can be interpreted as an indication that Dr. Bloch still stands outside the consensus of the subspecialty; he is being told that he has not demonstrated a theory that both takes into account current concepts and also allows him to go beyond the current line of work. Although Dr. Bloch's proposal was not successful, the strategy of downplaying the model and emphasizing his awareness of structure-function studies seems to have been the only strategy that would have had a chance. Dr. Bloch's comment was that he would have to "talk to them through more publications"; that is, he would have to establish himself as a known contributor to the field before applying again.

Before Dr. Crews's decision was reached, the study section scheduled a site visit at his lab to observe its work. Such a visit illustrates the consensus-forming function of the proposal process. Site visits can be scheduled by the executive secretary of the section (the NIH administrator) to resolve differences or doubts on the panel; they are usually made in cases of applications that are close to being funded. In some cases, the fact of the site visit would indicate a seriously split panel trying to reach some sort of agreement. But Dr. Crews's interpretation is that the administrator thought that some members of the panel were just unenthusiastic about the proposal, so it might not get the good priority score necessary for funding by NIH under current budget conditions. If this is the case, his strategy of emphasizing the broad implications of his work was probably wise because the panel's conception of him as an ambitious researcher turns out to be more important than their awareness of his controversial relation to his research community.

The site visit was, in a way, a second proposal, this time presented orally, with the lab itself as the most persuasive illustration. Dr. Crews prepared by going over his proposal carefully with a number of colleagues, and he planned to temper somewhat the tone of the submitted version of the proposal. He knew that one of the visitors would be a well-known researcher on mammals who would be a critic of his theory He said that he did not want them to think he was claiming to have the last word on the relations between hormones and sexuality. As it turned out, he spent most of his presentation demonstrating that his lab was capable of such a large project. He showed a detailed notebook of experimental prospectuses drawn up by his assistants to demonstrate his careful quality control. He emphasized the lab's publications over the last five years to demonstrate its capacity to handle so many projects. There was no arguing over controversial theories; he wasn't even sure afterward which of the visitors had been his critic. In the visit, as in the written proposal, persona and relation to the literature and the discipline are crucial. Dr. Crews consults with colleagues, adjusts his tone, prepares still more textual evidence to present himself as a competent researcher and as an accepted contributor to the literature, all to enable this group to come to an agreement within itself. If his proposal had been rejected due to opposition by one powerful reviewer, this view of proposal writing as a consensus-making process would be meaningless. Instead we see still more mechanisms to allow the researcher to shape his or her persona and to make the decision representative of the subspecialty as a group.

The Uses and Limits of Rhetoric

I have argued that the proposal-writing process shapes both the writers and, to a lesser degree, the discipline. The writers, who are doing work they see as being on the boundary of two fields, move toward a presentation of themselves as good members of those fields, and present their work in terms of its interest to other researchers who might tend to reject it. There is a tension in both lines of argument. As we have seen, self-presentation requires a difficult balance—not too meek, not too assertive—that cannot always be arrived at by studying some generalized portrait of the good scientist. The image seems to depend partly on the type of research proposed. Both these researchers decide to present themselves in ways we might not expect. The researcher who wants to verify his model of the origin of life presents himself as the skeptical servant of the mountains of data printed out by his computer program. The researcher who wants to spend five more years in painstaking studies of thousands of snakes and lizards presents himself as a theoretician studying a new conceptual framework. There is a similar tension in their attempts to present their work as interesting, for they must show their work is original and yet show that it is entirely in accordance with the existing discipline. So they use citations, or significant vocabulary, or on occasion directly claim they can make a contribution. But here too they are limited; for instance, words like *new, fundamental* and *important* are all but forbidden, and even *interesting* seems to provoke some readers. Claims of originality are risky, and criticisms of opposing views can seldom be explicit. Both authors have written letters defending their work against the criticisms of hostile reviewers; comparing these to their proposals, one sees how careful they have been with tone. When decorum is no longer demanded by the proposal format and the evaluating audience, they are unabashedly enthusiastic about their projects. They have not lost the sense they had at the beginning that they are in hot pursuit of the secrets of life, though in their proposals they conceal their excitement.

But I have argued that the contexts of their projects are changed by the process, even if their enthusiasm is not. Dr. Bloch, as I have pointed out, reorients his studies to provide mathematical analyses of the possibility of function accounting for the homologies he observes. His research is no longer just a proof for his ideas on the origin of life; it is now also a fairly elaborate method for comparing structures of molecules. Dr. Crews makes no such methodological changes, but he has to think, whenever he writes a proposal, about what his work can contribute to fairly distant lines of research on other species and about how his theoretical models relate to those used by most researchers. Finding conventional terms for unconventional research is not just an exercise in rhetoric—it changes the research.

Of course the success or failure of the proposal also changes the research. But funding does not always determine if a research program continues. Dr. Bloch continues to write articles about tRNA-rRNA homologies, but he is following a line of work that requires less money. He has no funding for laboratory work of his own in this area, so he continues to analyze the published data for significant patterns. He did not get a post-doc with whom to develop the theory, but he found a collaborator in, of all areas, statistical mechanics, who is interested in developing the mathematical description of these homologies. A number of researchers have responded this way to cutbacks, moving into less expensive lines of research, but not abandoning the research program altogether. If Dr. Crews were not funded, it would mean cutbacks in the lab, but he has other grants for other projects to work on.

The proposal process also changes the field in a more fundamental way, by challenging the terms in which the subspecialty defines itself (Callon, 1980). Both these researchers see themselves as working at the edge of a specialty or on the border between two subspecialties; Dr. Bloch talks about "the establishment" in molecular biology, and Dr. Crews refers to the "prevailing paradigm." When the study section gives a proposal like one of these a priority number below the payline, they draw the line that marks the edge of their specialized field. When it approves such research, it redefines that line. To a large degree, both researchers accept the assumptions and criteria by which this decision is made; they disagree with the panel only about how these criteria apply to their own work. Because they are part of the system, we should ask not whether the system is "fair" to individuals, but how it serves the scientific discipline.

Representative Conlan, whom I quoted earlier, is not alone in asking whether the peer review process "stifles new ideas." A favorable reviewer of one of Dr. Bloch's proposals concludes, "Provocative ideas are always in short supply, and there is truth to the criticism that the present funding system often fails to nourish them." But the funding system exists to select as well as to nourish, and here the powerful consensus that Representative Conlan calls "incestuous" may serve to stabilize the economy of the discipline. For example, to approve either Dr. Bloch's proposal or Dr. Crews's would be to define large new research programs, beyond what these individuals propose, to study the origin of primitive RNA through homologies in present-day tRNAs and rRNAs, or to look for relations between hormonal cycles, mating behavior, and ecological factors in a wide variety of species. Such redefinitions of a field require changes in careers and institutions, and are enormously costly in time and money. In some cases, such as the line of neuroendocrinology Latour and Woolgar have studied, such costs may prove to be worthwhile. In this case, some reviewers might argue that there is too much left to be done on conventional structure-function studies, or on hormonal studies based on the simpler paradigm, for attention to be diverted to other lines of work, even if these other lines of work turn out to be important someday. If husbanding of resources for a consistent line of work is a function of funding decisions, it is not surprising that the proposals focus on who the writers are, whether they can do what they say, and whether, if they do it, they will have much effect on other researchers.

If the rhetoric of the proposal is not given by some ideal list of persuasive or communicative techniques, or by an ideal scientific persona, or by the characteristics of the project itself, but instead depends on a complex process involving both the researcher and the discipline, then it will vary with each discipline and with the writer's relation to the discipline. Thus the cautious tone adopted by Dr. Bloch, appropriate for his situation as a newcomer, would be disastrous for Dr. Crews, who is well established in his specialized field. They learn the rhetoric of their discipline in their training as graduate students and post-docs, but they relearn it every time they get the referees' reports on an article or the pink sheets on a proposal. Dr. Bloch learns where his data receive a good response; Dr. Crews finds how his assertions affect a researcher who works on mammals. Finally, they come to assume most of this knowledge of the discipline as something natural. But we need to make it explicit and conscious to open it to people outside the discipline.

To do this, I think we could borrow from Dr. Crews's work, observing the behavior of reptiles. He noted in the margin of my "Methods" section, "You're an ethologist." Like ethologists, we should not only observe and categorize the behavior of individuals, we should also consider the evolution of this behavior in its ecological context, and comparisons to behavior of other species in other environments. I agree with Dr. Crews that atypical subjects may provide the best means of reexamining received ideas about behavior, but I do not think we are ready yet for what Dr. Crews sees as "A Natural History of Grant Writing." This is not just because scientists are more complicated than lizards or garter snakes, or because they will not stay in glass cages until we can perform an assay, but because our language, institutions, and authority are intertwined with theirs. When Dr. Crews saw how I interpreted my data, he decided I was more of a "seat-of-the-pants ethologist." That, I think, is all one can be in the study of scientific writing now.

Appendix: Texts of Summaries

Dr. Bloch's Abstract

Version 1

(1) A search is being conducted for sequence homologies and for homologies of the reverse complementary sequences among tRNAs and rRNAs. (2) The results of these searches are being compiled in order to compare the distributions of the sequences among different regions of the molecules.
(3) The purpose is to search for evidence of common origins of these classes of RNA.
(4) A model is proposed for the evolutionary origin of the protein synthetic mechanism that predicts a common origin of the different classes of RNA. (5) The model is based on a synthesis of a multifunctional RNA through a series of alternating syntheses: elongation through looping back, replication via templating, then repetition of the this cycle [sic], starting with a primordial tRNA with a simple anticodon region. (6) The result would be a molecule with extensive internal complementarity, doted with codons and anticodons, capable of assuming configurations that would permit it to serve as message and structural RNA, and alternatively as gene.
(7) The model predicts extensive homologies between the primordial tRNA and rRNAs. (8) Homologous sequences in present day tRNAs and rRNAs are being found.
(9) An attempt is being made to sort out the relative importance of function

and common descent as explanations for the homologies, by studies of the commonality of the homologies and their placements within and among the RNAs of the different classes.

Version 2

(1) Ribosomal RNA is peppered with tracts that are homologous with regions found among the different transfer RNAs. (2) The matches are too frequent and extensive to be attributed to coincidence. (3) Their distributions and patterns suggest a common evolutionary origin for the two classes of molecules. (4) Function as an explanation for their existence appears unlikely but cannot be ruled out. (5) Different domains have been conserved in different classes of organisms. (6) Our work will continue to identify examples of these homologies by searching for them among a variety of organisms. (7) The search was prompted by a model for the origin of a primitive multifunctional RNA molecule. (8) In the model, a short RNA with a codon or anticodon near the 3' end undergoes successive rounds of elongation by self-priming (looping back) and self-templating, giving rise to an RNA in which codons are held in contiguous configurations by secondary folding. (9) The subsequent split of message, transfer, and ribosome functions is thought to follow acquisition of the cellular habit. (10) The model suggested the existence of homologies among present day t- and r-RNAs and this prediction is being realized. (11) The interpretation of the homologies is of importance. (12) A multidimentional test for evolutionary convergence has been designed and is being used to determine whether the homologies do indeed reflect common origin rather than function. (13) Filling out the rRNA map, through continued accumulation of homologies, should permit the reconstruction of a primordial RNA molecule.

Version 3

(1) A large minority of tRNAs from all species of organisms studied have stretches whose base sequences are identical or nearly so to stretches found in rRNAs. (2) They are too frequent and too extensive to be attributed to coincidence. (3) Factors contributing to these matches might be shared functions at the RNA or DNA levels, or common origins. (4) The latter might be of recent derivation through recombination and transfection, or relics of ancient origin. (5) The matching sequences are distributed without discernable pattern among the molecules and among species. (6) Their frequent appearance, often unique to interspecies comparisons, indicates that they need not result from selection for interaction in a common cellular environment. (7) They are also thought to be conserved vestiges of ancient origin. (8) The occurrence of overlapping sets of homologies within species, and confirming overlays among species (homologies found in independent searches in different organisms that occupy equivalent positions on the rRNAs, and assign similar base sequences) suggest that their continued identification should

permit the reconstruction of an RNA that is ancestral to both tRNAs and rRNAs. Such a "synthesis" should help to provide an understanding of the early evolution and current functions of the transcription-translation mechanisms.

Dr. Crews's "Specific Aims"

Version 1

I propose to work in the area of reproductive biology, concentrating on the regulation of reproduction by internal and external stimuli in seasonally breeding vertebrates. Specifically, I will continue my studies of two reptile species that differ markedly in their reproductive physiology.

The green anole lizard is similar to many laboratory and domesticated mammals and birds in that the peak gonadal activity (gamete maturation accompanied by a substantial increase in the circulating level of sex steroid hormones) is *associated* with mating. Species that exhibit such a reproductive tactic frequently have a functional association between sex hormones and sexual behavior. Previous research with the green anole lizard has shed new light on ecological and evolutionary adaptations of the neuroendocrine mechanisms controlling sexual behavior and reproductive physiology. In contrast, the red-sided garter snake, as well as many other vertebrates including some mammals, exhibits a *dissociated* reproductive tactic. In these species, production of gametes and maximal sex hormone secretion are temporally dissociated from mating behavior. In the garter snake, gametes are produced in late summer only after the breeding season is ended; the gametes are then stored until the next mating period. Thus, unlike those species with associated reproductive tactics, mating in the red-sided garter snake occurs when the gonads are completely regressed and circulating levels or sex hormones are low. This implies that the causal mechanisms of mating behavior, at least at the physiological level, must be fundamentally different in species with dissociated reproductive tactics. Recent studies of the red-sided garter snake indicate that this is the case.

The observation that gonadal and behavioral cycles can be dissociated is itself not new, but the implications of this observation have not been fully appreciated. I present here a systematic and comparative series of studies that will focus on specific questions involving the causal mechanisms and functional outcomes of sexual behavior in these two species. From this comparison will emerge a new perspective on the many species, life histories, and sex differences observed in vertebrates. In addition to contributing to our understanding of related areas of reproductive biology, including gamete storage and animal husbandry, this research will yield insight into fundamental reproductive processes.

Version 2

In general I am interested in the biopsychology of reproduction, or more precisely the regulation of reproduction by internal and external stimuli in seasonally breeding invertebrates. The general objectives of my research are to (i) investigate how the environment regulates reproduction, (ii) determine how reproductively relevant stimuli are perceived and integrated in the central nervous system, (iii) demonstrate how the information regulates internal reproductive state, and (iv) examine how changes in internal state influence the expression of behavior. To this end, I use a comparative approach that combines and integrates the physiological, morphological, organismal, and ecological levels of analysis. The emphasis on laboratory and field experiments reveals the causal mechanisms and functional outcomes of reproductive behavior on each level without obscuring the relations among the levels. Moreover, the laboratory and field studies are complementary. The field has proven to be a valuable testing ground for hypotheses; similarly, the laboratory is the only possible arena for determining the physiological bases of phenomena observed in the field.

The specific objective is to examine the causal mechanisms and functional outcomes of the two major annual reproductive tactics—associated and dissociated—exhibited by higher vertebrates. In many seasonally breeding vertebrates, gamete production and maximum secretion of sex steroid hormones precedes immediately or coincides with courtship and copulatory (mating) behavior. This annual pattern may be termed the *associated* reproductive tactic, or prenuptial gametogenesis (Figure 1). A markedly different annual pattern is exhibited in many vertebrates, including some mammals, in which the gametes are produced only after the breeding season has ended; the gametes are then stored until the next breeding period. In these species, mating occurs when the gonads are not producing gametes and blood levels of sex steroid hormones are basal. This pattern may be referred to as a *dissociated* reproductive tactic, or postnuptial gametogenesis (Figure 1).

I will focus on one representative species of each reproductive tactic. The green anole lizard is similar to many laboratory and domesticated mammals and birds in showing the associated tactic. In contrast, the red-sided garter snake shows the dissociated pattern. In many instances a direct comparison of these two species will be made, whereas in other instances gaps in our knowledge must be filled before conceptually valid comparisons can be made. Thus, some of the proposed experiments deal only with one species or tactic. Ultimately, however, my goal is to compare the two tactics at as many levels of organization as are feasible and reasonable. Such a broad approach is crucial if important generalities underlying vertebrate reproductive processes are ever to emerge. My proposed studies will contribute directly to our understanding of related areas of reproductive biology, including gamete storage and animal husbandry.

References

Bloch, D. (1983). tRNA-rRNA sequence homologies: Evidence for a common evolutionary origin? *Journal of Molecular Evolution, 19*, 420-428

Callon, M. (1980). Struggles and negotiations to define what is problematic and what is not: The sociologic of translation. In K. Knorr, R. Krohn, & R. Whitley, (Eds.), *The social process of scientific investigation. Sociology of the sciences* (Vol. IV, 197-219). Hingham, MA: Kluwer Academic.

Cole, J., & Cole, S. (1979). Which researcher will get the grant? *Nature, 279*, 575-576.

Cole, S., Cole, J., & Simon, G. (1981). Chance and consensus in peer review. *Science, 214*, 881-886.

Cole, S., Rubin, R., & Cole, J. (1977). Peer review and the support of science. *Scientific American, 237*(4), 34-41.

Cooper, C., & Odell, L. (1976). Considerations of sound in the composing processes of published writers. *Research in the Teaching of English, 10*, 103-115.

Crews, D. (1975). Psychobiology of reptilian reproduction. *Science, 189*, 1059.

Crews, D. (1984). Gamete production, sex hormone secretion, and mating behavior uncoupled. *Hormones and Behavior, 18*, 22-28.

Gilbert, N., & Mulkay, M. (1984). *Opening Pandora's box: A sociologic analysis of scientists' discourse.* Cambridge: Cambridge University Press.

Kenward, M. (1984, May 31). Peer review and the axe murderers. *New Scientist*, p. 13.

Knorr-Cetina, K. (1981). *The manufacture of knowledge: An essay on the constructivist and contextual nature of science.* Oxford: Pergamon.

Latour, B., & Woolgar, S. (1979). *Laboratory life: The social construction of scientific facts.* Beverly Hills, CA: Sage.

Mandel, H. (1983). Funding more NIH research grants. *Science, 221*, 338-340.

Myers, G. (1984). *The social construction of two biology articles.* Paper presented at the Conference on College Composition and Communication. New York, March.

National Institutes of Health (1983). *Proceedings of the 1983 meetings of NIH scientific review groups.* Washington, DC: Department of Health and Human Services.

National Institutes of Health (1984). *Application for public health service grant.* Washington, DC: Department of Health and Human Services.

Van den Beemt, F., & LePair, C. (1983). *Appraisal of peer review.* Paper presented at the meeting of the Society for Social Studies of Science, Blacksburg, VA. November.

Social Context and Socially Constructed Texts

The Initiation of a Graduate Student into a Writing Research Community

by Carol Berkenkotter, Thomas N. Huckin, and John Ackerman

In the last few years researchers using various empirical and hermeneutic techniques have studied the difficulties that young adult writers confront as they enter the university culture (North; McCarthy) and more specifically their major fields (Herrington; Faigley and Hansen). These studies suggest that students entering academic disciplines need a specialized literacy that consists of the ability to use discipline-specific rhetorical and linguistic conventions to serve their purposes as writers. Academic disciplines have been characterized as *discourse communities* (Bizzell "Cognition"; Herrington; Porter); however, these communities are not nearly as tangible as the *speech communities* that Shirley Brice Heath described in her study of the children of Trackton and Roadville. Academic or professional discourse communities are not necessarily located in specific physical settings, but rather their existence can be inferred from the discourse that members of a disciplinary subspecialty use to communicate with each other. In this sense, the discourse that one group of like-minded people use *defines* the community and is its product as well.

In this essay we follow a skilled adult writer, Nate, entering a research community (and by implication, a discourse community) by examining the introductions he wrote to research papers over the first year and a half of his tenure in a doctoral program. We view these introductions as evidence of the writer's socialization into this particular community, and suggest that they provide valuable information regarding the writer's ability to instantiate into text the "institutionalized norms" (Fahnestock and Secor) of his audience. Elsewhere we have discussed the story of this student's initiation into the rhetoric program at Carnegie Mellon University (1988). In this essay we foreground microlevel evidence of his socialization: his increasing mastery of

Reprinted from *Textual Dynamics of the Professions: Historical and Contemporary Studies of Writing in Professional Communities.* Ed. Charles Bazerman and James Paradis. Madison: U of Wisconsin P, 1991. 191-215. Used with permission.

the community's linguistic, rhetorical, and topical conventions, as seen in the introductions to three papers.

The data that we report on here are part of a study that was conducted at Carnegie Mellon during the 1984-85 academic year. One of the authors (CB) was a participant observer in the rhetoric program, attending classes with students, interviewing faculty and students, and collecting case study data from two first-year doctoral students. (One of these students dropped out of the study at the beginning of 1985.) This data, which consisted of Nate's written self reports chronicling his experiences in the program, weekly taped interviews, copies of papers the students wrote, as well as CB's field notes, were reduced and translated into a narrative of Nate's progress as a writer during his first year. This part of the data analysis was carried out by CB and JA. The remaining author (TH), using a series of linguistic measures, independently analyzed the papers Nate wrote between September 1984 and November 1985.[1]

Background of the Study

The theoretical and methodological assumptions on which the study was based are derived from sociolinguistics and from research in the sociology of science. Recent research on scientific publication views texts as socially mediated products and revision as a process of social negotiation (Bazerman, "The Writing"; Gilbert and Mulkay; Knorr-Cetina; Latour and Woolgar; Myers; Yearly). In different ways these studies demonstrate how researchers advance knowledge claims within the linguistic conventions of scientific discourse—conventions which codify audience expectations.

The ways in which linguistic behaviors are derived from community context has also been documented by another group of researchers studying the development of school literacy in young children (Dyson; Heath; Schultz, Florio, and Erickson). These studies suggest that the cognitive components of language acquisition are developed within and therefore are intimately connected to the language user's home (i.e., cultural community) environment. As language users travel from one community context to another—from home to public (or private) school, from high school to college, from college to graduate or professional training, from graduate school to the work force—they must master new ways of speaking, reading, and writing, ways that are appropriate within each community. The application of this knowledge constitutes what Dell Hymes has called "communicative competence."

Through a synthesis of the above research perspectives with the findings from our data, we developed four assumptions that inform the discussion of these findings:

---

[1] Our goal in analyzing Nate's enculturation and growth as a writer was to bring multiple perspectives and methodologies into play. Our analysis is based on close familiarity and participation in the CMU discourse community, on the relative detachment and objectivity afforded by the linguistic methods, and on the triangulation of our observations and interpretations. The assumptions and procedures of this eclectic methodology are elaborated in our 1988 article.

1. Members of a research community share a "model of knowing" (Miles and Huberman, 20). This model of knowing is embedded in the research methodology that incoming students in graduate programs learn and is encoded in the language that community members use.

2. A research community extends beyond a student's graduate school to include researchers at other institutions. The vanguard of these researchers constitutes an "invisible college" (Crane, 34-40, 49-56), wherein they share their work with one another through publications in professional journals and through papers delivered at professional meetings.

3. Papers and publications are among a research community's *communicative forums*; significant issues are raised, defined, and debated within these forums. In this sense, to publish and to be cited is to enter the community's discourse.

4. Graduate students are initiated into the research community through the reading and writing they do, through instruction in research methodology, and through interaction with faculty and with their peers. A major part of this initiation process is learning how to use appropriate written linguistic conventions for communicating through disciplinary forums.

The Rhetoric Program at Carnegie Mellon

Carnegie Mellon is a private technical university known for its strength as a research institution. Several departments, including cognitive psychology and computer science, are ranked among the foremost in the country. The research reported here was conducted in the English Department, specifically the rhetoric program, which has been in existence as a doctoral program since 1980. Carnegie Mellon's Ph.D. in Rhetoric is one of a number of doctoral programs in rhetoric and composition that have been developed within English departments in the last several years. David W. Chapman and Gary Tate, in a 1986 survey of 123 doctoral programs in English, identified 53 institutions claiming to offer a specialization of composition/rhetoric. They point out that of these institutions, only sixteen have more than ten doctoral students enrolled, and only three universities actually offer a doctorate in rhetoric: Louisville, Carnegie Mellon, and Texas Woman's (129).

The Ph.D. in Rhetoric at Carnegie Mellon was developed under the aegis of Richard Young, who did a good deal of innovative hiring during his tenure as department head between 1978 and 1983. The current program enables students to enter a field that draws on the expertise of researchers and scholars in a number of disciplines. Rhetoric program faculty include cognitive psychologists, classical and contemporary rhetoricians, a linguist, a speech communication specialist, and a computer scientist. The rhetoric program also has strong ties with the Psychology Department, and it is quite common for English Department students to engage in directed research with psychology faculty. As students proceed through their graduate work, they take several courses in historical rhetoric and contemporary rhetorical theory. But the spine of the program is the training that graduates receive in empirical research methodology.

This training is quite rigorous. Students take an introductory course, "The Process of Research" (team taught in 1984-85 by a rhetorician and a cognitive psychologist), in which they are introduced to the principles of what faculty members call "rhetorical research." They read an introductory textbook on research in the social sciences, learn how to formulate research questions, learn the principles of experimental research design, and receive basic instruction in statistics. As a next step, students often choose to take advanced quantitative research courses in which they learn more about experimental research design and statistical procedures. Students also learn the technique of protocol analysis (gathering and analyzing data from subjects who "think aloud" while performing writing and reading tasks). Second-year students are encouraged to take courses on information processing theory in order to learn the intellectual model and theoretical assumptions that underlie protocol analysis methodology.

The rhetoric program's interdisciplinary curriculum appears to be aimed at producing an intellectual hybrid: a scholar familiar with historical and contemporary rhetorical theory, who can communicate through such forums as *College English* and *College Composition and Communication*, yet also a competent researcher, who can write social science expository prose for educational research publications such as *Research in the Teaching of English* and *Written Communication*. Students therefore need to become knowledge-able about invention theory as well as ANOVA tables, Aristotle and Ong as well as Campbell and Stanley, experimental design confounds and the Pearson product-moment r as well as contemporary writing pedagogy. Course work often includes carrying out research projects, giving oral presentations, and writing "publishable" or "national conference"–quality papers. With these assignments many faculty members in the rhetoric program attempt to introduce graduate students to the major communicative forums for research and scholarship.

Since students' assignments frequently require them to write using a knowledge of the conventions of empirical research reporting, we wondered to what extent students whose background was, as Nate's, in English studies would be hindered by writing in an unfamiliar genre. Because writers in different disciplines use different rhetorical and linguistic conventions, we would expect to see a student such as Nate experiencing considerable difficulty without direct instruction in writing about research. Indeed, there is considerable research that suggests that mastering the conventions of the research report is a formidable task (Faigley and Hansen; Hill, Soppelsa, and West; Selinker, Todd Trimble, and Trimble).

Research on the Structure of Article and Thesis Introductions

In this study we were concerned with the subject's ability to write introductions, the composing of which creates a special set of problems for the student who is learning the conventions of expository prose in the natural and social sciences. John Swales and Hazem Najjar suggest that:

> Introductions to research articles or papers have become in the last few years an important proving ground for our current capacity to understand the process and product of specialized academic writing. The extensive case studies of Latour & Woolgar (1979), Knorr-Cetina (1981) and Gilbert & Mulkay (1984) provide solid evidence for the complexity of the compositional process at the Introduction stage. All three studies show that writing an introduction to a research article is not simply a wrestling with words to fit the facts, but is also strongly modulated by perceptions of the anticipated reactions of peer-colleagues. Knorr-Cetina's analysis of the evolving drafts of a single paper . . . show(s) how the first draft's bold announcement of a new method ultimately becomes the reporting of a comparative analysis; how the early exuberance of the primary researchers turns into the careful understatement of a wider group; and how dangerous knowledge-claims are made safe as insurance against potential damage to the research laboratory's reputation if difficulties subsequently emerge. (175-76)

Swales, Graham Crookes, and Tony Dudley-Evans, analyzing introductions in scientific and social science publications and graduate student theses, found introductions to exhibit a structural schema which can be broken down into a series of rhetorical "moves." The number and the complexity of these moves depends on such variables as space constraints (in professional journals), the nature of the research and the research field (Dudley-Evans, 132), and whether the writer composes in a professional or a training (university) context.

Swales examined the introductions to forty-eight articles in the natural and social sciences, and found that most of them contained a sequence of four rhetorical moves through which a scientist creates a *research space* for his work. Using these moves, the writer: (1) establishes the field in which he or she is working, (2) summarizes related research in the area of concern, (3) creates a research space for the present study by indicating a gap in current knowledge or by raising questions, and (4) introduces the study by indicating what the investigation being reported will accomplish for the field ("Structure of Introductions," 80-92; *Article Introductions*, 178-80). An article by Cynthia L. Selfe in *Research in the Teaching of English* includes an illustration of this four-move schema (figure 8.1).

As Swales's model predicts, this writer immediately identifies the research context in which she will later place her own study by defining the terms that constitute the general research area and naming the researchers who coined the term "writing apprehension." She then establishes a historical context by enumerating previous studies. In three sentences, through highly condensed summarizing, she presents an overview of the field. Having established this overview, she is ready to make the next rhetorical move by

---

1. Establishing the Field:

The term "writing apprehension," originally coined in 1975 by Daly and Miller (1975b), refers to a generalized tendency to experience "some form of anxiety when faced with the task of encoding messages."

2. Summarizing Previous Research:

Much of the early research in writing apprehension was concerned with defining the theoretical construct of writing apprehension and establishing the validity of the Writing Apprehension Test (WAT), an instrument designed to measure that construct (Daly & Miller, 1975b, 1975c). Later research has explored the correlative and predictive functions of the WAT. Specific studies have connected scores on WAT with choice of academic majors and careers (Daly & Shamo, 1976, 1978), scores on self-concept and self-confidence measures (Daly, 1979), and performance on various assessments of writing skill and writing quality (Daly, 1978a, 1978b; Daly & Miller, 1975a, 1975d).

3. Creating a Research Space by Indicating a Gap:

To date, however, no substantive research has been done to define the relationship between writing apprehension and the processes students employ as they compose. It is not even certain, for example, how or to what extent the theoretical construct of writing apprehension is evidenced during the act of composing, whether, in other words, there are definable differences between the composing process [sic] of high and low apprehensives.

4. Introducing Present Research:

The current study was designed to address this particular question.

The research project reported in this paper had three main goals:

  1. To record the predrafting processes of several high and several low writing apprehensives engaged in academic writing.
  2. To analyze the predrafting processes of both groups.
  3. To examine the results of this analysis for evidence of differences related to writing apprehension.

Figure 8.1. Illustration of four rhetorical moves in article introductions (after Swales 1981)

raising issues and questions that have not been addressed in the literature. Swales points out that the onset of this third move is often marked by a contrastive connector like "however" and/or some negative element that will be found in the thematic sentence-initial position. In this instance, the writer uses both features, combining "however" with the negative construction "no substantial research" in the thematic position of the first sentence of that move. A second negative, "It is not even certain," appears in the thematic position in the following sentence, linking new information to that in the previous sentence. By identifying two issues that have not yet been addressed—"defining the relationship between writing apprehension and the processes students employ as they compose," and "whether there are definable differences between the composing process[es] of high and low apprehensives"—the writer creates a niche or "research space" for her own study. This she introduces in the next sentence, "The current study was designed to address this particular question," and presents her purpose by enumerating the three goals of the research project she is to report.

The regularity with which these four moves appear in scientific journal article introductions suggests that they constitute the basic schema. However, as Swales himself has noted, many variations can and do occur. In separate studies, Bazerman and Huckin have shown that scientific journal conventions change over time. And Crookes, in a follow-up study of Swales 1981 using the same three categories but half as many articles, found that there were only five cases (out of 24) which had a clear 1-2-3-4 sequence of moves. Four cases had only a Move 2 and Move 4. And seven of the eight social science articles had five or more moves. It seems that in the "softer" sciences the writer is often compelled to address not a single problem but multiple problems. These problems emerge from the summary of previous research (Move 2). Each is addressed, in turn, by a separate Move 3. Thus there is a characteristic reiteration of Moves 2 and 3, resulting in an overall 1-2-3-2-3-2-3-4 sequence or something similar.

In a study of master's theses, Dudley-Evans found this longer reiterative pattern to be so common as to constitute a virtual schema unto itself. He examined the introductions of seven theses in plant biology, ranging in length from 320 words to 4,640 words, and found that Swales's four-move schema was not adequate to describe their rhetorical complexity. In all of these theses, which were rated "satisfactory" to "good" by a plant biology professor, the writers went to far greater lengths to establish and justify the research topic than was done in Swales's journal articles. Dudley-Evans proposed a six-move schema to describe these introductions:

Move 1: Introducing the Field
Move 2: Introducing the General Topic (within the Field)
Move 3: Introducing the Particular Topic (within the General Topic)
Move 4: Defining the Scope of the Particular Topic by:
    (i)   introducing research parameters
    (ii)   summarizing previous research
Move 5: Preparing for Present Research by:
    (i)   indicating a gap in previous research
    (ii)   indicating a possible extension of previous research
Move 6: Introducing Present Research by:
    (i)   stating the aim of the research
        or
    (ii)   describing briefly the work carried out
    (iii) justifying the research.

Figure 8.2. A Six-move schema of rhetorical moves for master's theses in scientific fields (Dudley-Evans, 1986)

Although Dudley-Evans does not venture an explanation for the differences between journal article introductions and thesis introductions, we suppose that the latter are more elaborate because students are expected to display their knowledge in a more comprehensive way, and to presuppose less knowledge on the part of the reader, than are writers of specialized journal articles.

We found the Dudley-Evans' student-oriented schema more appropriate than Swales's professional-oriented one for the study at hand, since the subject was a graduate student learning the conventions of research report writing. It should be noted that neither Swales's nor Dudley-Evans' models should be taken as prescriptive. They do, however, provide us with an analytical framework for gauging Nate's development of formal, text-based schemata which enabled him to communicate with others in his field through professional forums.

Entering the Conversation of a Writing Research Community by Acquiring Genre Knowledge

The research described above suggests that writing the introduction to a research report involves bringing into play a considerable amount of procedural as well as content knowledge. Because such introductions contain a great deal of information (sometimes as many as thirty summaries of related research presented as brief "gists") in a relatively small space, writers must master both the technique of summarizing and the procedures that will enable them to summarize according to their rhetorical purposes. Learning to use the conventions of the article introduction may well constitute the most difficult part of research writing, especially for novice researchers.

The first-year student we chose to study entered the Carnegie Mellon program with substantial experience as a writing teacher, as an expressive writer, and as a creative writer. Nate had received a B.A. and an M.Ed. in English and in Curriculum and Instruction and had taught freshman composition for six years prior to entering the program, so he brought considerable experience and linguistic expertise to graduate school. His background, however, like that of many students who entered the Ph.D. program from English departments, had not included training in the genres of social science expository writing that were the preferred form of academic discourse in many of his courses. Nate had not written experimental research papers or literature reviews and therefore was not familiar with the conventional structure of the research report in the sciences and social sciences, i.e., introduction, methods, results, discussion. He therefore could not have been expected to know, for example, where in such a report, writers place their key findings (Swales and Najjar); nor could he have been expected to possess or to utilize the procedural knowledge described above. On the other hand, Nate could be observed over a period of several months becoming familiar with his professors' research agendas and with the disciplinary issues being discussed in the classrooms, hallways, and offices, at department colloquia, conferences, and other gatherings. At the same time he was also learning social science research methodology and immersing himself in the professional journals and technical reports which essentially constituted the textual counterpart of his new field of study. Thus, not only was he learning how to converse within the immediate context of a graduate program, but he was also learning the conventions appropriate to a larger research network.

We hypothesized that the attendant changes appearing in Nate's writing can best be understood from the sociolinguistic perspective of language operating in a "multidimensional space." Richard A. Hudson, paraphrasing Robert B. LePage, argues that writers can and do belong and respond to more than one community at once, and that a writer "chooses" to address a community with corresponding linguistic and topical conventions (13-14). For a writer entering a new community, as was the case with Nate, this choice was hardly clearcut or final. The texts chosen for analysis were introductions to end-of-term project reports written in Nate's first three semesters. These reports served as mileposts in that they represented the culmination of a semester's thinking on the given research topic and the writer's compiled linguistic and substantive knowledge in his new discipline. Since these texts are introductions to papers that Nate wrote for course assignments rather than articles submitted for professional journals or theses, we cannot expect him to exhibit a command of the conventions that Swales or Dudley-Evans describe. Yet, in spite of the obvious differences in school and professional contexts, constraints, and purposes for composing, this writing increasingly shows signs of the adoption of the conventions of his newly adopted community.

Thus the introductions to Nate's research reports can be viewed not only for presence of the rhetorical features that mark acceptance in a national community of researchers but for facility with and dependence on topics and language from both his past and from his immediate social context. In these introductions we shall see Nate integrating new topical and rhetorical information with old, the latter derived from his teaching background and familiarity with literary forms of discourse.

The first introduction is from a report on a survey that Nate conducted three months after he entered the program. This survey was completed in his first research methods course, which all students entering the rhetoric program were required to take. His professors told the class that the research questions from which they developed their surveys should grow from a "felt difficulty," that is, an intensely felt issue, question, or problem. (The sentences have been numbered for later reference.)

TEXT 1
How and Why Voice is Taught: A Pilot Survey
Problem
The English profession does not agree on what a "writer's voice" means or how the concept should be used to teach writing, equating it to personal style, literary persona, authority, orality, or even grammar. (1) When teachers, writers, and researchers comment on the

phenomenon of voice, they usually stay on a metaphorical level. (2) Voice is "juice" or "cadence." (3) The concept appears to be too illusive and too closely tied to personal rhetorical philosophy, disallowing a generally accepted definition for common usage. (4) A novice writing teacher, then, might say "You don't know what it is. (5) I don't understand it. (6) How or why should I teach it?" (7)

It should be taught. (8) Most experienced teachers and accomplished writers recognize that in spite of the wide range of definitions the concept of voice is somehow central to the composing process. (9) Some believe that without voice, true writing is impossible. (10) Until the profession understands the phenomenon or in some way addresses what these experts are saying, a paradox exists, and the novice writing teacher confronts a mixed message. (11) Voice should not remain just another eccentricity in an already idiosyncratic profession. (12)

Background

Who are these "accomplished" teachers, writers and thinkers who uniquely honor a writer's voice? (13) Aristotle, Coleridge and Moffet [sic] have acknowledged the impact of the "self" on an audience. (14) Donald Murray and other contemporary rhetoricians state without reserve that this *self*, the writer's voice, is "at the heart of the act of writing." (15) From my experience writing and teaching writing I know that a writer's voice can spirit a composition and, if the voice is misplaced or confused, can drive a teacher or writer batty. (16) If I say to my class "No, No the voice is all wrong here," or "Yes, I can hear you now," I might induce the kind of *authority* I seek, but I am probably sending one of those strange undeciferable teacher-messages that students rightfully ignore or misinterpret. (17) I am liable to get talk-writing or emotions unbound. (18) Like the accomplished experts and theorists, I tacitly know that voice is important, but I am not necessarily equipped to translate this importance for my students. (19)

Are there other teachers who face or at least perceive the same dilemma? (20) I sense that there are, but a hunch is not good enough. (21) Since I have invested time and energy searching the question of voice, I worry that my observations and suspicions are egocentric. (22) Before I tire myself and my colleagues with a series of inquiries and experiments, I must decide if a problem actually exists. (23) Therefore I composed a pilot survey to tell me if I should continue my study of voice and in what direction. (24) The survey, a questionnaire, was aimed at other writing teachers in the Pittsburgh area. (25) By asking if, how, and why voice is taught I hoped to understand the boundaries of my questions and my universe. (26)

This text is a good example of a writer working in a "multidimensional linguistic space" in the sense that in it we can identify traces of the writer's past experience and interests merging with new research methods, problems, and rhetorical forms. Nate had entered the rhetoric program in part because he wanted to learn research methods to help him answer questions growing out of his experience as a freshman writing teacher. He chose to survey ways that college-level writing teachers used the concept of voice. Nate's view that writers have a "personal voice" was central to his teaching philosophy and guided his participation in a National Endowment for the Humanities seminar the summer before he entered the Ph.D. program. Thus, the introduction to his survey reveals the pedagogical values he brought to the rhetoric program, implicit in his claim that an understanding of "voice" is essential to an understanding of the writing process. At the same time the introduction was his first presentation of research to social science-oriented readers who would expect to see a term like "voice" defined operationally.

That Nate seems to be addressing more than one audience in this paper is suggested by the vocabulary and genre features he uses. He mixes terminology suitable for social science expository writing ("phenomenon," "paradox," "acknowledged," "pilot survey") with colloquialisms like "batty," "liable to," and "hunch." He talks in neutral language about "a series of inquiries and experiments" and then changes register and talks in a more personal vein about "the boundaries of my questions and my universe."[2] Although he appears to be following a social science text schema by labeling segments of the introduction "Problem" and "Background," his use of these subheadings seems imitative rather than based on true genre knowledge. His problem statement consists of a series of assertions about the importance of teaching and researching voice.

Nate's aim here appears to be persuasive; he wishes to convince his readers that it is important to begin to isolate the phenomenon of voice in order to characterize and thus define it. In sentences 13-19 he attempts to elaborate on the problem, first by referring to such diverse authorities as Aristotle, Coleridge, Moffett, and Murray. Instead of including citations to specific works, however, he mentions these four names only in passing; most of the support he marshals for his claims comes from personal testimony. By not placing his research within a larger disciplinary frame of reference, he cannot offer his audience a warrant in the form of citations which designate an established field to which his present study will contribute (Toulmin, 97-107). From the perspective of his immediate audience, Nate's persuasive strategies would likely be ineffective, since he neither bases his claims on shared knowledge nor uses conventions that will enable him to establish warrants for his claims. From the perspective of his NEH or freshman compositon writing communities, on the other hand, his strategies would probably be quite effective.

A comment in one of Nate's self reports shows he was aware of his new role in a research community and a change in his writing:

---

[2] A more detailed account of Nate's register shifts can be found in Berkenkotter, Huckin, and Ackerman (1988).

I always intended to be sensitized to the scientific canon, something I accept like my father's lectures on handshakes, something I just need to do if for no other reason than you have to know something from the inside before you can fairly criticize it.

Yet the warrants behind the claims in his report rest in his shared experience with fellow teachers and writers and not in explicit connections with previous research or scholarship. Although this writing does not create a "research space" in the way Swales describes, we can still say the text is socially constructed. It reflects Nate's recent participation in a linguistic community where the rhetorical moves of social science are less attractive and personal appeals and experience are more common. Readers from Nate's previous community would (and did) find his claims accurate and without need of further substantiation. What interests us here is that this writing, though originating with a personal "felt difficulty," was a first attempt at social science prose. Nate responded (predictably) by relying mostly on the wealth of substantive and linguistic knowledge that he brought to the program.

Writing for a Local Audience in the Rhetoric Program

Six months later in the program, Nate wrote an introduction to a research report for his "Process of Composing" course. This report detailed a pilot study he conducted using protocol research methodology. Nate began this introduction as he had Text 1, by introducing a problem that his research was to address. However, Text 2 reflects a new area of personal inquiry and research. Here we see him drawing on newly acquired theoretical knowledge of cognitive psychology as well as on issues that he was being exposed to in his coursework.

TEXT 2

Reframing: The Role of Prior Knowledge in the Process of Reading to Write

Introduction

The Problem

It is nearly impossible to ignore the remarkable efforts by researchers and theorists over the last 15 years to understand the composing processes of writers. (1) It is equally remarkable to consider how little is known about the reading process, especially as a companion process to writing. (2) Many of the academic exercises our students encounter or the competencies we aspire for them embrace both domains. (3) Only recently have researchers begun to study relationships between reading and writing processes, focusing primarily on how reading affects the development of a writer (Smith, 1982; Scardamalia and Bereiter, 1984). (4)

One reason for this seeming oversight may rest in our shortsighted image of the writer. (5) Romantic philosophies and practices urge self-determinism; and writing is seen as a lonely struggle, the writer armed only with a blank legal pad, introspection, and the admittedly noble cause of writing to discover a universe. (6) Though I do not argue the place or nature of expressive writing, I do argue that another image of the writer is equally viable. (7) Writers collaborate, for one thing, with other writers (Ede and Lunsford, 1984) and with other language communities. (8) Among others, Patricia Bizzell (1984) draws our attention to the price paid for ignoring the conventions and genres of an academic community. (9) Working from that image, the writing in college is social, and assignments include the artful manipulation of texts and task, of plans and intentions, of community and self. (10)

If composing is multi-dimensional, what processes must a writer manage in order to move gracefully from the act of critical reading into the act of critical writing? (11) And if "grace" is not possible, what constraints interrupt and alter the process for a writer who must first read to write? (12) In this report and proposal I describe what I am calling reframing, one cognitive component in the process of reading to write. (13) To reframe means to map semantic schemas from prior knowledge onto key propositions in freshly encountered material. (14) Readers reframe to create manageable "gists" dependent on experience related to the subject domain and their representation of the task. (15) Reframing is best understood as a constructive act of reading: a lessening of informational loads, a creating of plans and a shaping of content—all of which drive the draft that soon follows. (16)

Text 2 differs in many ways from Text 1. Although Nate and his classmates were asked to begin with an "interesting feature" in the protocol data that they had collected, an assignment that appears to invite a personal perspective, Nate writes with much less a sense of a "felt difficulty" and without personal testimony. Here, his writing is "collaborative" in that this text refers to issues he and his peers had discussed in the immediate context of the graduate course. For example, in the second paragraph Nate alludes to an alternative "image of the writer" and cites examples (lines 7 and 8) from scholarship on "collaboration" and "academic communities." Comments from Nate's self reports and his professor's positive reception of this argument suggest that Nate had successfully entered into a local conversation. This conversation would, however, exclude many readers. Sentences 14-16, for example, are written in language that would have been understood by Nate's professor, but is jargon ("semantic schemas," "key propositions," "informational loads," etc.) to readers unfamiliar with psycholinguistics. Nate also appears to be using a more situationally appropriate register in Text 2 than he had in Text 1. Instead of colloquialisms like "hunch" and "batty," we find him employing more formal lexical choices, which include "encounter," "aspire," "viable," and "admittedly." Finally, the I-centered focus of Text 1 seems to be giving way to a broader, more communal perspective: whereas the first-person singular pronoun was used heavily in Text 1 (19 times), here there is a 4-4 split between the first-person singular and the first-person plural.

Genre features also point to Nate's growing identification with a disciplinary community. Indeed, this text exhibits the sequence of rhetorical moves Dudley-Evans observed in the introductions to graduate plant biologists' theses (although not in the detail that appeared in those texts). In sentence 1 Nate introduces the general field, "the composing processes of writers" (Move 1). In sentences 2 and 3 he introduces the general topic within the field, "the reading process, especially as a companion process to writing" (Move 2). Sentence 4 introduces the particular topic, "relationships between reading and writing processes" (Move 3). In sentences 4-10 he defines the scope of the particular topic by introducing research parameters and summarizing previous research (Move 4). Sentences 11-12 prepare for present research by raising questions (Move 5). And in sentences 13-16 he introduces the present research (Move 6) by describing briefly the work carried out (but see discussion below).

Text 2 occupies a transitional position between Texts 1 and 3. On the one hand, Nate can be said to be constructing an argument in this introduction that will enable him to create a "research space" for his study. Not having received formal instruction in the rhetorical moves of introductions, he has apparently picked them up, at least superficially, from his reading: he displays all four of Swales's moves and all six of Dudley-Evans', in the right order. On the other hand, he does not situate the field and the topic in the kind of detail that would be called for in a thesis (Moves 1-3). Further, his attempt to summarize previous research (Move 4), though more focused than in Text 1, is still somewhat vague and discursive. Move 5 is clear enough, yet coming on the heels of weak Moves 1-4, it might not be fully expected. Move 6 is also quite clear, but it does not adequately describe the work actually carried out in this study (case studies using protocol analysis).

Although Nate's assignment was actually to write a proposal for more research based on his pilot study, as if he were seeking funding, his argument would not succeed in the eyes of a reviewer outside his research seminar. First, he does not provide readers outside of the seminar with enough explicit detail. Second, and more important, he does not establish his authority by citing previous publications and acknowledging established arguments within an existing research forum. If Nate's report were submitted to a journal referee or grant reviewer, we could expect the reader to puzzle over what is assumed to be shared knowledge. For example, he does not establish a connection between his comments on collaboration and social contexts (sentences 8-10) and the material which follows in the last paragraph. It would not immediately be clear how the questions posed in sentences 11-12 relate to the discussion in the preceding paragraph. However, for Nate's *immediate* audience, his professor and even other members of his research seminar, this argument is much less elliptical. The antecedents to the propositions on collaborative writing, social contexts, and critical reading and writing are traceable to earlier drafts, comments by his professor and classmates, and class discussion as evidenced by Nate's self reports during the semester. We suggest that Text 2 is transitional because it exhibits the outward signs of the rhetorical devices of a social science subspeciality, with a system of warrants, claims, and rhetorical structures, while at the same time is clearly a collaborative, local construct, dependent upon the shared knowledge of a limited set of readers.

Writing to Join a Conversation Among Composition Researchers

Text 3 is the introduction to a research report Nate wrote in December 1985, after having been in the rhetoric program for a year and a half. The immediate occasion of the report was a term project for a "Computers and Rhetorical Studies" course. Nate also used this introduction for a shorter paper that he wrote for a psychology course on human problem-solving. Thus the paper was written for two immediate readers—his rhetoric professor, whose background was in computer science, and a senior psychology professor. As we shall see, however, Text 3 reflects not only Nate's immediate rhetorical situation, but also his intellectual identification with the research agenda of the professor of his "Process of Composing" course, for whom he wrote Text 2. Through that professor he became familiar with studies by researchers beyond his local university setting who were asking questions about the interactions between reading and writing processes (as seen in his references to Smith, Langer, and other researchers). In this sense, Nate was not only fulfilling course assignments with this project, he was also writing to participate in a local dialogue and enter into the professional conversation of a research subspeciality.

This text deals with the same topic as Text 2: how writers use background knowledge when writing from source materials. It is the first time in his graduate career that Nate has been able to run a follow-up study and write a second paper on the same topic; hence it is interesting to compare these two texts. Like Text 2, this introduction displays the sequence of six rhetorical moves described by Dudley-Evans. Sentences 1 and 2 introduce the general field, "relationships between writing and reading processes" (Move 1). Sentences 3 and 4 narrow the topic to "how reading and writing facilitate each other" (Move 2). Sentences 5-8 narrow the topic further to "the role of experiential knowledge" (Move 3). Overlapping with Move 3 is Move 4, in which Nate defines the scope of his topic by summarizing previous research (sentences 6-8). He then prepares for present research (Move 5) by indicating how previous research by Judith Langer can be extended (sentences 9-12). Finally, he introduces the present research (Move 6) with a lengthy discussion of aims and justification (sentences 13-27).

TEXT 3
Toward a Generative Computer Environment:
A Protocol Study
The Problem

Although reading and writing have received national attention with the advent of the literacy crisis, only recently have researchers begun to study relationships between reading and writing processes. (1) That research has focused primarily on how reading affects the development of young writers (Smith, 1982; Scardamalia and Bereiter, 1984). (2) There is little research at all that looks specifically at how reading and writing facilitate each other (for a speculative study see Petrosky, 1982). (3) This dearth is especially curious in the light of the amount of academic learning that depends on simultaneous expertise in both modes of expression.* (4)

> *It is increasingly accepted that reading, along with writing, is a constructive act where the reader, like the writer, uses goals, knowledge, and strategies to make meaning. (This note belongs to Nate's text.)

Dead center in the reading-to-write question is the role of experiential knowledge. (5) Accomplished writers (who are surely accomplished readers) admonish novice writers for straying too far from topics nourished by experience or substantial study (Murray, 1981 & McPhee, 1984). (6) Similarly, research overwhelmingly supports our intuitions that background knowledge significantly affects the construction of meaning in a text (Anderson, 1977; Goodman and Goodman, 1978; Harste, Burke and Woodward, 1982; and Langer, 1984). (7) What advice, then, do we give our students—when they continually face reading and writing assignments demanding facility with both text-based and experience-based knowledge? (8)

The Study

Judith Langer (1985) partially answered that question by analyzing the effects of text-based topic knowledge on 10th grade writing. (9) She found, via a free-association test, a direct and positive relationship between her subjects' ability to hierarchically display the meaning of a passage and the ability to compose later a "coherent" draft. (10) Following Langer's lead, this study explores how topic knowledge affects academic writing and, more specifically, how experiential knowledge becomes the major variable in a reading and writing scenario. (11) Although Langer's study begins with much the same question for research, important distinctions must be noted. . . . (12) (Here Nate elaborates on differences between his project and Langer's. We have omitted this passage for the sake of brevity.)

The primary goal of this study is to describe how experts use experiential knowledge to invent original, effective organizational patterns in their plans and drafts. (13) Bonnie Meyer (1984) has documented a reader's affinity for hierarchical text plans, or what might be called the traditional mental representations that guide comprehension in print. (14) Since Aristotle we know that rhetorical discourse follows common logical patterns. (15) From years of exposure to these basic plans—antecedent/consequent, comparison, description/response, time-order—a writer who is first a reader might naturally turn such a plan into a traditional albeit unoriginal plan for writing. (16) However, a writer becomes "noteable" when he or she strategically deviates from these norms (Elbow, 1984), creating what is essentially an organic, experience-based plan that improves upon time-worn organizational patterns. (17) Stephen White (1985), through extensive product analyses of personal narrative assignments, has begun to document how students successfully create autonomous, experience-based text structures. (18) This study seeks to explore this phenomenon as well, tracing the decisions and variables that speed the process. (19)

An exploratory study need not be run blind. (20) Findings from previous research and protocol analyses suggest the following list of predictable behaviors in the reading-to-write scenario. (21) A subject might:

Balance text-based and experiential knowledge successfully to complete the task—
 using both to form a coherent, organized, and original design for the draft.
 choosing a personal organizing principle inherent in the recollection to structure the paper and otherwise structure the key issues in the texts.
 choosing one of Meyer's text-specific organizational patterns to structure a draft, adding substance with experience-based elaborations. (22)
Lean on experiential knowledge and lose sight of the task—
 selecting only those issues in the reading that comfortably match experience, ignoring other germane issues.
 ignoring the texts altogether, digressing into a narrative or personal elaboration which distorts the task.
 misrepresenting key points in the texts by illogically attaching personal background knowledge. (23)
Rely on text-based knowledge exclusively, ignoring any and all related experience. (24)

These predictions in effect create a working hypothesis on the range of behaviors possible in a reading-to-write assignment. (25) Coupled with the findings here they will form a data base on which a model of expert behavior can be built. (26) That model and a computer tutorial based on that model are the long range goals of this research and should offer substantive answers to the educational question of how can facility with experiential and text-based knowledge be taught. (27)

However, Text 3 differs from Text 2 in significant ways. It elaborates more on every one of the six rhetorical moves and is more than twice as long. Where Text 2 devotes four sentences to introducing the topic (Moves 1-3), Text 3 devotes eight. Where Text 2 discusses four previous studies (Moves 4-5), Text 3 discusses twelve. Most important, where Text 2 introduces present research (Move 6) by simply stating a thesis, Text 3 introduces present research via an elaborate, hierarchically organized series of hypotheses. Clearly, Nate has not only become aware of the standard rhetorical moves of this genre, he has also learned how to use them to better effect. Text 3 draws more on information reported in antecedent texts by other researchers than does Text 2. It is also more sensitive to the possibility that, without the necessary evidence and warrants, some readers may not accept the claims the writer is about to make. Although there remain a few "off-register" metaphorical expressions such as "dead center," (5) and "nourished" (6) most of the prose in this text is cast in the neutral, "objective" style that characterizes the research writing that Nate had been reading in the fields of psycholinguistics, cognitive psychology, and educational research. Readers may want to flip back a few pages and compare the style of this text to the more informal, "oral" style in Text 1. Here Nate is projecting a more "scientific" *persona*. In fact, one of the most striking differences between Text 1 and Text 3 is the transformation of the relationship between persona and subject matter. In Text 3 the writer directs the reader's attention toward the issues under discussion, rather than to his own sensibility as he had done in Text 1. Even in Text 3, the writer had occasionally adopted the first-person pronoun. For example, in sentence 7 of that text he had asserted, "Though I do not argue the place or nature of expressive writing, I do argue that another image of the writer is equally viable." In contrast to the twenty-three first-person singular pronouns in Text 1 and the four first-person singular pronouns in Text 2, here Nate avoids the first-person singular pronoun altogether. The frequent use of first person, the informal oral style, and the metaphorical constructions in Text 1 created the sense of the writer's personal involvement with the object of study. In Text 3 the writer's expression of a personally "felt difficulty" has been replaced by a "neutral" description of a "significant" research issue. The writer documents the significance of this issue by using citations. For example, the string of citations that appear in sentence 7 refers anaphorically to subject and verb of the sentence ("research . . . supports") and serves to instantiate the writer's claim that "research supports our intuitions that background knowledge significantly affects the construction of meaning in a text." Nate's use of this technique as well as his "socially appropriate" persona and style are signs of his increasing command over the conventions of writing about research.

Text 3 would probably be the most difficult of the three introductions to decipher for readers outside of the community of specialists to whom Nate was writing. To many readers Nate's meaning would appear to be obfuscated by a thicket of jargon. One encounters throughout a technical terminology familiar primarily to a specialized readership of cognitive psychologists and psycholinguists. Some examples of this terminology are: "experiential knowledge" (5, 11, 13), "experience-based knowledge" (8), "experienced-based plan" (17), "autonomous experience-based text structures" (18), "text-based knowledge" (8), "text-based topic knowledge" (9), "topic knowledge" (11), "hierarchically display(ed) meaning" (11), "reading and writing scenario" (11), "hierarchical text plans" (14), and "mental representations" (14). Nate's use of this terminology suggests that he is able to speak in the discourse of a specialized readership. His use of this lexicon also indicates that he is building a conceptual framework that will allow him to interact with other members of this specialist community, to identify important research issues and problems, and in a general sense, to share (although perhaps not to be cognizant of) the community's epistemological assumptions.

The differences between these three texts written over three consecutive semesters suggest some summary inferences regarding the manner in which Nate appears to have migrated toward the specialist's perspective. Text 3 is "intertextual" in a way that Texts 1 and 2 are not. It is heavily indebted to concepts and terminology in the literature that Nate cites (de Beaugrande and Dressler, 10-11; Porter, 35). While Text 3 gains strength through this intertextuality, it remains collaborative as well, since it is staged within a local conversation and is directed at an immediate readership. In Text 1 the writer had been an isolated newcomer inquiring whether anyone shared his "dilemma." In Text 2, we see the embryonic researcher learning a theoretical model and research methodology reflected in the terminology he is beginning (albeit somewhat awkwardly) to use. By Text 3 Nate has assimilated a literature and a lexicon and therefore is more comfortably able to speak in the discourse of his subspecialty.

Conclusion

In his case study of two biologists revising to accommodate their referees' criticisms, Myers raises the questions, "How does a researcher learn all [the] complex conventions of the scientific article? What part do such negotiations play in the education of a doctoral student, or in the choice of problem or shifts of specialty?" ("Texts as Knowledge Claims," 628). From the changes appearing in the three texts above, we can infer some of the complex social negotiations that writers engage in as they prepare to enter an academic field. Although we are reluctant to generalize from our findings to other students entering academic discourse communities as graduates, we would like to offer the following observations and speculations.

First, it appears that, for students with backgrounds similar to Nate's, making the transition from *composition teacher* to *composition researcher* (i. e., from practitioner to specialist) involves a difficult passage from one academic culture to another. Developing communicative competence requires that they master the ways of speaking, reading, and writing which are indigenous to the new culture.

Second, although many students entering interdisciplinary doctoral programs with an emphasis on empirical research like the one at Carnegie Mellon will be reading in new and unfamiliar fields, students with prior training in the sciences or social sciences may be more likely to bring previously developed procedural schemata for writing about research than those with backgrounds in literary studies or composition pedagogy. We base this observation partly on Nate's predictable difficulty mastering the conventions and language of social science reporting and partly on observational data from the earlier study (1988) which indicated that most entering graduate students struggled to gain competence with either key issues or the locally preferred conventions for reading and writing. Though far from conclusive, the earlier study and our analysis here raise the question of what type of training or teaching experience best prepares a graduate student to enter a community of writing researchers.

Finally, we suggest that the development of *academic* communicative competence (or academic literacy) involves the ability to adapt one's discourse as the situation requires. In this study we saw a writer struggling in his first assignments to use a comfortable voice and style to address an uncomfortable and unfamiliar writing assignment. As his training progressed, he learned through exposure, practice and reinforcement to use a different voice and style. Some theorists have proposed that similar struggles characterize undergraduates' writing instruction and experiences (Bartholomae). How much information regarding the discoursal expectations of those who teach, write, and read in the sciences, the social sciences, and the various humanities needs to be made explicit to students in their undergraduate and graduate curricula? At what level of sophistication should such information be presented? In what instructional contexts should it be provided?

Like many sophisticated language users, Nate was able to adapt his discourse over time to achieve various intellectual social and professional ends. We do not mean to imply that he was a linguistic chameleon, as is a professional journalist who may infiltrate a wide range of discourse communities (Swales, *Article Introductions*, 7). Nor did Nate, in the process of becoming a composition researcher, abandon his previous writing community of friends and teachers. Rather, he brought bits and pieces of his experience as writing teacher to his new role as an apprentice researcher.

This is not to say that his passage does not raise some interesting questions for scholars interested in the growth of knowledge in composition studies. How, for example, do the sociopolitical constraints that govern the "manufacture of knowledge" (Knorr-Cetina) in this emerging field affect a graduate student's choice of research program? To what extent are the issues that concern composition teachers subsumed by the agendas of mentors as they join powerful research or scholarly enterprises, such as the one that we studied? How will the increasing graduate specialization in rhetorical studies and educational research affect the development of the canon within composition studies? We raise these questions because composition studies is a young field bound to be affected by the above factors.

Socialization studies such as the one we have reported above may also raise pedagogical questions that will concern composition teachers and scholars: What does learning the multiple registers and codes of various academic communities entail both cognitively and socially for undergraduate students? How does acquiring specialized literacy affect the graduate writer's world view, or his or her ethnic and gender identity? Finally, to quote Nate, what does it mean to the undergraduate or graduate student to become "sensitized to the scientific canon," or the literary canon, or the canons of the many subspecialties within these broad fields of inquiry?

It is to Nate that we turn to provide, if not an answer, an insight:

I just need to do it if for no other reason than you have to know something from the inside before you can fairly criticize it.

Bibliography

Bartholomae, David. "Inventing the University." In *When a Writer Can't Write*, ed. M. Rose, 134-65. New York: Guilford, 1985.

Bazerman, Charles. "Modern Evolution of the Experimental Report in Physics: Spectroscopic Articles in *Physical Review*, 1893-1980." *Social Studies of Science* 14 (1984): 163-95.

Bazerman, Charles. "Scientific Writing as a Social Act: A Review of the Literature of the Sociology of Science." In *New Essays in Technical and Scientific Communication: Research, Theory, Practice*, ed. P. V. Anderson, R. J. Brockmann, and C. R. Miller, 156-84. Farmingdale, N.Y.: Baywood, 1983.

Bazerman, Charles, "What Written Knowledge Does: Three Examples of Academic Discourse." *Philosophy of the Social Sciences* 11 (1981): 361-82.

Bazerman, Charles. "The Writing of Scientific Non-fiction: Contexts, Choices, Constraints." *Pre/Text* 5 (1984): 39-74.

Berkenkotter, Carol, Thomas Huckin, and John Ackerman. "Conversations, Conventions and the Writer: Case Study of a Student in a Rhetoric Ph.D. Program." *Research in the Teaching of English* 22 (1988): 9-44.

Bizzell, Patricia. "Cognition, Convention, and Certainty: What We Need to Know about Writing." *Pre/Text* 3 (1982): 213-43.

Bizzell, Patricia. "College Composition: Initiation into the Academic Discourse Community" [Review of *Four Worlds of Writing* and *Writing in the Arts and Sciences*]. *Curriculum Inquiry* 12 (1982): 191-207.

Chapman, David W., and Gary Tate. "A Survey of Doctoral Programs in Rhetoric and Composition." *Rhetoric Review* 5 (1987): 124-86.

Crane, Diana. *Invisible Colleges*. Chicago: University of Chicago Press, 1972.

Crookes, Graham. "Towards a Validated Analysis of Scientific Text Structure." *Applied Linguistics* 7 (1986): 57-70.

de Beaugrande, Robert, and Wolfgang Dressler. *Introduction to Text Linguistics*. London: Longman, 1981.

Dudley-Evans, Tony. "Genre Analysis: An Investigation of the Introduction and Discussion Sections of MSc Dissertations." In *Talking about Text*, ed. M. Coulthard, 128-45. Birmingham, Eng.: English Language Research, 1986.

Dyson, Anne H. "Emerging Alphabetic Literacy in School Contexts: Toward Defining the Gap Between School Curriculum and Child Mind." *Written Communication* 1 (1984): 5-55.

Fahnestock, Jeanne. "Accommodating Science: The Rhetorical Life of Scientific Facts." *Written Communication* 3 (1986): 275-96.
Fahnestock, Jeanne, and Marie Secor. "The Rhetoric of Literacy Criticism." Paper delivered at the Penn State Conference on Rhetoric and Composition, July 1982.
Faigley, Lester, and Karen Hansen. "Learning to Write in the Social Sciences." *College Composition and Communication* 34 (1985): 140-49.
Gilbert, Nigel G., and Michael Mulkay. *Opening Pandora's Box: A Sociological Analysis of Scientists' Discourse.* Cambridge: Cambridge University Press, 1984.
Heath, Shirley Brice. *Ways with Words: Language, Life, and Work in Communities and Classrooms.* New York: Cambridge University Press, 1983.
Heath, Shirley Brice. "What No Bedtime Story Means: Narrative Skills at Home and at School." *Language in Society* 11 (1982): 49-76.
Herrington, Anne. "Writing in Academic Settings: A Study of the Contexts for Writing in Two College Chemical Engineering Courses." *Research in the Teaching of English* 19 (1985): 331-61.
Hill, S., B. F. Soppelsa, and G. K. West. "Teaching ESL Students to Read and Write Experimental-Research Papers." *TESOL Quarterly* 16, 3 (1982): 333-48.
Huckin, Thomas. "Surprise Value in Scientific Discourse." Paper presented at the Conference on College Composition and Communication, Atlanta, Ga., 1987.
Hudson, Richard A. *Sociolinguistics.* Cambridge: Cambridge University Press, 1980.
Knorr-Cetina, Karen D. *The Manufacture of Knowledge: An Essay on the Constructivist and Contextual Nature of Science,* Oxford: Pergamon, 1981.
Latour, Bruno and Steve Woolgar. *Laboratory Life: The Social Construction of Scientific Facts.* Beverly Hills: Sage, 1979.
McCarthy, Lucille P. "A Stranger in Strange Lands: A College Student Writing Across the Curriculum." *Research in the Teaching of English* 21 (1987): 233-65.
Miles, Matthew B., and A. Michael Huberman. "Drawing Valid Meaning from Qualitative Data: Toward a Shared Craft." *Educational Researcher* 13 (1984): 20-30.
Myers, Greg. "The Social Construction of Two Biologists' Proposals." *Written Communication* 2 (1985): 219-45.
Myers, Greg. "Texts as Knowledge Claims: The Social Construction of Two Biology Articles. *Social Studies of Science* 15 (1985): 593-630.
North, Stephen M. "Writing in a Philosophy Class: Three Case Studies." *Research in the Teaching of English* 20 (1986): 225-62.
Porter, J. E. "Intertextuality and the Discourse Community." *Rhetoric Review* 5 (1986): 34-47.
Selfe, Cynthia L. "The Predrafting Processes of Four High- and Four Low-Apprehensive Writers." *Research in the Teaching of English* 18 (1984): 45-64.
Selinker, Larry, R. Mary Todd Trimble, and Louis Trimble. "Presuppositional Rhetorical Information in EST Discourse." *TESOL Quarterly* 10, 3 (1976): 281-90.
Shultz, Jeffrey J., Susan Florio, and Frederick Erickson. "Where's the Floor? Aspects of the Cultural Organization of Social Relationships in Communication at Home and in School." In *Children in and out of School: Ethnography and Education,* ed. P. Gilmore and A. A. Glatthorn, 88-123. Washington, D.C.: Center for Applied Linguistics, 1982.
Swales, John. *Aspects of Article Introductions.* Aston Research Reports No. 1. Aston, Eng.: University of Birmingham, 1981.
Swales, John. "Research into the Structure of Introductions to Journal Articles and its Application to the Teaching of Academic Writing." In *Common Ground: Shared Interests in ESP and Communication Studies,* ed. R. Williams, J. Swales, and J. Kirkman, 77-86. Oxford: Pergamon, 1984.
Swales, John, and Hazem Najjar. "The Writing of Research Articles: Where to Put the Bottom Line?" *Written Communication* 4 (1987): 175-91.
Toulmin, Stephen. *The Uses of Argument.* Cambridge: Cambridge University Press, 1958
Yearly, Steven. "Textual Persuasion: The Role of Social Accounting in the Construction of Scientific Arguments." *Philosophy of the Social Sciences* 11 (1981): 409-35.

Bibliography Supplement

This bibliography supplements the works cited in the notes and bibliographies of the reprinted articles. It contains some significant recent research and some important articles not contained in the individual bibliographies.

Anderson, Worth, Cynthia Best, Alycia Black, John Hurst, Brandt Miller, and Susan Miller. "Cross-Curricular Underlife: A Collaborative Report on Ways with Academic Words." *College Composition and Communication* 41 (1990): 11-36.

Anson, Chris M., and L. Lee Forsberg, "Moving Beyond the Academic Community: Transitional Stages in Professional Writing." *Written Communication* 7 (1990): 200-31.

Bazerman, Charles, and James Paradis, eds. *Textual Dynamics of the Professions*. Madison: University of Wisconsin Press, 1991.

Bazerman, Charles. *Constructing Experience*. Carbondale: Southern Illinois University Press, 1994.

Bazerman, Charles. *The Informed Writer*. Boston: Houghton, 1981.

Becher, Tony. *Academic Tribes and Territories: Intellectual Enquiry and the Cultures of Disciplines*. Bristol, PA: Open University Press, 1989.

Becker, Howard. *Writing for Social Scientists*. Chicago: University of Chicago Press, 1986.

Berkenkotter, Carol, and Thomas N. Huckin. *Genre Knowledge*. Hillsdale, NJ: Erlbaum, 1994.

Bizzell, Patricia. *Academic Discourse and Critical Consciousness*. Pittsburgh: University of Pittsburgh Press, 1992.

Clark, Burton R. *The Academic Life: Small Worlds, Different Worlds*. Princeton: Carnegie Foundation for the Advancement of Teaching, 1987.

Clark, Burton R., and Guy Neave. *Encyclopedia of Higher Education*. London: Pergamon, 1992.

Clarke, John H., and Arthur W. Biddle. *Teaching Critical Thinking*. Englewood Cliffs, NJ: Prentice Hall, 1993.

Clifford, James, and George Marcus, eds. *Writing Culture*. Berkeley: University of California Press, 1986.

Connors, Robert. "The Rise of Technical Writing Instruction in America." *Journal of Technical Writing and Communication* 12 (1982): 329-54.

"English and Other Teaching." Editorial. *Nation* 19 Mar. 1908: 253-54.

Fulwiler, Toby. *The Journal Book*. Upper Montclair, NJ: Boynton, 1987.

Geertz, Clifford. *Local Knowledge: Further Essays in Interpretive Anthropology*. New York: Basic Books, 1983.

Geertz, Clifford. *Works and Lives: The Anthropologist as Author*. Stanford: Stanford University Press, 1988.

Geisler, Cheryl. "Exploring Academic Literacy: An Experiment in Composing." *College Composition and Communication* 43 (1992): 39-54.

Gillham, Bruce, ed. *The Language of School Subjects*. London: Heinemann Education, 1986.

Glick, Milton D. "Writing Across the Curriculum: A Dean's Perspective." *WPA: Writing Program Administration* 11 (1988): 53-58.

Graham, Joan. "What Works: The Problems and Rewards of Cross-Curricular Writing Programs." *Current Issues in Higher Education* 3 (1983-84): 16-26.

Greene, Stuart. "The Role of Task in the Development of Academic Thinking through Reading and Writing in a College History Course." *Research in the Teaching of English* 27 (1993): 46-75.

Haring-Smith, Tori, ed. *A Guide to Writing Programs: Writing Centers, Peer Tutoring Programs, and Writing Across the Curriculum*. Glenview, IL: Scott Foresman, 1987.

Hedley, Jane, and Jo Ellen Parker. "Writing across the Curriculum: The Vantage of the Liberal Arts." *ADE Bulletin* 98 (1991): 22-28.

Herrington, Anne J. and Charles Moran, eds. *Writing, Teaching, and Learning in the Disciplines*. New York: MLA, 1992.

Herrington, Anne J. and Deborah Cadman. "Peer Review and Revising in an Anthropology Course: Lessons for Learning." *College Composition and Communication* 42 (1991): 184-99.

Huot, Brian. "Finding Out What They Are Writing: A Method, Rationale and Sample for Writing-across-the-Curriculum Research." *WPA: Writing Program Administration* 15 (1992): 31-40.

Kantor, Kenneth J. "The English Curriculum and the Structure of the Disciplines." *Theory into Practice* 22 (1984): 174-81.

Kinneavy, James. "Writing Across the Curriculum." *Teaching Composition: 12 Bibliographic Essays*. Ed. Gary Tate. Texas Christian University Press, 1987. 353-77.

Langer, Judith A., and Arthur N. Applebee. *How Writing Shapes Thinking: A Study of Teaching and Writing*. NCTE Research Report No. 22. Urbana: NCTE, 1987.

Language for Life. (The Bullock Report). London: HMSO, 1977.

MacDonald, Susan Peck. "A Method for Analyzing Sentence-Level Differences in Disciplinary Knowledge Making." *Written Communication* 9 (1992): 533-69.

MacDonald, Susan Peck. *Professional Academic Writing in the Humanities and Social Sciences*. Carbondale: Southern Illinois University Press, 1993.

Maimon, Elaine P. "Cinderella to Hercules: Demythologizing Writing Across the Curriculum." *Journal of Basic Writing* 2 (1980): 3-11.

Maimon, Elaine P. *Writing in the Arts and Sciences*. Boston: Little Brown, 1981.

Maimon, Elaine. "Talking to Strangers." *College Composition and Communication* 30 (1979): 364-69.

Matalene, Carolyn. *Worlds of Writing*. New York: Random, 1989.

McLeod, Susan H., and Margot Soven, eds. *Writing Across the Curriculum: A Guide to Developing Programs*. Newbury Park, CA: Sage, 1992.

McLeod, Susan H., ed. *Strengthening Programs for Writing Across the Curriculum*. San Francisco: Jossey, 1988.

McLeod, Susan. "Defining Writing across the Curriculum." *WPA: Writing Program Administration* 11 (1987): 19-24.

Moffett, James. *Active Voice: A Writing Program across the Curriculum*. Upper Montclair, NJ: Boynton, 1981.

Moss, Andrew, and Carol Holder. *Improving Student Writing: A Guidebook for Faculty in All Disciplines*. Dubuque, IA: Kendall/Hunt, 1988.

Myers, Greg. "The Rhetoric of Irony in Academic Writing." *Written Communication* 7 (1990): 419-55.

Myers, Greg. *Writing Biology*. Madison: University of Wisconsin Press, 1990.

Nash, Walter, ed. *The Writing Scholar: Studies in Academic Discourse*. Written Communication Annual 3. Newbury Park, CA: Sage, 1990.

Nelson, John S., Allan Megill, Donald N. McCloskey. *The Rhetoric of the Human Sciences: Language and Argument in Scholarship and Public Affairs*. Madison: University of Wisconsin Press, 1987.

Prior, Paul. "Contextualizing Writing and Response in a Graduate Seminar." *Written Communication* 8 (1991): 267-310.

Ronald, Kate. "On the Outside Looking in: Students' Analyses of Professional Discourse Communities." *Rhetoric Review* 7 (1988): 130-49.

Rosenberg, Vivian M. "Writing Instruction: A View from across the Curriculum." *Journal of General Education* 36 (1984): 50-66.

Schumacher, Gary M., and Jane Gradwohl Nash. "Conceptualizing and Measuring Knowledge Change Due to Writing." *Research in the Teaching of English* 25 (1991): 67-96.

Simons, Herbert W., ed. *Rhetoric in the Human Sciences*. Newbury Park, CA: Sage, 1989.

Simons, Herbert W., ed. *The Rhetorical Turn: Invention and Persuasion in the Rhetoric of Inquiry*. Chicago: University of Chicago Press, 1990.

Sipple, Jo-Ann M. "A Planning Process for Building Writing-across-the-Curriculum Programs to Last." *Journal of Higher Education* 60 (1989): 444-57.

Stanley, Linda, and Joanna Ambron, eds. *Writing Across the Curriculum in Community Colleges*. San Francisco: Jossey-Bass, 1991.

Swales, John. *Genre Analysis*. Cambridge: Cambridge University Press, 1990.

Swanson-Owens, Deborah. "Identifying Natural Sources of Resistance: A Case Study of Implementing Writing Across the Curriculum." *Research in the Teaching of English* 20 (1986): 69-97.

Tchudi, Stephen N. *Teaching Writing in the Content Areas: College Level*. Washington, D.C.: National Education Association, 1986.

Thaiss, Christopher, and Charles Suhor, eds. *Speaking and Writing, K-12: Classroom Strategies and the New Research*. Urbana: NCTE, 1984.

Thaiss, Christopher, ed. *Writing to Learn: Essays and Reflections on Writing Across the Curriculum*. Dubuque, IA: Kendall/Hunt, 1983.

Walvoord, Barbara Fassler. *Helping Students Write Well: A Guide For Teachers in All Disciplines*. New York: MLA, 1986.

Walvoord, Barbara, and Lucille McCarthy. *Thinking and Writing in College*. Urbana, IL: NCTE, 1990.

White, Edward. *Developing Successful College Writing Programs*. San Francisco: Jossey-Bass, 1989.

Young, Art, and Toby Fulwiler, eds. *Writing Across the Disciplines: Research into Practice*. Portsmouth, NH: Boynton, 1986.

Index